Income Mobility, Racial Discrimination, and Economic Growth

Income Mobility, Racial Discrimination, and Economic Growth

John J. McCall
University of California
Los Angeles
The Rand Corporation

Lexington Books
D.C. Heath and Company
Lexington, Massachusetts
Toronto   London

Library of Congress Cataloging in Publication Data

McCall, John Joseph, 1933-
    Income mobility, racial discrimination, and economic
growth.

    Bibliography: p.
    1. Income—United States.   2. Poor-United States.
3. Discrimination in employment—United States.   I. Title.
HC106.6.M22   339.4'6'0973   73-11212
ISBN 0-669-90852—5

Published simultaneously in Canada.

Printed in the United States of America.

International Standard Book Number: 0-669-90852-5

Library of Congress Catalog Card Number: 73-11202

Contents

List of Figures

List of Tables

Preface

Over the last few years there has been a plethora of books and articles on poverty, income distribution, racial discrimination, and unemployment. The reader is entitled to know what distinguishes this book from previous work on these topics. It contains, I believe, two major innovations, one empirical and the other theoretical.

This volume presents an empirical study of income mobility with special emphasis on poverty dynamics. Almost all previous empirical treatments of poverty have been limited to cross-sectional income data, that is, income data on individuals or families for a particular time period. The persistence of poverty has been measured by analyzing consecutive cross-sections of income data. Income distribution studies have relied on similar cross-sectional data. The conclusions of these studies with respect to the persistence of poverty and the degree of income inequality in the United States must be regarded as highly tentative, because the data on which they are based do not permit the investigator to trace the income behavior of individuals over time. Consequently, those individuals who are poor in one cross-section, say for 1965, may be the same group that was poor in a previous cross-section, say for 1964, or they may be a completely different group. The impossibility of differentiating between these polar extremes follows immediately from the inability to identify the temporal income profiles of individuals. Obviously, policy implications are critically dependent on which of the polar extremes is closer to the truth. Occupancy of the lower end of the income distribution by the same individuals year after year calls for entirely different policies than does a distribution exhibiting substantial yearly changes in the poverty population.

In this study I use longitudinal data, which permits identification of the temporal income profiles of individuals and thereby the measurement of the persistence of poverty over time. I analyze movements into and out of poverty in the United States during the ten-year period, 1957-66. The analysis is based on a unique and hitherto untapped longitudinal file of Social Security data that includes information on race, age, sex, and estimated annual earnings for over one million individuals. Movements within a more finely partitioned income distribution are also estimated using these data. The conventional "snapshot" or static view of the income distribution is contrasted with the "motion picture" or dynamic analysis conducted here. These results are new and give added insight into the problems of poverty and income mobility in the United States.

The theoretical part of the volume develops a stochastic theory of unemployment and racial discrimination. In the past, most theories of unemployment have neglected the role of information and job search in explaining labor-market behavior.[1] Here this neglect is remedied and labor-market behavior is interpreted within a probabilistic setting. Almost all previous research on racial discrimination involved the construction of static models that assumed perfect information. A novel feature of this book is the introduction of a model of racial discrimination that incorporates uncertainty and explicitly considers both the cost of searching for employment by potential employees and the cost of searching for productive employees by employers.

At this point I feel compelled to face up to a profound ethical problem accompanying formal research on such topics as poverty and racial discrimination. What emotional stance should the writer adopt when discussing the consequences of human frailty and bad luck? Poverty and racial discrimination in the United States cry out for a passionate and sympathetic portrayal. Instead, I shall adopt a cool and dispassionate stance and analyze these problems from a purely economic perspective. First, any attempt to convey the plight of our society's casualties would be intolerably arrogant. I possess neither the experience nor the literary talent such an endeavor requires. James Agee possessed both of these prerequisites and still voiced deep misgivings about his ability to communicate the desperate conditions surrounding rural poverty in the 1930s.

It seems to me curious, not to say obscene and thoroughly terrifying, that it would occur to an association of human beings drawn together through need and chance and for profit into a company, an organ of journalism, to pry intimately into the lives of an undefended and appallingly damaged group of human beings, an ignorant and helpless rural family, for the purpose of parading the nakedness, disadvantage and humiliation of these lives before another group of human beings, in the name of science. . . . And it seems curious still further that, with all their suspicion of and contempt for every person and thing to do with the situation, save only for the tenants and for themselves, and their own intentions, and with all their realization of the seriousness and mystery of the subject, and of the human responsibility they undertook, they so little questioned or doubted their own qualifications for this work. . . .

As it is, though, I'll do what little I can in writing. Only it will be very little. I'm not capable of it; and if I were, you would not go near it all.[2]

The second reason for adopting an analytic approach is that emotion frequently impedes economic understanding. One of the greatest benefits of economics is its ability to make sharp distinctions between outcomes and intentions. It is a paradox of the human condition that some of man's most elevated accomplishments have their foundation in greed and self-interest, whereas the noblest of virtues have frequently produced disastrous outcomes. As we will see, many of the early efforts at poverty alleviation failed to recognize this paradox and, although rooted in good intentions, caused greater suffering among the poor.

Research for this study was supported by the National Science Foundation, the Office of Economic Opportunity and The Rand Corporation. The opinions expressed herein are those of the author and should not be construed as representing opinions or policy of any agency of the U.S. government. The author is indebted to K.J. Arrow, Y. Ben-Porath, S. Carroll, R. Clower, A. Cook,

E. Durbin, B. Ellickson, B. Fox, J. Hirshleifer, L. Jacobson, M. Kosters, R.A. Levine, J. Merck, T. Ozenne, A. Pascal, S.J. Press, E. Scheuer, F. Sloan, F. Welch, and C. Wolf for their valuable comments and suggestions. The calculations reported herein are based on programs designed by R. Ayanian, H. Chiou, K. Hall, T. Ozenne, and J. Wharton.

This book is dedicated to my parents.

1

Introduction to the Problems of Poverty, Racial Discrimination, and Economic Growth

Introduction

Poverty and racial discrimination are two of the most important problems confronting our society. The main objective of this book is to develop a methodology that will enhance our understanding of these related phenomena and lead to the design of practical policies for their alleviation and control, with economic growth being the most prominent control variable.

The empirical part of this volume studies income mobility with special emphasis on poverty dynamics and its relation to economic growth. Almost all previous empirical studies of poverty have been limited to cross-sectional income data, that is, income data on individuals or families for a particular time period. Here I use longitudinal data, which permits an individual's income behavior to be tracked over time. Those who are temporarily poor can be distinguished from those who remain in poverty year after year. A Markovian model is constructed to analyze movements into and out of poverty in the United States during the ten-year period, 1957-66. The analysis is based on Social Security data that includes information on race, age, sex, and estimated annual earnings for more than one million individuals. These data are also used to measure the behavior of the income distribution over the same ten years. The dichotomous (poor-non-poor) distribution is repartitioned into twelve earnings categories and a more general analysis of income dynamics is conducted. The empirical results that emerge from a standard cross sectional analysis are contrasted with those obtained from this longitudinal study. A summary of the empirical findings is reported in Chapter 3.

While the Social Security data are unique in their coverage and content, they are deficient in several important respects. An extensive discussion of these limitations is set forth in Chapter 3. For now it should be noted that the time series is short, the data are for individuals and not for families, only income covered by Social Security is estimated, and no information is available on education. These limitations make it impossible to conduct my analysis in the traditional human-capital setting and accounts to some extent for the eclectic character of this study.

No new theory of the income distribution is presented here, but I do develop a theory of income mobility for low-income individuals. This descriptive model of the incidence and persistence of poverty is based on a simple probability process—the Markov chain. In spite of its simplicity, the Markovian model does

1

seem to encompass the basic causative forces generating that multifarious sequence of events called poverty dynamics. An integral part of the theory of poverty dynamics is a model of racial discrimination. This model is based on recent research in the economics of information and job search.[1] Economic growth is the fundamental link between the poverty model and the discrimination model. When searching for productive employees, employers will attempt to use relatively costless information devices to assess potential employees' marginal products. Race, sex, and education are cheap screening devices. Considering racial discrimination in this context, the employer will hire white employees rather than nonwhites who otherwise have the same apparent abilities. This choice is based on the prior assessment that the employer has regarding the relative productivities of whites and nonwhites—namely, that the probability of a success given whiteness is greater than the probability of success given nonwhiteness.[2] However, in the face of persistent economic growth, the correlation between easily observed characteristics of newly hired employees and their subsequent performance should weaken; the unemployed pool will contain more and more marginal workers. Accordingly, the firm will begin experimenting and hire employees with different attributes. For example, it may begin hiring black employees, the assumption being that they will be more productive than their unemployed white counterparts. Thus the overall effects of sustained economic growth should be a reduction in racial discrimination and an increase in employment and incomes of the employable poor, especially those who are black. Chapter 2 presents a full discussion of this model.

The Social Security data are also used to measure changes in the earnings distribution from 1957 to 1966, by extending the dichotomous (poor-nonpoor) analysis of poverty dynamics to a more finely partitioned earnings distribution. The behavior of the earnings distribution over the ten-year period is summarized by conventional measures that include the mean, the variance of log income, the coefficient of variation, and the Gini concentration ratio. These measures are compared with those calculated for nonlongitudinal data. Comparisons of the relative performance of different demographic classes are also highlighted throughout both the empirical study of poverty dynamics and the empirical study of the earnings distribution. These empirical studies are contained in Chapters 4 and 5 and Appendix A.

In the development of a normative model of movements into and out of poverty, the emphasis shifts from describing poverty dynamics to improving the income behavior of individuals by controlling critical variables. This normative analysis presumes that there is agreement as to what constitutes poverty and, furthermore, that poverty should be reduced or eliminated. Although this presumption does raise the ethical issue of the "correct" income distribution, achieving a consensus with respect to poverty alleviation is much less difficult than having society agree on the "optimal" amount of income inequality. The former requires only agreement with respect to the lower tail of the income distribution, and the latter, of course, entails the entire income distribution. Here it is assumed that there is a sufficient consensus with respect to poverty alleviation to justify a normative analysis.

The practical implications of utilizing alternative control variables to ameliorate poverty are investigated. One of the most significant variables affecting poverty dynamics is the rate of change of gross national product. An extensive empirical analysis of the relation between economic growth and poverty is conducted. Some tentative conclusions regarding preferred rates of economic growth are drawn. Two other variables that are assumed to have substantial influence on movements into and out of poverty are expenditures on income maintenance and training. An empirical study of the relative effectiveness of these two variables is not possible at this time because of data limitations. Therefore, the allocation of a fixed budget between expenditures on these two variables is studied for different levels of effectiveness. The allocation is made to minimize the weighted proportion in poverty in the long run, where those in dire poverty receive a higher weight than those who are less poor.

Fundamental Issues in the Analysis of Poverty

Definition of Poverty

The first problem in analyzing poverty is to decide what distinguishes the poor from the nonpoor. Many people with enormous monetary wealth are clearly destitute relative to nonmonetary criteria. Throughout this book the focus is on monetary or economic poverty. The reason for this restriction is not the unimportance of nonmonetary poverty, but rather its immeasurability. Indeed, the concept of economic poverty is arbitrary, with each definition posing measurement difficulties. The measure should be adjusted for family size, geographic location, and price-level changes. Many have argued for a relative measure such as 50 percent of median family income, the argument being that material well-being is not absolute but relative to the affluence of the society to which the family belongs. A fixed poverty line (either absolute or relative) may also give misleading results when the number of crossings enters the improvement criterion. Many families can move out of "poverty" with little real improvement when most of these families were just below the poverty line in the previous period. Similarly, very few crossings need not mean that improvement is slight when there are many families in dire poverty in the previous period who make significant positive movements but not sufficient to cross the poverty threshold.

Perhaps the most appealing definition of poverty was advanced by H. Watts.[3] His definition considers the individual's or family's permanent level of command over resources. Society determines some minimum acceptable level of this permanent income from human and financial wealth. The minimum depends on family size, location, time, and so on. A family's condition is measured by the ratio of its permanent income to this threshold. Unfortunately, this definition is almost always impossible to measure.

The poverty index proposed by the Social Security Administration has received the widest use. Their starting point is the cost of providing a nutritionally adequate diet for families of various sizes. Multiplication by three converts this minimum food budget into the poverty index. The poverty budget for a nonfarm family of four was $3410 in 1967. In my analysis of poverty, information was available only on an individual basis. Three different poverty lines are studied: $1500, $3000, and $4500.

Characteristics of the Poor

In Appendix A, I examine the behavior of the poverty population over the ten-year period, 1957-66. This analysis is summarized in Chapter 3. Table 1-1 previews some of the characteristics of the poverty population for the year 1966. It differs from Appendix A in that the unit of measure is the family rather than the individual, and the poverty line (for a nonfarm family of four) is $3350. Of the 30 million people who would be designated poor by these criteria, 13 million were under 18 years old. Almost two-thirds were either over 65 or under 18. Over two-thirds of the poor were white. Nevertheless, the incidence of poverty was much greater among the nonwhite; the probability of being poor was .41 for nonwhites and .13 for whites. About five-sixths of the poor were members of families. However, the incidence of poverty was much higher for unrelated individuals than for family members. The proportion of poor among the former group was .40, and the comparable measure among the latter group was .14. Similarly, there were many fewer farm poor, 2.5 million, than nonfarm, 27.5 million, but the incidence was much higher among the farmers, .23, compared with the nonfarmers, .15. Finally, more than half the poor were located in cities, but the probability of being poor was higher for rural than for urban dwellers, .19 versus .14, respectively.

Demographic Changes in the Poverty
Population, 1957-67

In a recent book, Lampman describes the various demographic changes that occurred in the U.S. population during the period 1957-67.[4] This is roughly coincident with the time period to be analyzed in Appendix A. These demographic changes are presented as an introduction and supplement to the analysis of Appendix A. Lampman tried to ascertain whether the underlying

Table 1-1
Selected Characteristics of the Poor and Nonpoor, 1966

Characteristics	Number (Millions) Poor	Nonpoor	Percentage Distribution Poor	Nonpoor
Age Total	30.0	163.9	100.0	100.0
Under 18 years	13.0	57.4	43.5	35.0
18-21	1.6	10.4	5.3	6.4
22-54	7.4	68.7	24.7	41.9
55-64	2.5	14.7	8.5	9.0
65 and over	5.4	12.6	18.0	7.7
Race Total	30.0	163.9	100.0	100.0
White	20.4	150.2	68.3	91.6
Nonwhite	9.5	13.7	31.7	8.4
Family Status Total	30.0	163.9	100.0	100.0
Unrelated individuals	5.1	7.6	17.1	4.6
Family members	24.9	156.3	82.0	95.4
Head	6.1	42.8	20.3	26.1
Spouse	4.1	38.5	13.5	23.5
Other adult	2.1	17.7	7.2	10.8
Child under 18	12.6	57.3	42.0	35.0
Type-of-Residence Total	30.0	163.0	100.0	100.0
Farm	2.5	8.5	8.2	5.2
Nonfarm	27.5	155.4	91.8	94.8
Rural	11.2	46.7	37.3	28.5
Urban	18.8	117.2	62.7	71.5

Source: President's Commission on Income Maintenance Programs (1969).

demographic forces during the 1957-67 period were producing changes in the population that culminated in a more poverty-prone population in 1967. This is precisely what did happen.

The incidence of poverty among large families and unrelated individuals is much higher than for intermediate-sized families. The distribution of low income families by size is shown in Table 1-2 for the years 1957 and 1967. The number of poverty-prone families increased during this period. For example, the number of unrelated individuals increased from 10.3 million to 13.1 million and the number of families with seven or more increased from 2.6 million to 3.4 million. However, the incidence of poverty declined for each size category.

Lampman looked at several other demographic changes during 1957-67 and concluded that "poverty was reduced *in spite of* (1) relatively rapid increases in

Table 1-2

Distribution and Frequency of Low-Income Consumer Units, by Size of Unit (Selected Years)

Size of Consumer Units (No. of Persons)	Number in Group (Millions)		Number of Low-Income Units[a] (Millions)		Incidence of Low Income (%)	
	1957 (1)	1967 (2)	1957 (3)	1967 (4)	1957 (5)	1967 (6)
1	10.3	13.1	4.4	4.0	43	30
2	14.3	16.9	2.5	1.9	17	11
3	9.5	10.3	1.2	0.8	13	8
4	8.8	9.5	1.0	0.6	11	6
5	5.5	6.2	0.8	0.4	15	6
6	2.9	3.5	0.7	0.4	24	11
7 or more	2.6	3.4	1.0	0.7	38	21
Total consumer units	54.0	62.9	11.6	8.8	21.5	14.0
Total persons	168.3	195.0	32.2	22.6	19	12

[a]Low-income units are defined as those below variable minimum incomes for the several family sizes with $2000 (1947 prices) for a family of 4 as a base.

Source: Data for 1957 are obtained from R.J. Lampman, Joint Economic Committee Study Paper No. 12, *The Low Income Population and Economic Growth.* Data for 1967 are derived from U.S. Bureau of the Census, *Current Population Survey*, Ser. P-60.

those family sizes where poverty is most common, (2) an unfavorable change in the ages of family heads, (3) a relative decrease in the number of families headed by persons in the labor force and (4) a disproportionate increase in the nonwhite population."[5] The deleterious effects of these demographic changes on the size of the poverty population were more than compensated for by the remarkable economic growth during this period.

Programs to Alleviate Poverty

Poverty reduction has been the goal of many government-sponsored programs. Urban renewal, farm subsidies, and minimum-wage legislation were all originally intended as highly effective programs for ameliorating poverty, but the actual effects were quite different from the intended effects. The beneficiaries of the urban renewal and farm subsidy programs were mainly nonpoor with, in some cases, a direct income transfer going from the poor to the nonpoor. Minimum-wage legislation has been argued by many to produce similar perversities. Some recent empirical studies lend support to these dire predictions.[6] The main lesson to be learned from these programs is that good intentions are not sufficient for achieving desired outcomes. In the political arena, the relation between the goal of poverty reduction and its achievement is complex and uncertain. Naive programs that are not fully appreciative of these complications are doomed to subversion.

The recent academic and governmental literature on poverty regard training and income maintenance as the two most promising means for reducing poverty. In fact, the primary weapon for waging the War on Poverty has been the provision of various types of training for enhancing productivity. In some programs (Headstart, for example), the nexus with productivity is rather weak, but even these programs have been defended on grounds of economic efficiency. Most subsidies for training programs have been furnished by the federal government. Cost-benefit analysis has been used almost exclusively to evaluate alternative training programs; that is, cost-benefit comparisons have been used to measure the relative efficiency both of projects within programs and of different programs.[7] Projects and programs with low cost-benefit ratios tend, of course, to be favored. This emphasis on efficiency has to some extent obscured the distributional goals of the War on Poverty. If training programs are to be the main device for eliminating poverty and these programs are evaluated solely on the basis of efficiency, then, obviously, mobility from poverty will tend to be restricted to those who are most easily trained and probably least poor. It is possible that poverty could be eliminated through training, but the cost-benefit ratios would be quite high and the overall cost would be enormous. Furthermore, if this policy were followed in an optimal—with respect to efficiency—fashion until poverty were eliminated, the first to leave poverty would be the most able (and probably the least poor), and the last to leave would be the least able (and probably the poorest). With any reasonable training budget, only the most able would escape poverty.

In his extensive survey of the economic effectiveness of education as a poverty alleviative, Ribich found that traditional cost-benefit analysis *always* yielded cost-benefit ratios greater than unity.[8] His book, when read in tandem with the Coleman Report, must certainly diminish enthusiasm for education as a solution to the poverty problem.[9] However, the conclusions of both of these reports are highly tentative and because of severe data limitations can only be provisionally accepted. There seems little doubt that training and education programs, perhaps very different and more specialized than those we are familiar with, will continue to be major instruments in antipoverty policy. The advice Ribich gives to policymakers is consistent with this prediction.

Thus, while it cannot be stated with certainty that improved education (of the kind and scope examined) results in income gains to the poor that are less than costs, it is useful to discuss policy implications that might follow under the assumption that a heavy emphasis on general education is not the most efficient way to approach poverty alleviation. Even this presumption does not lead to hard and fast rules about the direction of policy. Any one of several alternative policy attitudes can be adopted.

First, a policy maker could feel that the alleviation of poverty is only one of many benefits. The intangible benefits of education (social and private) may be considered much more important than the goal of generating income gains.

Second, he may feel that large amounts of transfers and other direct help are simply out of the question. The handout connotation of such approaches may result in a near-absolute constraint.

Finally, one could argue that education and direct help expenditures should be designed to work in close tandem. A somewhat heavier emphasis, than now exists, on direct help programs could be justified, but with the proviso that they be tied closely to education programs.[10]

A variety of income maintenance schemes have been advocated to alleviate poverty. The major differences among these plans are their overall cost and their effect on the recipients' incentive to seek employment. For example, consider the income maintenance plan recommended by the President's Commission on Income Maintenance. For a family of four the guaranteed family income, Y_g, is $2400 and the rate, α, at which other income, Y_o, is taxed is set at 50 percent. Under these conditions the family of four receives an income supplement, Y_s, until a total income, Y^*, of $4800 is earned. Table 1-3 displays the variation in the income supplement as increasing amounts of other income are earned. When there is no other income, the family receives the full income supplement, $Y_s = Y_g = 2400. When the family's other income reaches $3000, the supplement is reduced to $900. This is equivalent to a tax of 50 percent on the $3000 of other income. Finally, the income supplement is zero when other income exceeds $4800. The following algebraic relation links these variables:

$$Y^* = Y_s + Y_o = Y_g - \alpha Y_o + Y_o = Y_g + (1 - \alpha) Y_o.$$

All income maintenance proposals are variations of this simple plan, depending on just two parameters, the tax rate, α, and the guaranteed income, Y_g.

Table 1-3
Variation in Income Supplement as a Function of Other Income ($\alpha = .5$, $Y_g = 2400$)

Other Income (Y_o)	Income Supplement (Y_s)	Total Income (Y^*)
0	2400	2400
500	2150	2650
1000	1900	2900
1500	1650	3150
2000	1400	3400
3000	900	3900
4000	400	4400
4800	0	4800

Changes in these parameters give rise to changed work incentives for the family and changes in the total cost of the transfer plan.[11] The major advantages of income maintenance are its simplicity, directness, and ease of administration. The only requirement for participation is that earnings be less than the prescribed amount. The main argument against the program is that it

establishes a system under which taxes are imposed on some to pay subsidies to others. And presumably, these others have a vote. There is always the danger that instead of being an arrangement under which the great majority tax themselves willingly to help an unfortunate minority, it will be converted into one under which a majority imposes taxes for its own benefit on an unwilling minority. Because this proposal makes the process so explicit, the danger is perhaps greater than with other measures. I see no solution to this problem except to rely on the self-restraint and good will of the electorate.[12]

A Guide for the Reader

Very few will wish to read this book from cover to cover. Those who are mainly interested in the empirical results of the study of poverty dynamics should begin with Chapter 3, skim the last half of Chapter 2, and then skip to Chapter 5 and Appendix A. Readers whose major concern is with the dynamics of the income distribution should concentrate on the first half of Chapter 2 and Chapter 4. Readers who wish a theoretical discussion of labor-market phenomena should go directly to Appendix B. If racial discrimination is the topic of concern, the reader should specialize on the first half of Chapter 2 and those sections of Chapters 4, 5, and Appendix A that contain black/white comparisons.

2

A Theory of Income Mobility, Racial Discrimination, and Economic Growth

Introduction

The distribution of resources among members of an economy is one of the most important topics in economics. This importance has been recognized by many of the great economists, including Ricardo and Mill as well as most prominent contemporary economists (see Bronfenbrenner, 1971). Contemporary interest in the theory of income distribution has been stimulated by the recent concern for the poverty population of the United States. Nevertheless, an adequate theory of income distribution awaits construction. The traditional emphasis on the functional distribution of income—that is, the distribution of income among the various factors of production—produced few significant theorems; and these have little, if any, relevance to the distribution of income among individuals or households. The major contributions to the personal distribution of income have been made by economists and others who have developed probabilistic theories of income distribution.[1] These theoretical constructs are virtually devoid of economic content.[2] Almost without exception, these theories begin with an extremely simple probabilistic model of income mobility and then invoke a central limit theorem to obtain a steady-state income distribution that more or less approximates empirically derived income distributions.

The following line of argument is basic to these theories. In pursuing his economic welfare an individual is buffeted by a sequence of random variables or shocks over which he has little if any control. These include changes in his mental and physical health, climatic fluctuations, political upheavals, and so on. The participant in economic activity is reduced to Brown's dust particle,[3] and the same methods used to describe the motion of the dust particle are used to interpret the individual's income mobility. Let $\epsilon_1, \epsilon_2, \ldots$ denote the sequence of random shocks. The effect of these random variables on the individual's income or wealth is assumed proportional to his current level of income (wealth). More precisely, the increase in income (wealth) caused by the $i + 1^{st}$ shock, ϵ_{i+1}, is the product of ϵ_{i+1} and some function of the current level of income (wealth) w_i:

$$w_{i+1} = w_i + \epsilon_{i+1} f(w_i).$$

A continuous approximation gives:

11

$$\epsilon_1 + \epsilon_2 + \dots + \epsilon_n = \int_{w_0}^{w_n} \frac{dt}{f(t)} = F_n(w) ,$$

where $w = w_n$ is the accumulated income (wealth) after n shocks.

The ϵ's are independent random variables and, by the central limit theorem, t॥ random variable comprising their sum is approximately normally distributed, t॥ approximation improving with larger n. Thus $F_n(w)$ tends to normally as increases. In the special case where $f(t) = t$, the effect of each shock is direct proportional to current wealth and log w is normally distributed; that is, displays a lognormal distribution. Obviously, this is a very gross characterizatia of the probabilistic models of the income distributions. The argument has bee subjected to a number of subtle and imaginative modifications. However, mo of these theories are similar in their strong reliance on the central limit theore and their weak dependence on economic theory.

The impetus for creating these probabilistic theories of the income distrib tion is twofold. First, the income distribution is after all a special kind ‹ probability distribution. Second, the empirical manifestations of this distrib tion have been remarkably stable, they are truncated at zero, achieve an ear maximum, and have long tails. This shape of the income distribution is simil across developed and underdeveloped countries, and states; is relatively invariaı to the measure of income, wages, total income, or total wealth; does not deper on the unit of measure, individual or household; and has not shown dramat changes over time. These empirical regularities cry out for an explanation, and is not surprising that the first tentative explanations should be proposed ᴉ those most familiar with probability distributions. A detailed probabilist derivation of the Pareto, lognormal, or some more exotic distribution is ä important first step in understanding the distribution of income. Nevertheles these purely mechanistic arguments give little solace to the economist wh wishes an economic theoretic explanation of income distribution, an explanatic that replaces the passive dust particle with an intelligent decisionmaker wh continuously adapts his behavior to the changing environment.

The human-capital approach to income distribution is the most significaı attempt to provide an economic theoretic explanation of the income distribu tion. See Becker (1967) and Mincer (1972). For example, if the percentaṣ differences in the earnings of two individuals is a simple linear function of yea in school, then a symmetric distribution of schooling implies an earninꞬ distribution that is positively skewed.[4] Where the probabilistic models wei mostly stochastic with little economics, human-capital models are primaril composed of deterministic economic theory with little reference to the underlᵧ ing stochastic process. A balancing of these two theories of income distributic would appear to be very rewarding.

The income distribution of a particular society in some sense measures tʰ degree of inequality that is characteristic of that society. This is perhaps one of the major reasons for the renewed interest in income distributions. In the empirical part of the book, several of the most familiar measures of inequality will be applied to the Social Security data.

Although the general shape of the income distribution is robust against alternative definitions of income, the same is not true of inequality measures and their interpretation. The first problem is that most measures of income are annual rather than lifetime quantities. Accordingly, much of the observed dispersion of income may be due to its variation over the life cycle. The value of leisure may differ substantially among individuals. Since leisure is not included in most income measures, the measured inequality may differ greatly from the actual degree of inequality. Individuals also have different attitudes toward uncertainty, some being more risk averse than others. Few if any measures of inequality have taken account of these risk effects. The amount of education, the willingness to accept risk, and the attitude toward leisure are all matters of individual choice affecting the measures of income inequality. Presumably, one is much less concerned about these determinants of measured inequality than about the inequality caused by discrimination and monopoly. Unfortunately, given the available data, these causes are impossible to disentangle.[5]

The absence of any solid theory of the income distribution means, of course, that there are major obstacles to adequately explaining its observed behavior either over time or across different countries (states) at a fixed point of time. In particular, it is difficult to formulate hypotheses about the relationships between income inequality and economic growth. It is almost impossible to say anything meaningful about the optimal level of income inequality. The subtle relations among economic incentives, income inequality, and per capita income, while the topics of much speculation and controversy,[6] have not been subjected to any systematic theoretical analysis. Empirical studies of twentieth-century data tend to show a negative relationship between income inequality and economic growth in the more developed countries.[7] In Chapter 4 I will show how the conventional measures of income inequality behave where applied to the ten-year longitudinal Social Security data. No attempt will be made to construct a general theory of the income distribution. In the remainder of this chapter, I will try to develop a theory of income mobility that is applicable to individuals with low incomes. Following is a quick sketch of the basic argument underlying this theory.

The initial response of firms to the increases in product demand that accompany overall economic growth will be to make more intensive use of their employed resources with little added investment in either human or physical capital. New employees will be hired for whatever period the employer expects the increase in demand to persist. Initially, this expected period tends to be short and, therefore, the firm will be reluctant to provide these new employees with any extensive training. Furthermore, the firm will hire individuals with those characteristics that in the past have been strongly and positively correlated with desired work performance. For example, if the firm has previously had good work performance from high school graduates who are white males with some minimum level of experience, then the firm will ensure that its new employees also possess these attributes. As the firm realizes that the increase in its demand is more permanent than transient, it will alter its investment and hiring strategies. Durable assets will be purchased and, more importantly, the firm will begin to invest in human capital, that is, it will take actions like intensive training (general and specific) that will increase the productivity of its employees (new and old).

Finally, as economic growth persists the previously perceived relationship between employee productivity and easily observed employee attributes should diminish. For example, the pool of unemployed white male high school graduates will be composed mainly of marginal workers who for one reason or another are very unproductive. As a consequence, some firms will modify their selection criteria and experiment with alternative screening mechanisms. Firms will begin to expect that the productivities of black employees exceed those of their white counterparts and commence hiring blacks. In this way, a reduction of discrimination in general and racial discrimination in particular would be a natural outcome of sustained economic growth. The diminution of racial discrimination would be accompanied by an increase in black employment and black income.

The remainder of this chapter presents a formal model of the preceding argument. First, the hiring behavior of employers is presented within a search-theoretic framework. The focus of this theory is the relationship between economic growth and racial discrimination. A Markov model of poverty dynamics is then developed with special attention to the relationship between the income mobility of the poor and economic growth.

Racial Discrimination and Income Mobility: The Role of Information and Search

Even a cursory study of poverty in the United States reveals the special economic problems confronting nonwhites. The proportion of poor who are nonwhite far exceeds the proportion of nonwhites in the total population. Indeed, if attention is restricted to the "stayers" in poverty (those who remain in poverty year after year regardless of such exogenous factors as economic growth), it has been estimated that nonwhites constitute 40 percent of this group (see Miller, 1966).

It is clear that ever since blacks were brought to the United States, they have incurred a variety of injustices ranging from slavery to racial discrimination. The effects of these injustices have been cumulative and difficult to disentangle.

Discrimination appears in a variety of ways and in several distinct fields, primarily in education and training, housing, and occupation (see Thurow, 1969, and Pascal, 1967). The economic analysis described herein could be applied to any one of these fields. It could also be applied to other groups who are subject to discriminatory practices such as women and the aged. For specificity, this section will present an economic analysis of discrimination as it occurs in the job market for nonwhites.[8] A novel feature of this study is the introduction of a model of racial discrimination that incorporates uncertainty and explicitly considers both the cost of searching for employment by potential employees and the cost of searching for productive employees by employers. The major application of the model is to assess the relation between economic growth and racial discrimination.

In the literature on job market discrimination, a question that frequently arises is whether the economic value of discrimination accruing to the discriminator (or in the case to be discussed here, the employer) is positive or negative. If positive, would it pay the minority group to engage in retaliatory discrimination? A static economic model can usually provide the answers to such questions. Different answers are given depending on which static model is used. If discrimination does not pay economically, then one can estimate its cost. Employers may then decide that the cost is too high and reduce discrimination without altering their attitudes toward nonwhites. If discrimination does pay economically, then different policies may be required to reduce it. It will be argued here that in the presence of uncertainty, discrimination may be economically justified for both the white employer and the nonwhite employee.

The employer discriminates on the basis of color if, when presented with two individuals, one nonwhite and one white, who are otherwise equally qualified (on the basis of such variables as education, experience, age, sex, and so on) for a single job occupancy, he does not flip a fair coin and choose the nonwhite if a head appears and the white if tails (or vice versa). If the probability of a head is less than one-half, he discriminates against nonwhites; if this probability exceeds one-half, he discriminates against whites. Employees discriminate if they do not search for employment with the same intensity in firms and industries that are similar with respect to such variables as distance from home, wage rates, and so on, and only differ in the proportions of nonwhites in their labor forces.

It may pay employers to discriminate because information concerning the productivity of a potential employee is quite costly. They may, therefore, use color as a cheap screening device in the same way that they use a high school diploma. They do this because they believe the probability an employee will be productive given that he is nonwhite is less than the corresponding conditional probability for whites. In the same way, assuming similar jobs across firms, it may pay nonwhites to restrict their job searching activities to firms that have a relatively high proportion of nonwhite employees, the belief being that this proportion is a good measure of employer discrimination.[9]

Although the value of discrimination tends to be positive, the theory presented here assumes that the value is a function of the business cycle. A changing economic environment is assumed to induce employers to engage in experiments—for example, to hire nonwhites during the tight labor markets that accompany persistent economic growth. The outcomes of these experiments may alter whatever incorrect attitudes they might have toward nonwhites, and discrimination could decline in a very natural way. Similarly, the beliefs of nonwhite employees regarding the intensity of discrimination in certain industries would never be altered unless they or someone in their information network were employed by these industries.[10] Again in periods of tight labor markets, employees are also assumed to be experimenting with new industries and revising their beliefs concerning discrimination intensities. Both of these illustrations indicate that discrimination by both employers and employees can be explained on purely economic grounds when uncertainty is explicitly considered, and, furthermore, changes in the economic environment may cause both employers and employees to alter the beliefs that give rise to discriminatory practices.

Racial Discrimination and Income Mobility: The Employer Search Process

In most models of racial discrimination, it is assumed that employers have perfect information about prices, marginal products, and all other relevant economic variables. Employers who produce in an environment that is characterized by uncertainty and costly information do not actually possess such information. For example, the prior assessment of potential employees' marginal products could be very costly. Hence, when searching for productive employees, the employer will attempt to utilize relatively costless information devices. Cheap information sources such as age, race, sex, and education will very probably be used as screening devices. This is especially true in surplus labor markets.

Considering only racial discrimination within this context, the employer will hire white employees rather than nonwhite employees with the same apparent abilities. This choice will be based on the prior assessment that the employer has regarding the relative productivities of whites and nonwhites, namely that the probability of a success given that the employee is white is greater than the probability of a success given that the employee is nonwhite. The employer also has prior evaluations of the discrimination intensities of his white work force and their effect on total production.

Both sets of prior assessments will remain unaltered until the employer begins hiring nonwhites. This will increase in tight labor markets when the apparent quality differentials between whites and nonwhites outweighs the information provided by the nonwhite filter. More specifically, the prior assessment of the quality of the white unemployed labor pool will be revised downward as samples from this pool contain more individuals who have failed to make it in other firms. At some point, then, experiments with nonwhite employees will commence and employers may revise their prior assessments. If their experience with nonwhites is favorable, then presumably the use of color as a screening device will diminish when the labor market becomes less tight.

As an illustration, suppose there are two possible states of nature:

S_1 = Nonwhites inferior (in production) to whites with comparable (easily observed) characteristics.

S_2 = Nonwhites as productive as their white counterparts.

Suppose also that the employer's prior probability distributions over these two states of nature are

$$P'(S_1) = .9$$

and

$$P'(S_2) = .1 .$$

The employer hires a nonwhite and observes one of two outcomes;

Z_1 = Nonwhite is inferior (in production)

or

Z_2 = Nonwhite is productive as white.

Let the probability of observing each of these outcomes, given S_1 and S_2, be given by:[11]

$$f(Z_1 \mid S_1) = .8 \qquad\qquad f(Z_1 \mid S_2) = .2$$
$$f(Z_2 \mid S_1) = .2 \qquad\qquad f(Z_2 \mid S_2) = .8$$

If a Z_2 is observed, the employer's posterior assessments of S_1 and S_2 are by Bayes rule:

$$P''(S_1 \mid Z_2) = .7$$

and

$$P''(S_2 \mid Z_2) = .3 .$$

If employers' prior distributions are adjusted in this way and nonwhites are at least as productive as their white counterparts, then racial discrimination should diminish over time. This should be manifested by improvements in the income mobility of nonwhites.

To provide a more theoretical framework for analyzing employer searching behavior, I shall discuss several alternative models. The first model of employer search is a variant of the elementary search model contained in Appendix B with marginal products replacing wages. In the second model of employer search, the employer is able to discriminate among prospective employees on the basis of some easily measured (inexpensive) characteristics such as age, race, or sex. Given his beliefs about the costs of search—that is, the cost of measuring marginal products—and the distribution of marginal products for each distinguishable group, he chooses the group from which he will sample. He then proceeds to search according to the elementary search model.

In an adaptive model of search in the presence of racial discrimination, the employer is assumed to be uncertain about the marginal productivities of both white and nonwhite potential employees. An employee is successful if his marginal product exceeds some critical value; otherwise he fails and is discharged. The employer is assumed to have prior distributions over the proportion of nonwhites who will be successful and the proportion of whites who will be successful. He will hire a white or a nonwhite depending on the relative expected gain. Each white (nonwhite) observation provides the employer with an opportunity to revise his white (nonwhite) prior distribution.

The Elementary Employer Search Model

For a given wage offer, let the cost of experiment, the marginal product, and the probability density function of marginal products be denoted by k, m, and φ, respectively. The optimal search strategy for the employer is:

accept applicant   if $m \geqslant \eta$

reject applicant   if $m < \eta$

where η is the solution to

$$k = \int_{\eta}^{\infty} (m - \eta) \; \varphi \; (m) dm = G(\eta) .[12]$$

Choosing the Best Group for Search

Suppose the population from which the employer can search is decomposable into n subgroups on the basis of some easily measured characteristic such as age, race, or sex. Let k_i, m_i, and φ_i be the cost of search, the marginal product, and the probability density function of subgroup i. Using these values, the employer solves the preceding equation for η_i, $i = 1, \ldots, n$. The employer then searches in that subgroup with the highest η_i. For example, if the employer is discriminating between whites and nonwhites, he may believe that the cost of search k_n in the nonwhite market is higher than the cost of search k_w in the white market. Furthermore, his beliefs about the marginal products of nonwhites may be such that $G_w(\eta) > G_n(\eta)$. These beliefs are depicted in Figure 2-1. Given these beliefs, it is clear that $\eta_w > \eta_n$, and the employer will limit his search to the white market. If the employer pursues an adaptive policy, he may change his beliefs about white marginal products and switch to the nonwhite market.

A Simple Adaptive Model

In this formulation it is assumed that an employee is successful if his marginal product exceeds some critical value, m^*; otherwise he fails and is discharged. The employer has prior probability distributions over the two unknown parameters, p_1 and p_2, where p_1 is the proportion of prospective white employees whose marginal product exceed m^*, and p_2 is a similar measure for nonwhites. These prior probability distributions are based on both the past experience of the employer and his subjective assessments. Obviously, his

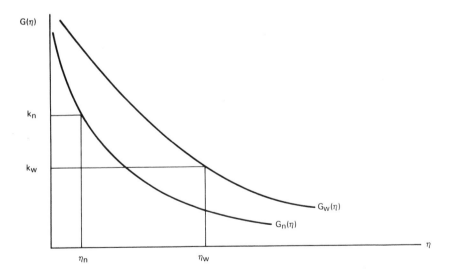

Figure 2-1. Employer Search in White and Nonwhite Labor Markets

subjective assessments will tend to dominate his nonwhite prior distribution if he has had only limited experience with nonwhite employees.

The employer is also assumed to have estimates of the costs of determining whether white and nonwhite marginal products exceed m^*. Let these costs be denoted by c_1 and c_2, respectively. They include the cost of search and the costs incurred while a decision is being made with respect to the employee's productivity. Clearly, c_1 and c_2 are also random variables, and presumably the employer will be revising his estimates of them in the same way as for p_1 and p_2. For simplicity, it will be assumed that these revisions are occurring, but the adaptive method will not be spelled out. These costs should therefore be interpreted as expected costs given all previously relevant information, and for this reason they will be denoted by $\bar{c}_1$ and $\bar{c}_2$.

The employer is assumed to minimize the cost per success.[13] For example, if he hires n individuals, he wants the ratio of total expected cost to expected number of successes, nc/np, to be as small as possible.[14] That is, he will hire whites or nonwhites so as to

$$\mathop{\text{MIN}}_{1,2}\left(\frac{\bar{c}_1}{p_1} \, , \, \frac{\bar{c}_2}{p_2}\right).$$

For analytical simplicity, it is assumed that the prior distributions over p_1 and p_2 are both beta with parameters (r_1, n_1) and (r_2, n_2) respectively.[15] The density functions for p_1 and p_2 are given by

$$\phi(p_i) = K_i p^{r_i - 1} (1 - p)^{n_i - r_i - 1} , \; i = 1, 2,$$

where K_i is a normalizing constant.

The employer's adaptive decision rule is simply:
Sample from labor market 1(2) if

$$\frac{\bar{c}_1}{\int_0^1 p_1 \, \phi_1(p_1) \, dp_1} \quad \mathop{(>)}^{<} \quad \frac{\bar{c}_2}{\int_0^1 p_2 \, \phi_2(p_2) \, dp_2}$$

where ϕ_1 and ϕ_2 are the updated posterior success distributions for whites and nonwhites, respectively.

Presumably, in periods of tight labor markets ϕ_1 will shift to the left, that is, the number of qualified whites who are currently searching for employment diminishes as the white unemployed labor pool becomes dominated by those who have tried and failed. Under these conditions, it will no longer be economical to use such simple screening devices as race, and employers will begin sampling from the nonwhite distribution.[16] If this is true, employable nonwhites should enjoy relatively (to their white counterparts) higher incomes in periods of sustained economic growth.

Another version of this model assumes that the employer is aware of the nonstationarity of the hiring process over the business cycle and adjusts his prior distributions accordingly. In the previous model, information about employees was the only factor influencing the employer's prior distributions. Adjustments to shifting productivity parameters would be more rapid if the employer knew the nature of the shifting process.

For simplicity, assume that only the white productivity parameter changes with the business cycle and that the employer adjusts to this phenomenon in the following manner. If the economy is growing, his prior distribution on p_1 is ϕ_1'; if the economy is declining, his prior distribution is ϕ_1''. In a growing economy, new information is fed into ϕ_1' in order to calculate the posterior distribution; in a declining economy, the posterior distribution is calculated by incorporating new information into ϕ_1''. As before, all of this is done in Bayesian fashion, with prior and posterior distributions members of the beta family. The same switching rule is used as before except that now the employer's behavior is directly influenced by the business cycle.

This remains a simple model of adaptation, but it could easily be generalized to accommodate more complex physical phenomena. For example, both white and nonwhite productivity parameters could be changing and in a much more complicated manner than the zero-one process discussed here. At this point, however, further generalizations of this model do not seem warranted.

Racial Discrimination and Income Mobility: The Employee Search Process

The searching activities of individuals for job vacancies is very similar to the employer's search process. One of the costs of search incurred by nonwhites is the probability that they will be rejected because of their color. These probabilities vary from industry to industry and among firms. If this probability is above a critical level for a particular firm or industry, then not applying for a job is the best policy for nonwhites.

More specifically, let

c = cost per period of search
x = random variable denoting the job offer, $x \geqslant 0$
$\phi(x)$ = the probability density function of x.

The cost, c, is incurred simultaneously with the offer, x. Costs of search include purely economic components such as transportation costs and the value of foregone alternatives, as well as psychic components, such as the frustration accompanying rejection and the discrimination (by race, age, and sex) present in many employment markets. Here the focus will be on the racial discrimination component of this cost. When the random variable, x, takes on a value of zero, this means that the firm did not make a job offer. The cost of search is an increasing function of the probability that $x = 0$; that is, the higher this probability, the greater the chance of rejection.

The cost of search tends to be larger for nonwhites than for whites because of racial discrimination. In addition, the wage distribution, $\phi(x)$, for nonwhites tends to be inferior to that of whites because of discrimination. Such factors could account for the disproportionate number of nonwhite dropouts.

In the tight labor markets that accompany sustained economic growth, employers should discriminate less. The cost of search should decline and $\phi(x)$, the wage distribution, should shift to the right with less mass being concentrated at zero.[17] Consequently, more nonwhites will be employed and this in turn will favorably influence their income mobility. More precisely, the number of nonwhite dropouts will decline; that is, it will now pay them to search for employment. One would also expect that nonwhites would enter new industries and occupations. This, however, is an empirical question in that nondiscriminating industries may benefit more from economic growth. However, nonwhites would probably begin to search in industries where search was previously uneconomical.

Markovian Models of Poverty Dynamics

In this section I discuss those properties of Markov chains that are most pertinent to the analysis of poverty dynamics. The design of a simple modified Markov model of poverty dynamics is followed by a discussion of hypothesis testing within this modified Markov model.

Elementary Markov Models

In the study of income mobility in general, and poverty dynamics in particular, considerable reliance is placed on the theory of Markov chains (see Solow, 1951). A Markov chain is one of the simplest dependent stochastic processes. The fundamental assumption is that the probability of an individual moving from state i in period t to state j in period $t + 1$ depends only on i, j, and t and is denoted by $p_{ij}(t)$. The behavior of the individual before period t has no influence on the transition probability, $p_{ij}(t)$. The future manifestations of a Markov chain are completely determined by the present state of the system and are independent of the past.

More precisely, the stochastic process $X(t)$ is a Markov chain if $X(t)$ assumes only a finite number of values as t runs over the positive integers *and* the following condition (Markov property) is satisfied:

$$P[X(t_n) = x_n \mid X(t_1) = x_1, \ldots, X(t_{n-1}) = x_{n-1}) \qquad (2.1)$$

$$= P[X(t_n) = x_n \mid X(t_{n-1}) = x_{n-1}]$$

The conditional probabilities $P[X(t_n) = j \mid X(t_{n-1}) = i] = p_{ij}(t)$ are called the transition probabilities of the Markov chain. If the transition probabilities are independent of t,

$$p_{ij}(t) = p_{ij}, \text{ for all } t, \qquad (2.2)$$

the chain is said to be stationary.[18]

Many of the properties of Markov chains can be illustrated with a simple two-state example. In the context of this chapter, an individual may occupy one of two states, poverty or nonpoverty. If an individual is poor in the period n, the probability of transiting to nonpoverty in period $n+1$ is p_1. On the other hand, if the individual is nonpoor in period n, the probability is p_2 that his income drops below the poverty level in period $n+1$. The probability of being in poverty at the initiation of the stochastic process ($n = 0$) is π_o. Let X_n be the random variable denoting the state of the system at period n. The state of poverty (nonpoverty) corresponds to $X_n = 0(X_n = 1)$. The transition probabilities of this two-state model are:

$$
\begin{aligned}
P(X_{n+1} = 1 \mid X_n = 0) &= p_1 \\
P(X_{n+1} = 0 \mid X_n = 0) &= 1 - p_1 = q_1 \\
P(X_{n+1} = 1 \mid X_n = 1) &= 1 - p_2 = q_2 \\
P(X_{n+1} = 0 \mid X_n = 1) &= p_2 .
\end{aligned}
\qquad (2.3)
$$

The transition probabilities of a Markov chain can be compactly described by the transition probability matrix

$$
\mathbf{P} = \begin{array}{c} \\ 0 \\ 1 \end{array}
\begin{pmatrix}
1 - p_1 & p_1 \\
p_2 & 1 - p_2
\end{pmatrix}
\qquad (2.4)
$$

The probabilities of being in poverty and nonpoverty initially are

$$P(X_O = 0) = \pi_0(0)$$

and

$$P(X_O = 1) = \pi_0(1) = 1 - \pi_0(0), \tag{2.5}$$

respectively. The initial distribution of the chain can be compactly represented by the vector

$$\pi_0 = [\pi_0(0), \pi_0(1)]. \tag{2.6}$$

Given the initial probability distribution π_0 and the transition matrix **P**, the probabilities of poverty and nonpoverty can be calculated for any future period n.

First note the following relations:

$$P(X_{n+1} = 0) = P(X_n = 0 \text{ and } X_{n+1} = 0) + P(X_n = 1 \text{ and } X_{n+1} = 0)$$
$$= P(X_n = 0)P(X_{n+1} = 0 \mid X_n = 0) + P(X_n = 1)$$
$$P(X_{n+1} = 0 \mid X_n = 1)$$
$$= P(X_n = 0)(1 - p_1) + P(X_n = 1)p_2$$
$$= (1 - p_1 - p_2)P(X_n = 0) + p_2. \tag{2.7}$$

The first equality is based on the addition rule for mutually exclusive events, the second on the definition of conditional probability, the third on the relations in (2.3), and the fourth on the relation $P(X_n = 1) = 1 - P(X_n = 0)$.

From (2.7) it is clear that

$$P(X_1 = 0) = (1 - p_1 - p_2)\pi_0(0) + p_2$$

since $P(X_O = 0) = \pi_0(0)$. Similarly,

$$P(X_2 = 0) = (1 - p_1 - p_2)^2 \pi_0(0) + p_2[1 + (-p_1 - p_2)].$$

On repetition of this argument, the general expression for $P(X_n = 0)$ is given by

$$P(X_n = 0) = (1 - p_1 - p_2)^n \pi_0(0) + p_2 \sum_{i=1}^{n-1} (1 - p_1 - p_2)^i. \tag{2.8}$$

Now since

$$\sum_{i=1}^{n-1} (1 - p_1 - p_2)^i = \frac{1 - (1 - p_1 - p_2)^n}{p_1 + p_2}$$

(2.8) can be rewritten (assuming $p_1 + p_2 > 0$)

$$P(X_n = 0) = \frac{p_2}{p_1 + p_2} + (1 - p_1 - p_2)^n \left(\pi_0(0) - \frac{p_2}{p_1 + p_2} \right) \qquad (2.9)$$

and

$$P(X_n = 1) = 1 - P(X_n = 0) = \frac{p_1}{p_1 + p_2} + (1 - p_1 - p_2)^n$$

$$\left(\pi_0(1) - \frac{p_1}{p_1 + p_2} \right) . \qquad (2.10)$$

As n gets large, the contribution of the second term on the right hand sides of (2.9) and (2.10) diminishes in importance, assuming as we will that $1 - p_1 - p_2 < 1$. In the limit (2.1) and (2.10) converge, respectively, to

$$\pi(0) = \lim_{n \to \infty} p(X_n = 0) = \frac{p_2}{p_1 + p_2} \qquad (2.11)$$

and

$$\pi(1) = \lim_{n \to \infty} P(X_n = 1) = \frac{p_2}{p_1 + p_2} \qquad (2.12)$$

both of which are independent of the initial state of the system.[19]

Equations (2.11) and (2.12) have the following implications within the poverty or nonpoverty setting. The probability that an individual is in poverty (nonpoverty) at some future date becomes less and less dependent on the initial state as the future state becomes more distant. In the limit, complete independence of the initial conditions is achieved.

In matrix notation, the distribution $\pi_n = [\pi_n(0), \pi_n(1)]$ of the Markov chain at period n is given by

$$\pi_n = \pi_{n-1} P$$

which on iteration reduces to

$$\pi_n = \pi_0 P^n , \qquad (2.13)$$

where P_n is the matrix of n step transition probabilities. The (i,j) entry of P^n, say $p_{ij}^{(n)}$, is simply

$$p_{ij}^{(n)} = p(X_n = j \mid X_0 = i) .$$

A Markov chain is said to be regular if *some* power of the Markov transition matrix is composed of only strictly positive elements. When the Markov chain is regular, an equilibrium or steady-state probability distribution, $\pi = [\,\pi\,(0), \pi\,(1)]$, exists and is the solution to

$$\pi = \pi P, \text{ and}$$

$$\pi\,(0) + \pi\,(1) = 1 \tag{2.14}$$

In the two-state example, this is a system of three equations in two unknowns and under the assumptions made has the following solution:

$$\pi\,(0) = \frac{p_1}{p_1 + p_2}$$

$$\pi\,(1) = \frac{p_2}{p_1 + p_2},$$

which are the same as the results obtained in (2.11) and (2.12).

In the income mobility milieu, the equilibrium distribution associated with a particular transition matrix can be interpreted as the proportion of individuals who will be in poverty at some future time when income mobility is regulated by that transition matrix. By its immediate indication of long-run effects, the equilibrium distribution is a convenient device for evaluating a specific transition matrix. If this long-run behavior is deemed unacceptable, different methods could be considered for altering the transition matrix. One can facilitate the choice among these different methods by studying their implications in terms of the equilibrium distribution. I shall return to the normative uses of Markov analysis below. For now I shall use a numerical example to illustrate the preceding methodology.

In a mythical society, suppose that movements between poverty and nonpoverty are controlled by the following Markov transition matrix:

$$\mathbf{P} = \begin{matrix} & \begin{matrix} 0 & \quad 1 \end{matrix} \\ \begin{matrix} 0 \\ 1 \end{matrix} & \begin{bmatrix} 3/4 & 1/4 \\ 1/10 & 9/10 \end{bmatrix} \end{matrix}, \tag{2.15}$$

where poverty and nonpoverty are represented by 0 and 1, respectively. Assume also that the initial distribution of the population between poverty and nonpoverty is

$$\pi_o\,(0) = .1 \text{ and } \pi_o\,(1) = .9 \tag{2.16}$$

that is, 90 percent of the members of this society begin in nonpoverty. Then from equation (2.9) the probability of being in poverty after n periods or, equivalently, after n moves according to transition matrix (2.15) is

$$P(X_n = 0) = 5/7 + (3/20)^n (1/10 - 5/7).$$ (2.17)

The corresponding probability for nonpoverty is

$$P(X_n = 1) = 2/7 + (13/20)^n (9/10 - 2/7).$$ (2.18)

From these relations it is clear that the steady-state distribution of poverty and nonpoverty differs markedly from the initial distribution. In the beginning only one-tenth of the population was in poverty, whereas in the long run five-sevenths of the population is destitute. The corresponding initial and steady-state probabilities for nonpoverty are nine-tenths and two-sevenths, respectively. The convergence of the initial distribution to the steady state is quite rapid. This is illustrated in Table 2-1 where Equations (2.17) and (2.18) are calculated for different values of n. After five iterations, the proportion in nonpoverty has declined from .90 to .36, after ten iterations to .29, and after fifteen iterations to .287, which is only .001 above the steady-state proportion. A society that was initially quite well off with respect to the incidence of poverty responds very badly to successive operations of the transition matrix (2.15). The movement from the favorable initial state to the unfavorable steady state can be prevented

Table 2-1
Convergence to Steady State When P and π are Given by Equations (2.15) and (2.16)

n	Proportion in Poverty	Proportion in Nonpoverty
0	.10	.90
1	.315	.685
2	.455	.545
3	.546	.454
4	.605	.395
5	.643	.357
6	.668	.332
7	.684	.316
8	.695	.305
9	.702	.298
10	.706	.294
15	.713	.287
∞	.714	.286

only by changing the transition matrix. This can be accomplished if the decisionmakers understand the process underlying the matrix *and* are able to control it.

A Modified Markov Model of Poverty Dynamics

It seems apparent that movements into and out of poverty cannot be adequately described by stochastic processes that generate movements without regard for past performance. The familiar Bernoulli process—in which, in this context, whether a person is to be poor or nonpoor is decided by flipping a coin—would provide an inadequate description of poverty dynamics. Individuals do not transit into and out of poverty in the haphazard manner of a Bernoulli experiment. Rather, their income movements possess a continuity that displays respect for the past. The Markov chain above is a stochastic process with at least a modicum of respect for the past. Future income movements are conditional on the present economic status of an individual. In his pioneering study of income dynamics, Solow (1951) demonstrated that Markov chain analysis gave a surprisingly accurate description of income mobility. Indeed, it is precisely this success that led to the adoption of the methodology exercised later in Chapter 4. Nevertheless, although simple Markov models are fairly accurate in their portrayal of income dynamics, they appear inappropriate for the study of poverty dynamics.

In theory the length of time in poverty or nonpoverty should have an important influence on the probability of moving to poverty or nonpoverty during the subsequent period. For this reason, a modified Markov process is used to describe movements into and out of poverty. In this modified process, I distinguish three different classes: stayers in poverty, stayers in nonpoverty, and movers. In this study the stayers in poverty are viewed as the backwash population, that is, those immune to economic growth; the stayers in nonpoverty are the affluent; and the movers are low-income individuals who are employable and, therefore, are affected by economic growth. The behavior of the movers is assumed to follow a simple first-order Markov process, and the stayers are assumed to remain in poverty or nonpoverty with probability 1. In addition to its theoretical appeal, this Markovian formulation proved to be a very convenient device for organizing the massive Social Security longitudinal file.

In the analysis here an individual can occupy three states: poverty, non-poverty, and uncovered; uncovered indicates that the individual has for one reason or another not been covered by Social Security for the period in question. Denoting poverty, nonpoverty, and uncovered by 1, 2, and 3, respectively, the law of motion for this process is given by:

$$p_{ij} = \begin{cases} s_i + (1 - s_i)\, m_{ii}, & i = j, \ i \neq 3 \\ (1 - s_i)\, m_{ij}, & i \neq j, \ i \neq 3 \\ m_{ij}, & i = 3 \end{cases}$$

In this process the proportions of stayers in poverty and nonpoverty are denoted by s_1 and s_2, respectively.[20] The mover matrix $\mathbf{M}$, is assumed to be a simple first-order Markov process:

$$\mathbf{M} = \begin{bmatrix} m_{11} & m_{12} \\ m_{21} & m_{22} \end{bmatrix},$$

where $0 \leqslant m_{ij} \leqslant 1$ and $\Sigma m_{1j} = \Sigma m_{2j} = 1$. The stayer matrix is simply

$$\mathbf{I} = \begin{bmatrix} 1 & 0 \\ 0 & 1 \end{bmatrix}.$$

The unknown parameters of this process are s_1 and s_2, the proportion of stayers in poverty and nonpoverty, respectively, and the transition probabilities, m_{ij}, of the mover matrix. These parameters cannot be estimated directly from longitudinal income data. An individual who remains in poverty (nonpoverty) for two consecutive periods may be a stayer or a mover. It is possible to estimate the the parameters, however, using some indirect methods devised by L. Goodman. When the sample size is large, Goodman suggests the following approximations to maximum likelihood estimators of the parameters[21]

$$\tilde{m}_{ij} = h_{ij} \ (i, j = 1, 2)$$

and

$$\tilde{s}_i = f_i \, (i = 1, 2),$$

where h_{ij} is the proportion of individuals in income class i in the initial period who were in income class j in the following period (considering *only* individuals in income class i in the initial period who *were not* continuously in the class for the next n periods), and f_i is the proportion of individuals in income class i in the initial period who *remained* in that class for the next n periods.

Hypothesis Testing in the Stayer-Mover Model

To illustrate the kinds of hypotheses that will be tested with the Social Security data, consider the following version of the poverty model. Two income states are distinguished, poverty and nonpoverty. There are also two race states (black and white), two sex states, and five age categories (25-34, 35-44, 45-54, 55-64, >64). The Markov process therefore has a total of 40 states. The 40x40 transition matrix decomposes into twenty 2x2 matrixes, a poverty-nonpoverty matrix for each of the twenty demographic classes. A stayer vector, (s_1^k, s_2^k), k = 1, 2, ..., 20, is associated with each of these twenty mover matrixes, where s_1^k and s_2^k are the proportions of individuals in class k who are in poverty and nonpoverty, respectively, and m_{ij}^k is the probability of going from state i to state j in one period given that the individual is a mover in class k.

In the recent literature on poverty, several authors have investigated the influence of the rate of change of gross national product (economic growth) on the poverty population. All agree that growth does indeed have a beneficial effect on the poverty population. These authors disagree, however, concerning the extent of this positive influence. Some claim that almost all groups participate in growth with, in some cases, the gains being greater for the nonwhite poor than for the white poor (see Gallaway, 1965, and Tobin, 1965). Others are less sanguine about the overall effects of growth. They have advanced the "backwash thesis," claiming that certain subgroups in poverty are so isolated from our society that their economic welfare is immune to aggregate growth.[22] Finally, some claim that sustained economic growth will, for all practical purposes, eventually eliminate poverty. Clearly, these hypotheses have different policy implications. If the "backwash thesis" is true, then the elimination of poverty requires special programs in addition to sustained economic growth. Now economic growth should manifest itself by increasing the transition probabilities from poverty to nonpoverty and from nonpoverty to nonpoverty and decreasing the transition probabilities from nonpoverty to poverty and from poverty to poverty. If the stayer-mover model is necessary even when these transition probabilities are changing, then the backwash thesis cannot be rejected.

The first hypothesis to be tested is the necessity of the stayer-mover model instead of the simple Markov model. Let the null hypothesis be that the simple Markov model is adequate. The alternative is that the stayer-mover model is required. Following Goodman (1961) let

f_i be the fraction of individuals in income class i in the initial period who remain in that class for the next n periods;

c_i be the number of individuals in income class i in the initial period who remain in that class for the next n periods;

w_i be the number of individuals in income class i in the initial period;

$f_i = c_i/w_i$;

$w_{ij}(t)$ be the number in class i in period t who were in class j in period $(t + 1)$;

$w_i(t)$ be the number in class i in period t;

p_{ii}^n be the expected proportion in income class i in the initial period who were in class i for n periods.

The expected value of f_i under the null hypothesis is simply

$$E(f_i) = p_{ii}^n ,$$

and the test can be based on the difference, d_i,

$$d_i = f_i - \overline{p}_{ii}^n ,$$

where

$$\overline{p}_{ii} = \frac{\sum\limits_{t=1}^{T} w_{ii}(t)}{\sum\limits_{t=1}^{T} w_i(t)}$$

and T is total number of periods.

The distribution of d_i is asymptotically normal with zero mean and variance that can be estimated by

$$S_{d_i}^2 = \frac{\overline{p}_{ii}^n (1 - \overline{p}_{ii}^n)}{w_i} - \frac{n\overline{p}_{ii}^{2n-1} (1 - \overline{p}_{ii})}{\overline{w}_i} ,$$

where

$$\overline{w}_i = \sum\limits_{T=1}^{T} w_i(t)/T.$$

Under the null hypothesis, the statistic

$$X_1^2 = d_1^2 / S_{d_1}^2$$

has a χ^2 distribution with one degree of freedom. The statistic

$$X = X_1^2 + X_2^2 ,$$

where X_2^2 is defined like X_1^2, is χ^2 with 2 degrees of freedom; it can be used to test the null hypothesis that both S_1 and S_2 are zero for each of the twenty demographic classes. If the null hypothesis is rejected, the stayer-mover model can be applied directly to the poverty-nonpoverty income distribution.

Hypotheses regarding the equality of transition rates for the twenty categories can, after a transformation of the data, be tested by the method of multiple comparisons used as an adjunct to the analysis of variance (see Scheffé, 1959). Similar methods can be used for testing the equality of the proportion of stayers in each category. Many interesting questions can be answered using these simple procedures. For example, is the proportion of stayers in poverty for the group of black males between the ages of 35 and 44 significantly different from the same proportion for white males in the same age group?

The hypothesis that two or more of the twenty sample matrixes are from the same underlying Markov chain can be tested using the likelihood ratio criterion.[23] For example, suppose that the following 2x2 arrays represent the number of individuals in each of the four transition categories—poverty to poverty, poverty to nonpoverty, and so on—for two different classes.

	Poverty	Nonpoverty
Poverty	n_{11}	n_{12}
Nonpoverty	n_{21}	n_{22}

	Poverty	Nonpoverty
Poverty	n'_{11}	n'_{12}
Nonpoverty	n'_{21}	n'_{22}

Let

$$\sum_j n_{ij} = n_i \text{ and } \sum_j n'_{ij} = n'_i$$

denote the total number of observations in row i for each group. The likelihood ratio is given by

$$\lambda = \frac{\prod_{i,j=1}^{2} \hat{p}_{ij}^{\,n_{ij}}}{\prod_{i,j=1}^{2} \hat{p}'_{ij}^{\,n'_{ij}}}$$

where

$$\hat{p}_{ij} = \frac{n_{ij}}{n_i}, \; \hat{p}'_{ij} = \frac{n'_{ij}}{n'_i} \; \text{and} \; \sum_j \hat{p}_{ij} = \sum_j \hat{p}'_{ij} = 1. \qquad 1.24$$

Under the null hypothesis that $p_{ij} = p'_{ij}$ all i, j, the statistic, $-2 \; ln \; \lambda$ is asymptotically χ^2 with one degree of freedom (see Mood and Graybill, 1963).

The adequacy of the first order Markov process in explaining the behavior of movers can also be tested using the likelihood ratio criterion, as described in Anderson and Goodman (1967). Let the null hypothesis be that the Markov process is first order and the alternative be that it is second order. Let p_{ijk} denote the probability of going to k at time t, given that the process was in state j at $t-1$ and in state i at $t-2$. The null hypothesis asserts the following equalities:

$$p_{1jk} = p_{2jk} = \ldots = p_{mjk} = p_{jk},$$

whereas the alternative hypothesis asserts that these probabilities are unequal. The likelihood ratio is given by

$$\lambda = \prod_{i,j,k=1}^{m} (\hat{p}_{jk}/\hat{p}_{ijk})^{n_{ijk}},$$

where

$$p_{jk} = \frac{\sum_{t=2}^{T} n_{jk}(t)}{\sum_{t-1}^{T-1} n_j(t)} \; \text{and} \; p_{ijk} = \frac{\sum_{t=2}^{T} n_{ijk}(t)}{\sum_{t=2}^{T} n_{ij}(t-1)}$$

are the maximum likelihood estimates for p_{jk} and p_{ijk}. Under the null hypothesis, $-2 \; ln \; \lambda$ is χ^2 with $m \, (m-1)^2$ degrees of freedom.

Using similar arguments, Anderson and Goodman (1967) also develop a likelihood ratio procedure for testing the hypothesis that the transition probabilities are constant, that is, that the Markov process is stationary. Once again I expect the transition probabilities to be nonstationary due to the influence of economic growth. Furthermore, I expect the nonwhite probabilities to be more nonstationary than the white probabilities, that is, nonwhites should be more sensitive to economic growth if the discrimination theory outlined above is correct.

Normative Markov Models

By its very nature, the purely descriptive model of the previous section adopts a passive attitude toward poverty. The normative model takes a different stance and interferes with the income dynamics of the poverty process. The object of this interference is to alter the poverty process in the most desirable way.

The decisionmaker is assumed to have a fixed budget per unit of time available for poverty alleviation. He can alter the poverty process by direct income transfers to the poverty stricken, by subsidizing the most 'suitable training program, or by some combination of the two. The best allocation depends on the criterion used to evaluate alternative combinations. The different criteria considered here are presented within the context of Markov renewal programming.

Two different criteria are investigated in a brief discussion of optimization within a Markov chain. First, the policy that minimizes the expected losses imposed on society is preferred. Second, based on a steady-state criterion, the preferred policy minimizes the steady-state proportion in poverty.

Two other criteria for evaluating semi-Markov decision models are based on expected discounted net benefits. They differ in that the first occurs over a finite horizon whereas the second has an infinite horizon policy.

Optimization in a Markov Chain

Consider the Markov mover matrix

$$\mathbf{M} = \begin{bmatrix} m_{11} & m_{12} \\ m_{21} & m_{22} \end{bmatrix},$$

where 1 and 2 denote poverty and nonpoverty, respectively. The Markov chain is completely ergodic[25] and hence

$$\pi = \pi M$$

with

$$\sum_i \pi_i = 1,$$

where π is a row vector with π_i the steady-state proportion in state i. Solving for the π_i in terms of the transition probabilities m_{ij} gives

$$\pi_1 = \frac{m_{21}}{m_{12} + m_{21}}$$

and

$$\pi_2 = \frac{m_{12}}{m_{12} + m_{21}}.$$

Following Howard (1960), a reward structure is associated with the various transitions. This is given by the matrix

$$\mathbf{R} = \begin{bmatrix} r_{11} & r_{12} \\ r_{21} & r_{22} \end{bmatrix}.$$

Finally, a set of decisions is available. Each decision has its own mover and reward matrixes. The object is to choose that policy yielding the highest expected rewards. The dynamic programming policy iteration methods developed by Howard can be used to solve this problem. The problem can also be formulated as a linear program.

The analysis of the poverty model with these methods does, however, pose a problem. Presumably, in the two-state model, if the individual is not in poverty, the only action available will be to do nothing. But the transition probabilities for an individual out of poverty may depend on the action taken for those in poverty. For example, the fact that a training program or income transfer will accompany a transit into poverty may affect the probability of moving into poverty as well as the probability of moving out. As an illustration, consider three alternatives for an individual in poverty: (1) do nothing, (2) invest X in training, and (3) invest X in income transfers. Nothing is done for those out of poverty. The hypothetical effects of the various alternatives on m_{ij} and r_{ij} are as follows:

		State 1		State 2
	m_{1j}^1	$= (3/5, 2/5)$	m_{2j}^1	$= (1/5, 4/5)$
Alternative 1	r_{1j}^1	$= (-15, 15)$	r_{2j}^1	$= (-5, 10)$
	m_{1j}^2	$= (2/5, 3/5)$	m_{2j}^2	$= (2/5, 3/5)$
Alternative 2	r_{1j}^2	$= (-25, 10)$	r_{2j}^2	$= (-5, 10)$
	m_{1j}^3	$= (1/5, 4/5)$	m_{2j}^3	$= (3/5, 2/5)$
Alternative 3	r_{1j}^3	$= (-25, 5)$	r_{2j}^3	$= (-5, 10)$

Howard's iteration procedure cannot be used to choose among these three policies because of the secondary effects that alternatives in state 1 have on the transition probabilities of state 2. When there are only a few alternatives, each can be evaluated by his value-determination procedure. In this simple example, alternative 1 is preferred.

This problem vanishes when a steady-state criterion is adopted. Let x be the amount spent on training and y the amount spent on income maintenance, and let $m_{ij}(x, y)$ be the relation between these expenditures and the transition probabilities. Given some constraint on amount spent per period, society could allocate between x and y to minimize

$$\pi_1 = \frac{m_{21}(x,y)}{m_{12}(x,y) + m_{21}(x,y)}$$

subject to

$$x + y \leqslant C.$$

Optimization in a Semi-Markov Process

A semi-Markov process is a generalized Markov process in which the transition time is not the same constant for each transition but is a random variable with a known probability distribution. The two-state poverty model can be used to illustrate this continuous time stochastic process. As before, let m_{ij} be the probability that an individual will move from state i to state j given that he is in state i. In the simple two-state model, the subscripts i and j are limited to 1 (poverty) and 2 (nonpoverty). In the Markov model, movements from i to j were accomplished in a fixed time interval. In the semi-Markov model the movement from i to j is a random variable, τ_{ij}, with probability density function, f_{ij}. For example, an individual transits from poverty to nonpoverty with probability m_{12}. The time for this transition is the random variable τ_{12} with probability density function, f_{12}. The stationary probabilities (π_1, π_2) for the imbedded Markov chain $[m_{ij}]$ are calculated as before. The more important stationary probability for the semi-Markov process is the proportion of time that is spent in transiting from state i. Let ρ_i denote this probability. Then

$$\rho_i = \frac{\pi_i \mu_i}{\Sigma \pi_i \mu_i},$$

where $\mu_i = \sum_j \mu_{ij} m_{ij}$ and $\mu_{ij} = E(\tau_{ij})$. As an example, let

$$M = \left\{ \begin{array}{cc} 2/3 & 1/3 \\ 4/5 & 1/5 \end{array} \right\}$$

$$\mu = \left\{ \begin{array}{cc} 3 & 9 \\ 20 & 5 \end{array} \right\},$$

then

$$\mu_1 = 3 \times 2/3 + 9 \times 1/3 = 5$$
$$\mu_2 = 20 \times 4/5 + 5 \times 1/5 = 17$$
$$\pi_1 = 12/17$$
$$\pi_2 = 5/17$$

and

$$\rho_1 = 12/29$$
$$\rho_2 = 17/29 .$$

The advantage of semi-Markov processes in describing poverty dynamics is that the transitions from poverty to nonpoverty and vice versa are not instantaneous, nor of fixed duration, but are random variables. For example, if an individual is in nonpoverty, the probability of a transition to poverty might be p_{21}, and the waiting time to reach poverty is a random variable τ_{21} with some known probability distribution. Presumably both p_{21} and the distribution of τ_{21} would depend on the individual's current level of affluence. This, of course, suggests that the income distribution should be partitioned into several classes. The semi-Markov process is easily generalized to accommodate this requirement.

In the normative or optimization model, the semi-Markov process can be interfered with by altering some of its parameters. In the two-state poverty model, the process can be improved either by changing the parameters of the imbedded Markov chain [m_{ij}] or by changing the waiting time distributions, F_{ij}. It is assumed that with a fixed budget the decisionmaker can choose any feasible combination of the two control variables—investment in human capital and direct income transfers. To simplify the discussion, the time between transitions is assumed to be a random variable possessing exponential distribution with parameter λ_{ij}. The parameter λ_{ij} is the transition rate of the process from state i to state j and, as usual, $\lambda_{ij} dt$ can be interpreted as the probability of going from i to j in a small interval of time dt, $i \neq j$. The λs are related to the stationary probabilities in the following way:

$$\pi_j(t+dt) = \pi_j(t)\left[1 - \sum_{i \neq j} \lambda_{ij} dt\right] + \sum_{i \neq j} \pi_i(t)\lambda_{ij} dt.$$

Let

$$\lambda_{ij} = -\sum_{i \neq j} \lambda_{ij},$$

and taking limits, this reduces to

$$\frac{d}{dt}\pi(t) = \pi(t)\Lambda,$$

where Λ is a differential matrix of λ_{ij}; that is, each row sums to zero. For the two-income-state poverty model,

$$\Lambda = \begin{vmatrix} \lambda_{11} & \lambda_{12} \\ \lambda_{21} & \lambda_{22} \end{vmatrix}$$

is the differential matrix for a particular group, where

$$\lambda_{11} = -\lambda_{12}$$

and

$$\lambda_{22} = -\lambda_{21}.$$

Let X_1 and X_2 denote, respectively, the rate of expenditure on human capital and income transfers for those individuals in poverty. A linear relation is assumed between these expenditures and the transition rates; that is,

$$\lambda_{12} = \alpha_0 + \alpha_1 X_1 + \alpha_2 X_2,$$
$$\lambda_{21} = \beta_0 + \beta_1 X_1 + \beta_2 X_2.$$

With a steady-state criterion, the object is to choose the combination of X_1 and X_2 that minimizes the stationary probability π_1. The process is assumed to be completely ergodic, implying that the steady-state proportions are constants and are independent of the initial conditions. Therefore, the two equations

$$\frac{d\pi(t)}{dt} = \pi(t)\Lambda = 0$$

and

$$\pi_1 + \pi_2 = 1$$

can be solved for π_1 and π_2:

$$\pi_1 = \frac{\lambda_{21}}{\lambda_{21} + \lambda_{12}}$$

and

$$\pi_2 = \frac{\lambda_{12}}{\lambda_{21} + \lambda_{12}}$$

The optimization problem can be stated as

$$\min_{X_1, X_2} \frac{\sum_{i=0}^{2} \beta_i X_i}{\sum_{i=0}^{2} (\alpha_i + \beta_i) X_i}, \quad X_0 = 1,$$

subject to $X_1 + X_2 \leqslant X$. This is a problem in linear fractional programming that can be solved using well-known methods (see Fox, 1966).

Actually, there are n such 2x2 differential matrixes, one for each of the n nonincome groupings. If N_k denotes the number in group k,

$$\pi_1 = \frac{\sum_{k=1}^{n} N_k \pi_{1k}}{\sum_{k=1}^{n} N_k}$$

represents the overall steady-state proportion in poverty where

$$\pi_{1k} = \frac{\sum_{i=0}^{2} \beta_{ik} X_{ik}}{\sum_{i=0}^{2} (\alpha_{ik} + \beta_{ik}) X_{ik}}.$$

The revised objective then is to minimize

$$\pi_1 (X_{11} X_{12}, \ldots, X_{1n}; X_{21} X_{22}, \ldots, X_{2n}),$$

subject to

$$\sum_{i=1}^{2} \sum_{k=1}^{n} X_{ik} \leq X.$$

It is important to distinguish between a movement from dire poverty to nonpoverty as opposed to a movement from not-so-poor to nonpoverty. Similarly, it is sometimes important to distinguish movements within the poverty category. These distinctions can be made by dividing the poverty category into m classes. The new criterion then would be to minimize the weighted average of the proportion in poverty, where the lowest income classes are assigned the largest weights. The m class criterion can be stated as

$$\text{Min} \sum_{i=1}^{m} W_i \pi_i$$

subject to

$$\sum_{i=1}^{2} \sum_{k=1}^{m} X_{ik} \leq X,$$

where π_1 is the stationary proportion in the lowest income class and π_m is the stationary proportion in the highest poverty class; $W_1 > W_2 > \ldots > W_m > 0$ and

$$\sum_{i=1}^{m} W_i = 1$$

and X_{1k} and X_{2k} are amounts spent respectively on training and income maintenance for income class k. The steady-state proportions are obtained from

$$0 = \pi \Lambda$$

and

$$\sum_{i=1}^{m+1} \pi_i = 1,$$

where Λ is an $(m + 1) \times (m + 1)$ differential matrix.

Policy iteration and linear programming can be used to solve semi-Markov decision problems when the decisionmaker maximizes discounted net benefits over an infinite horizon and a fixed amount to spend per period (see Jewell, 1963, and Denardo and Fox, 1968). Finally, if the War on Poverty is limited to a finite period, and k dollars can be spent over this time, then these funds can be allocated to maximize the present value of discounted net gains (see Miller, 1968).

3

Description of the Social
Security Data and a
Summary of Empirical
Findings

Introduction

The advantages of the longitudinal Social Security data for measuring income dynamics in general and poverty dynamics in particular have been emphasized above. This chapter critically appraises this unique data file, spelling out its limitations for analyzing income mobility. In order to achieve more perspective, the Social Security data are compared with the data source most frequently used for estimating income distributions—the Census Bureau's Current Population Survey. Several procedures are suggested which would mitigate the most glaring deficiencies of the Social Security data. Finally, with the data limitations freshly in mind, it seems most appropriate to briefly summarize the empirical results of this study both with respect to poverty dynamics and the personal income distribution. Such a summary comprises the final section of this chapter.

The Social Security Continuous
Work History Sample

The Social Security Continuous Work History Sample is maintained by the Social Security Administration as an aid in administering the Old Age Survivors Disability and Health Insurance system. This national 1 percent sample is obtained from employee-employer records and has been maintained since 1957. The sample includes information on race, age, sex, and estimated annual earnings for 984,500 individuals over the ten-year period, 1957-66. Table 3-1 is a detailed description of the sample information.

Month and year of birth, sex, and race information are obtained from the employee's application for a social security number. Geographic and industry data are obtained from the employer's application for an identification number and other related forms used periodically to update this information.

The 1-percent sample is obtained by designating certain digit combinations of individual Social Security numbers, comprising 1 percent of all Social Security numbers assigned. Since only "active" (i.e., records showing some reported earnings) cases are considered, the file actually represents about .7 percent of the total set of people who are assigned Social Security numbers at any time.[1] Social Security Administration statisticians have found no reason to doubt the representativeness of the sample as being 1 percent of the active Social Security

43

Table 3-1

Information Contained in the Continuous Work History Sample

Item	Information Shown
1. Employee Ident. number	Scrambled social security number
2. Sex	Male, female
3. Race	White, black, other than white or black (1963 and later), unknown (1962 and later), other than white or black, included in nonwhite unknown deleted
4. Month of birth	January-December, unknown
5. Year of birth	Last 3 digits of year, unknown
6. Year count	Number of years employee appears in file
7. Year	Last 2 digits of data year
8. Employer count	Number of employers in the year
9. Employer Ident. number	Scrambled employer identification number
10. Geographic code	Four-digit (1957-63) or 5-digit (1964 and later) SSA geographic code (State and county)
11. Industry code	Four-digit SSA industry code
12. Coverage group code	Agriculture, state and local government, non-profit, federal civilian, military household, reserves (1963 and later), tips (1966 and later) all other
13. Wage items	Number of debit wage reports reported by employer for employee
14. Annual wages	
15. First quarter wages	Amount of taxable wages (dollars and cents) reported for employee by employer in data year
16. Second quarter wages	
17. Third quarter wages	
18. Fourth quarter wages	
19. Total estimated wages (applicable to nonfarm for 1957-62 and farm and nonfarm for 1963-66)	Amount of total wages (dollars and cents) estimated as paid to employee by employer based on quarterly wage substitution method

cases.[2] The consistent use of certain digit combinations of the Social Security number to select cases into the sample assures the full chronology of a selected individual's work history.[3] Thus an individual who has been employed continuously since 1957, and whose earnings have been reported to Social Security, will have at least one record in each annual file. The number of records in each annual file is approximately one to one-and-a-quarter million. This represents slightly less than a million individuals each year. Thus the 1.153 million records estimated for 1965 will probably represent about .8 million individuals.

The year and the annual and quarterly taxable wages are obtained from the various reporting forms submitted by the employers. For quarterly reported workers, the annual wages are derived by summing the quarterly wages. For annually reported farm workers, the annual wages are shown on the employer report. These wages consist of reportable wages per employee from each employer taxable under the Federal Insurance Contributions Act or under state agreements with the secretary of Health, Education and Welfare. The reported wages are subject to the prevailing maximum as follows:

Year	Taxable Maximum Per Employer
1957-58	$4,200
1959-65	4,800
1966	6,600

These data are unique in their coverage and content. The single most important feature of this data file is the tracking of individual earnings over several years. As was noted above, this longitudinal property should increase our understanding of the dynamic behavior of individual earnings. However, these data also possess serious limitations for the analysis of earnings mobility.

Absence of Household Data. The data are collected for individuals rather than for households. Thus an individual may be earning very low wages and be a member of a relatively prosperous household or an individual may be earning relatively high wages (when considered by himself), while he and his large family are in fact destitute.

The Coverage Problem. Not all workers are covered by Social Security. Table 3-2 was compiled by the Social Security Administration based on data from the Bureau of the Census' Current Population Survey (June week). Table 3-2 shows the manner in which coverage has changed over the ten-year period 1957-66. "At the end of 1959, the major groups covered on a mandatory basis were: employees in non-farm industry and commerce; certain farm employees and domestic employees, Federal civilian employees not under a Federal retirement system; and self-employed persons, except doctors of medicine. Groups covered on an elective basis, individually or jointly, included ministers and employees of non-profit organizations and State and local governments. U.S. citizens employed outside the United States by foreign subsidiaries of American employers are covered at the option of the American company involved."[4] The estimated percentage distribution of workers in noncovered employment for December 1960 is displayed in Table 3-3.

Coverage poses an additional complication in that individuals move into and out of covered employment (and therefore the Social Security sample) over the time span being analyzed. Furthermore, movements from covered to uncovered employment can occur for a number of indistinguishable reasons. Among the

Table 3-2
Approximate Percentage Distribution of Total Employment by Type, 1957-66

				Type of Employment							
		Wage and Salary							Self-Employed[a]		
			Reported to SSA	Not Reported to SSA						Reported to SSA	Not Reported to SSA
Year	Total	Total		Total	Federal Civilian	State and Local	Railroad	All Other	Total		
1957	100.0%	85.3	73.8	11.5	3.1	3.6	1.8	3.1	14.7	11.2	3.6
1958	100.0%	85.4	74.8	10.6	3.1	2.8	1.5	3.3	14.6	11.1	3.5
1959	100.0%	85.6	75.2	10.4	2.9	2.7	1.5	3.3	14.4	11.0	3.4
1960	100.0%	86.1	76.2	9.9	2.9	2.6	1.4	3.1	13.9	10.7	3.2
1961	100.0%	86.3	76.5	9.8	3.0	2.5	1.2	3.2	13.7	10.5	3.2
1962	100.0%	86.8	76.9	9.9	3.0	2.6	1.2	2.9	13.2	10.2	3.0
1963	100.0%	87.3	77.3	10.0	3.0	2.9	1.1	3.0	12.7	9.8	2.9
1964	100.0%	87.9	77.9	9.9	3.0	2.7	1.1	3.0	12.2	9.4	2.8
1965	100.0%	87.8	78.5	9.3	2.9	2.5	1.0	2.9	12.2	10.5	1.7
1966	100.0%	88.8	79.4	9.4	3.0	2.6	1.0	2.8	11.2	9.7	1.6

[a]Not included in longitudinal file.
Note: Percentage figures may not add to 100 due to rounding.

Table 3-3
Distribution of Noncovered Employment (1960)

Employment Group	Percent
State and local governments	27.6
Federal civilian	24.0
Nonfarm employment	17.2
Domestic service	19.9
Farm self-employment	8.3
Nonprofit organizations	6.7
Farm wage workers	3.4
Others	1.9
Total (6.2 million persons)	100

most important are (a) if the maximum taxable income is earned in a prior quarter, the individual will appear as uncovered in the current quarter; (b) if the individual is unemployed or earns less than $50 he will appear as uncovered in the quarter; (c) if his employer fails to file a quarterly report (casual labor and domestics), he will appear as uncovered; (d) finally, if he in fact does move from covered to uncovered employment, he will appear as uncovered.

Absence of Nonwage Income. There is no information on income from nonemployment sources. An individual may appear to be poor on the basis of his wage income but be relatively affluent when his nonwage (dividends, interest, and so on) income is considered.

Estimation of Employment Income. Employment income must be estimated for individuals whose earnings exceed the taxable ceiling. Total estimated wages are derived from the taxable wages amounts reported on an individual employer basis as shown in Table 3-4.[5]

The Posting Problem. The wage reports included in the Continuous Work History sample are subject to a processing cutoff related to each reference year represented in the file. Specifically, all such wage reports that have been processed and posted to SSA's Master Summary Earnings Record through September of the year following the reference year are included. These files are not updated with items that may be posted after this cutoff. The effect of exclusions due to the cutoff is not significant with respect to overall totals in any given year; however, it is known to understate the number of workers with wages in four quarters and workers with wages at the taxable limit. It therefore tends to understate the wages of individuals with low earnings.

48

Table 3-4
Estimation of Employment Income

	Year	Type of Employer	Taxable Wages	Method Used to Derive Estimated Wages Field
1.	1957-58	nonfarm	< $4200	Taxable wages used.
2.	1957-58	nonfarm	≥ 4200	The quarter in which the taxable limit is reached is first determined (limit quarter). Then the wages in the next quarter prior to the limit quarter that shows as much or more wages than the limit quarter are substituted for the limit quarter and all subsequent quarters. If no other quarter has as much wages as the limit quarter, the limit quarter wages are substituted in subsequent quarters. The resulting sum of these quarterly wages is the estimate. *Exception:* if the limit quarter is the first quarter then the estimate is $27,000 for males and $24,000 for females.
3.	1957-58	farm	any	No estimate shown.
4.	1959-62	nonfarm	< 4800	Taxable wages used.
5.	1959-62	nonfarm	≥ 4800	Same as for item 2 except that for first quarter limit cases the estimate is $32,000 for males and $25,000 for females.
6.	1959-62	farm	any	No estimate shown.[a]
7.	1963-65	nonfarm	< 4800	Taxable wages used.
8.	1963-65	nonfarm	> 4800	Same as for item 5.[b]
9.	1963-65	farm	< 4800	Taxable wages used.
10.	1963-65	farm	≥ 4800	$8,000 for males; $7,300 for females.
11.	1966	nonfarm	< 6600	Taxable wages used.
12.	1966	nonfarm	> 6600	Same as item 2 except that for first quarter limit cases the estimate is $42,000 for males and $33,000 for females.
13.	1966	farm	< 6600	Taxable wages used.
14.	1966	farm	≥ 6600	$10,700 for males; $9,600 for females.

[a]Estimate can be made as follows: taxable wages < $4,200, use taxable wages; taxable wages ≥ $4,200, use $7,400 for males and $7,000 for females.

[b]Estimate can be made as follows: taxable wages < $4,800, use taxable wages; taxable wages ≥ $4,800, use $8,000 for males and $7,300 for females.

Other Limitations. Finally, most forms of human-capital analysis are rendered almost impossible due to the lack of information on educational attainment, occupation, and work experience.

Bureau of the Census Current Population Survey

The Current Population Survey (CPS) is a monthly sample survey collected by the Bureau of the Census. As a supplement to this sample, data are also collected each March on individual and family income. These income data are gathered from a subsample of the rotating monthly sample. The CPS consumer income estimates have been published each year since 1944. In 1961-63 the CPS interviewed 35,000 households each month; during March a subsample of 26,000 reported income information. The income distribution was partitioned into seventeen money income classes for both families and unrelated individuals. Using other information contained in the survey, it was possible to cross-classify income distributions by farm, nonfarm, color, age, marital status and family size, occupation and industry of head, sources of income, work experience, region and educational attainment.[6]

The major deficiency of CPS is its nonlongitudinal feature—different individuals and families are interviewed each March. In addition there is a problem of underreporting when comparing white and nonwhite incomes. The major source of unreported income, self-employment, is primarily composed of white workers. This is counterbalanced to some extent by the disproportionate number of nonwhite men who are missed by census interviewers (see Wohlstetter and Coleman, 1972).

As Schultz (1965) has indicated, budget data, linking the Social Security data with other data sources like CPS, could greatly enhance the usefulness of the Social Security file. For example, the Social Security longitudinal income distributions could be classified by occupation and educational attainment after links had been constructed between CPS and the SS data.

The absence of these budget data imposes fundamental constraints on the scope of this study. The data analysis can of course be carried out with both rigor and vigor. However, a gingerly and cautious stance will be adopted when deriving policy implications.

Since there is no information on education, occupation, or work experience, this study has little chance of making any significant contribution to the human-capital literature. Perhaps a more adventurous researcher could construct a theory in the human-capital tradition and test it with these Social Security data. I feel that the current status of these data does not warrant such an enterprise. Consequently, the models of income mobility developed here will appear relatively mechanistic to the human-capital theorist. I will try to compensate for this by relating, wherever possible, my findings to previous empirical work in the human-capital literature.

Analysis of Income Dynamics: A Summary

It seems appropriate at this point to briefly summarize the empirical findings of this study. This section reviews the empirical analysis of income mobility;

the following section is a similar survey of the empirical analysis of poverty dynamics.

The earnings distribution is partitioned into thirteen groups according to annual estimated earnings. These are: less than $1,000, $1000-1999, $2000-2999, $3000-3999, $4000-4999, $5000-5999, $6000-6999, $7000-7999, $8000-8999, $9000-9999, $10,000-15,000, greater than $15,000 and uncovered. The distribution is calculated for each of the ten years, 1957-66, for various subgroups of the sample. The analysis is based on a 10-percent sample of the Continuous Work History File. Within this sample there are individuals who reported income for each of the ten years and another set of individuals who reported income in at least one of ten years. The former group is called the full coverage group and the latter the reporting group.

For the reporting group, approximately 57 percent had covered earnings less than $3000 in 1957; by 1966 this percentage had declined to 46. At the same time mean income increased from $3080 to $4340. The Theil coefficient of inequality increased from .37 in 1957 to .41 in 1966.

For the full coverage group, average income increased from $3798 in 1957 to $6472 in 1966 and the Theil measure decreased from .26 to .23.

The average income for whites in the reporting group increased from $3224 in 1957 to $4563 in 1966. The average income for whites in the full coverage group rose from $3956 to $6739. Similar changes for the corresponding nonwhite groups were $1904 to $2772 for the reporting group and $2419 to $4149 for the full coverage group. The Theil coefficient increased for white and nonwhite reporting groups, .36 to .40 and .37 to .39, respectively. This coefficient declined for white and nonwhite full coverage groups, .22 to .19 and .26 to .21 respectively.

The earnings distributions were estimated by the lognormal and Pareto probability functions. The estimated parameters of these functions are presented together with "goodness of fit" measures, which are based on both the χ-square and Kolmogorov-Smirnov tests. In no case was the Pareto distribution superior to the lognormal in its ability to fit the empirical income distributions.

Three different methods are used to estimate the mobility of individuals within the earnings distribution. The first is based on an analysis of variance. The individual variance over the ten years is used as a crude measure of income mobility. Income mobility was also measured by stayer proportions and a tenth-order Markov transition matrix. A stayer proportion is the probability of remaining in a specified income category for the entire ten years, given occupation of that category in 1957. The i, j entry in the tenth-order Markov matrix is the probability of moving from income category i in 1957 to income category j in 1966. These mobility measures are also calculated for a variety of age, race, and sex subgroups. For example, the probability of a male white between the ages of 35 and 44 moving from a $6000-6999 income class in 1957 to an income class greater than $10,000 in 1966 was .35. The corresponding probability for his nonwhite counterpart was .24.

One of the main flaws in standard analyses of income distribution is the inability to calculate life-cycle income. Using total ten-year earnings as a surrogate for life-cycle income, the analyses revealed a significant reduction in the measures of inequality for the full coverage group. For example, the Theil measure declined from .24 (for the single year 1966) to .08 (for the ten years).

Analysis of Poverty Dynamics:
A Summary

This section summarizes the major findings of the empirical analysis of poverty dynamics. These empirical results together with their policy implications are reviewed first for males and then for females. For males:

1. The probability of remaining in a low earnings category all ten years given low earnings in 1957 was significantly greater than zero. This was true for both white and nonwhite males for all age groups, and for each of the three measures of low earnings, verifying the "backwash thesis" in that there is a significant proportion of prime working age males (covered by Social Security and employed) who are unaffected by economic growth. Clearly, if unemployed, uncovered, and discouraged male workers were added to the Social Security sample, the "backwash thesis" would receive much stronger support.

    Sustained economic growth is not sufficient for the elimination of low earnings. Alternative programs are needed—either an income maintenance program or one that invests in human capital (such as health and training programs).
2. The probability of remaining in a low-earnings category all ten years given low earnings in 1957 was significantly larger for male nonwhites than for male whites. This was true for all age groups and all earnings levels. This is just another indicator of the economic plight of the nonwhite male and suggests that if the nonwhite male's economic level is to be raised very much, it will require more intensive programs than stimulating the economic growth of the economy as a whole. The disproportionate number of nonwhites among the dropouts from the labor force is further justification for this recommendation.
3. The probability of remaining in a non-low-earnings category all ten years given high earnings in 1957 was significantly greater than zero. This was also true for both white and nonwhite males for all age groups and for each of the three measures of low earnings.
4. The probability of remaining in a non-low-earnings category all ten years given high earnings in 1957 was significantly greater for male whites than for male nonwhites. This was true for all age groups and all earning levels. This suggests that it is more difficult for nonwhite males to escape permanently from low-earnings levels than it is for whites. It is consistent with the much

observed phenomenon that causes nonwhite males to be disproportionately represented in dead-end occupations.

5. When the low-earning and non-low-earning stayers were deleted from the sample, male movers showed a strong systematic relationship between each of the low-earning and non-low-earning transition probabilities and g, the percentage change in GNP. More specifically, the low-earning to low-earning and non-low-earning to low-earning transition probabilities were decreasing functions of g, and the low-earning to non-low-earning and non-low-earning to non-low-earning transition probabilities were increasing functions of g. These relationships were highly significant for whites and nonwhites, all age groups, and all earning groups. This suggests that growth does have a strong positive influence on male workers who move about a given low-earnings level. These marginal workers constitute a substantial percentage of total covered workers. Monetary and fiscal decisionmakers should take cognizance of this powerful influence when they manipulate those decision variables that affect growth.

6. Economic growth had a stronger influence on nonwhite male movers than on white male movers; that is, the relative changes in the transition probabilities across each of these earnings levels were greater for nonwhites than for whites. In terms of the regression equations calculated between the transition probabilities and g, the absolute values of their slopes were always greater for nonwhites than for whites.

A buoyant economy is more beneficial for nonwhite movers than for whites. On the other hand, if the effects of growth are symmetric, a depressed economy would be more deleterious for nonwhites than for whites. These factors should also be considered by monetary and fiscal decisionmakers. This result is consistent with the hypothesis that employers discriminate less in tight labor markets and begin hiring from the nonwhite population.

Analysis of the female population produced the following results:

1. The probability of remaining in a low-earnings category all ten years given low earnings in 1957 was significantly greater than zero. This was true for white and nonwhite females, for all age groups, and for each of the three measures of low earnings.

The existence of a significant proportion of female stayers in L (low-earning status) requires more interpretation than in the case of males. Perhaps those who are stayers in L were mainly working wives who chose to work part-time. However, 24 percent of nonwhite families have a female head *and* the proportion of female stayers in L was significantly higher for nonwhites than for whites. In addition, with the exception of the youngest age group, the proportion of female stayers in N (non-low-earning status) was significantly greater for whites than for nonwhites.

2. Year-to-year transition matrixes were also calculated for the female movers, that is, all those who were not stayers in L, N, or U (uncovered). Both white and nonwhite females benefited trom growth. However, the relationships between the four L-N transition probabilities and percentage change in GNP were not nearly as strong as those for males. Differences between white and nonwhite female movers were also much smaller than for males.

3. The transition probabilities from U to L and from U to N were more closely associated with percentage change in GNP than the corresponding male probabilities. These results suggest that the labor participation rates for females identified as movers have a strong positive relation to growth.

4

An Empirical Study of
Income Dynamics

Introduction

This chapter studies the mobility of individuals within the income distribution over a ten-year period. As mentioned earlier, the earnings distribution is partitioned into thirteen groups according to annual estimated earnings. These are: less than $1000, $1000-1999, $2000-2999, $3000-3999, $4000-4999, $5000-5999, $6000-6999, $7000-7999, $8000-8999, $9000-9999, $10,000-15,000, greater than $15,000, and uncovered. This distribution is calculated for each of the ten years for various subgroups of the sample. In the interests of economy, this computationally complex analysis is based on a 10-percent sample of the Continuous Work History File. The data span the ten years 1957-66 and include information on race, age, sex, and estimated annual earnings for approximately 108,000 individuals. The unique features of these data are their longitudinal character—that is, a ten-year earnings profile can be estimated for each individual in the sample—and the relatively large sample size. Nevertheless, the data are not flawless. The time series is short, the data are for individuals rather than families, many people in the United States are in occupations not covered by Social Security, and, perhaps most important, there is no information on education.[1]

The earnings distribution is calculated for each of the ten years for various subgroups of the sample. Although the entire income distribution will be displayed for some key subgroups, many distributions will merely be summarized by conventional measures that include the mean, the median, the variance of log income, the coefficient of variation, the Gini concentration coefficient, and the Theil coefficient of inequality. Some of the more important relative performance comparisons of different demographic groups highlighted throughout these empirical studies are white versus nonwhite, male versus female, white male versus nonwhite male, and white female versus nonwhite female.

A median relative income distribution is also computed to give added insight into the behavior of the income distribution over the ten-year period. The earnings distribution is partitioned into thirteen classes based on the ratio of total earnings to median earnings. The classes are 0-.25, .26-.50, .51-.75, .76-1.00, 1.01-1.25, 1.26-1.50, 1.51-1.75, 1.76-2.00, 2.01-2.50, 2.51-3.00, 3.01-3.50, 3.51-4.00, and > 4.00. Median relative distributions are calculated for each year and for several important subgroups.

The earnings distributions were estimated by the lognormal and Pareto probability functions. The estimated parameters of these functions are presented together with "goodness of fit" measures, which are based on both the χ-square and Kolmogorov-Smirnov tests. For a discussion of these tests, see Hays and Winkler (1971). In no case was the Pareto distribution superior to the lognormal in its ability to fit the empirical income distributions.

Three different methods are used to estimate the mobility of individuals within the earnings distribution. The first is based on an analysis of variance. The individual variance over the ten years is used as a crude measure of income mobility. Income mobility was also measured by stayer proportions and a tenth-order Markov transition matrix. A stayer proportion is the probability of remaining in a specified income category for the entire ten years given occupation of that category in 1957. The i, j entry in the tenth-order Markov matrix is the probability of moving from income category i in 1957 to income category j in 1966. These mobility measures are also calculated for a variety of age, race, and sex subgroups.

One of the main flaws in standard analyses of income distribution is the inability to calculate life-cycle income. Using total ten-year earnings as a surrogate for live-cycle income, the analysis revealed a significant reduction in the measures of inequality for the full coverage group.

Following Atkinson (1970), the social welfare functions that are implicit in any normative interpretation of the different inequality measures are compared with a measure that explicitly considers the degree of inequality aversion present in the social welfare function.

Earnings Distributions, 1957-66

Within the total Social Security sample there are individuals who reported income for each of the ten years and another set of individuals who reported income in at least one of the ten years. Throughout this presentation, the former group is called the full coverage group and the latter is referred to as the reporting group. Obviously, the reporting group that comprises one earnings distribution for any particular year is always larger than the full coverage group associated with the other distribution for that year. Earnings distributions were calculated for both of these groups for each of the years 1957-66.

Table 4-1 presents the total distribution for the reporting group for the beginning year 1957 and for the ending year 1966. This distribution shifted to the right. For example, in 1957 approximately 57 percent had covered earnings less than $3000; by 1966 this percentage had dropped to 46. At the same time the mean (median) income had increased from $3080 (2570) to $4340 (3423). The total number in the reporting group increased from 62,822 in 1957 to 77,862 in 1966. As always there is considerable interest in the change in income inequality over this ten-year period. It is difficult to entertain specific hy-

Table 4-1
Total Earnings Distribution of Reporting Group, 1957 and 1966

	Median	1[a]	2	3	4	5	6	7	8	9	10	11	12	No. of Observations
1957	2,570	.257	.161	.146	.126	.116	.076	.047	.027	.016	.008	.014	.007	62,827
1966	3,423	.218	.132	.106	.103	.093	.077	.074	.054	.042	.030	.052	.019	77,862

[a]The earnings categories are: 1. < 1000, 2. 1000-1999, 3. 2000-2999, 4. 3000-3999, 5. 4000-4999, 6. 5000-5999, 7. 6000-6999, 8. 7000-7999, 9. 8000-8999, 10. 9000-9999, 11. 10,000-15,000, and 12. > 15,000.

potheses regarding the change in inequality because of the variety of conflicting influences at work during this period. The increase in sample size probably means that the 1966 sample is more heterogeneous and composed of more part-time workers than the 1957 sample. The age distribution was also undergoing significant changes during this period as was the distribution of education and experience. The coefficient of variation, the Theil coefficient of inequality, and the Gini coefficient all increased between 1957 and 1966.[2] For example, the Theil measure, T,[3] defined by

$$T(y) = \log N - \sum_{i=1}^{N} y_i \log \frac{1}{y_i} ,$$

where y_i is the proportion of total income earned by individual i, increased from .37 in 1957 to .41 in 1966.

I restrict my attention to those who reported earnings for each of the ten years, the full coverage group. From 1957 to 1966, average (median) earnings for these 35,073 individuals increased from $3798 (3375) to $6472 (5752), and the Theil measure of inequality decreased from .26 to .23. The homogeneity imposed by the full coverage requirement probably accounts for this decline. However, the coefficient of variation increased from .74 to .77. These conflicting views of inequality are based on the differing social welfare functions underlying the Theil measure and the coefficient of variation. The coefficient of variation attaches equal value to transfers at different points of the income distribution, and the Theil coefficient places more weight on changes at the lower end.[4] These discrepancies among inequality measures will be investigated later.

The distribution of earnings by race and sex are reported respectively in Tables 4-2 and 4-3 for the beginning and ending years. The average (median) income for whites (in the reporting group) increased from $3224 (2734) in 1957 to $4563 (3665) in 1966. The average (median) income for whites in the full coverage group rose from $3956 (3564) to $6739 (6036). Similar changes for the corresponding nonwhite groups were $1904 (1483) to $2772 (2166) for the reporting group and $2419 (2134) to $4149 (3776) for the full coverage group. The Theil coefficient increased for white and nonwhite reporting groups, .36 to .40 and .37 to .39 respectively. This inequality measure decreased for white and nonwhite full coverage groups, .22 to .19 and .26 to .21 respectively.

The average (median) income for females in the reporting group increased from $1777 (1487) in 1957 to $2438 (2019) in 1966. The average (median) income for females in the full coverage group rose from $2341 to $3726. Similar changes for the corresponding male groups were $3758 (3476) to $5488 (4880) for the reporting group and $4276 (4000) to $7373 (6627) for the full coverage group. The Theil coefficient increased for male and female reporting groups, .31

Table 4-2
Income Distributions by Race, 1957-68, Reporting Group

	Median	1[a]	2	3	4	5	6	7	8	9	10	11	12	Number of Observations
							White							
1957	2734	.24	.15	.14	.13	.12	.08	.05	.03	.02	.01	.01	.008	55987
1966	3665	.21	.13	.10	.10	.09	.08	.08	.06	.04	.03	.06	.02	68160
							Nonwhite							
1957	1483	.38	.22	.17	.10	.07	.03	.01	.003	.003	.001	.001	0	6840
1966	2166	.31	.17	.15	.12	.09	.06	.05	.03	.02	.01	.01	.002	9702

aSee Note a, Table 4-1 for earning categories.

Table 4-3
Income Distributions by Sex, 1957-68, Reporting Group

	Median	1[a]	2	3	4	5	6	7	8	9	10	11	12	Number of Observations
							Male							
1957	3476	.19	.13	.12	.13	.15	.11	.07	.04	.02	.01	.02	.01	41330
1966	4880	.16	.11	.08	.08	.09	.09	.10	.08	.06	.05	.08	.03	48554
							Female							
1957	1487	.39	.21	.19	.12	.05	.01	.004	.002	.001	.001	.001	0	21497
1966	2019	.32	.17	.15	.14	.10	.06	.03	.01	.006	.003	.003	.001	29308

aSee Note a, Table 4-1 for earning categories.

to .34 and .23 to .28, respectively. The same coefficient declined for male and female full coverage groups, .23 to .20 and .22 to .19 respectively.

The distribution of earnings was also calculated for different age cohorts (age as of 1960) by race and sex. Here I focus on differences between nonwhite and white males in the three age groups 25-34, 35-44, and 45-54. The results are displayed in Table 4-4. Table 4-5 presents comparable results for females.

Schultz (1969) has shown that for all males there is a pronounced tendency for the within-cohort inequalities to increase over time.[5] Mincer has suggested that these increases are due not only to the distribution of schooling levels within a cohort, which is assumed to remain fixed over time, but also to changes in the distribution of such postschool investments as on-the-job training.

For male whites in the 25-34 age group, the Theil coefficient decreased slightly from 1957 to 1966. For the reporting group the decline was from .22 to .19, and for the full coverage group the decline was from .16 to .15. For male whites in the 35-44 age group, inequality increases over time. For the reporting group, the Theil coefficient rises from .19 to .24, and an increase from .13 to .18 is registered by the full coverage group. For male whites in the 45-54 age group, income inequality also increases from .22 to .26 for the reporting groups and from .16 to .22 for the full coverage group.

For nonwhites the changes are somewhat different. For nonwhite males in the 25-34 age group, the Theil coefficient decreased for both the reporting group and the full coverage group, the former from .27 to .22 and the latter from .21 to .16. For nonwhite males in the 35-44 age group, almost no change took place in income inequality from 1957 to 1966. The reporting group's coefficient increased from .24 to .26, and the full coverage group remained constant at .17. For nonwhite males in the 45-54 age group, there was no change in either group's coefficient over the ten years. The coefficients for the reporting group and the full coverage group were .24 and .17 respectively. If in fact on-the-job training accounts for the inequality changes occurring in the white distributions, then nonwhites appear to be treated equally with respect to this investment variable; that is, on-the-job training for nonwhites is primarily a function of color and is relatively insensitive to other attributes.

Human-capital considerations should cause income inequality to increase with age. "Inequality could rise with age because it takes abler persons and those with favorable opportunities longer to reach their full earning power" (see Becker, 1967, p. 2). Table 4-6 shows the variation in the Theil coefficient across the different age groups in 1966. Overall there is a definite increase in inequality with age. Furthermore, the dependence is somewhat more striking for whites than for nonwhites. Since whites are more likely to have "favorable opportunities" than nonwhites, this result is not surprising.[6]

It is also interesting to note the change in the proportion of white and nonwhite males who were earning less than $3000 over this ten-year period of growth. For the white 35-44 age group, this proportion dropped from .25 to .15

for the reporting group and from .17 to .08 for the full coverage group. For nonwhites in the same age group, this proportion declined from .58 to .37 for the reporting group and from .47 to .23 for the full coverage group.

To enhance understanding of the dynamics of the earnings distribution, median relative earnings distributions were also studied. Table 4-7 reports the total median relative distributions for 1957 and 1966. This is done for both the reporting and fully covered groups. These two groups display very different behavior over the ten years. The proportion of those earning less than 50 percent of the median increased from .311 in 1957 to .312 in 1966 for the reporting group and decreased from .245 to .190 for the full coverage group. The corresponding changes for the class earning more than three times the median were from .051 to .064 for the reporting group and from .018 to .015 for the full coverage group. Further inspection of ten-year changes in median relative earnings confirms the impression created by the Theil inequality measure. The inclusion of all individuals with positive earnings in any one year gives rise to an earnings distribution with entirely different policy implications from the distribution that includes only those with positive earnings in every year. The ten-year changes in the former distribution lead to the conclusion that, relative to median earnings, there are no fewer poor and more wealthy. Any measure of inequality that heavily weights transfers at the lower end of the distribution would increase from 1957 to 1966. Recall that the Theil coefficient did increase for this distribution from 1957 to 1966. This characterization of the reporting distribution is relatively robust against alternate demographic decompositions (see Tables 4-8 through 4-15). Over these ten years the upper tail of these distributions gets fatter while the lower tail exhibits little change.[7] The ten-year changes in the full coverage distributions are quite different.[8] The lower tail of these distributions lose a significant amount of mass, and the upper tail gains mass or remains relatively constant. The Theil coefficient reflected these changes and declined from 1957 to 1966. Income distributions that are usually studied are more closely related to the reporting group than the full coverage group. Indeed, during this period most analysts have reported increasing inequality in the U.S. income distribution. The conflicting conclusions regarding changes in equality presented here suggest that empirical studies of the income distribution should be interpreted with the utmost caution, especially if they constitute the primary evidence for policy recommendations.

Lognormal and Pareto Estimates
of the Empirical Distributions

Both the lognormal and the Pareto distributions have been used extensively as estimators of income distributions. There are a variety of probabilistic and economic reasons to support this popularity. See Becker (1967), Champernowne

Table 4-4
Male Income Distributions by Race and Age, 1957-68

White Males
Reporting Group

	Median	1[a]	2	3	4	5	6	7	8	9	10	11	12	Number of Observations
								25-34						
1957	3462	.13	.15	.15	.16	.18	.12	.06	.03	.01	.006	.008	.002	8833[b]
1966	6876	.06	.04	.05	.07	.09	.09	.13	.11	.10	.08	.14	.04	8536
								35-44						
1957	4690	.09	.06	.10	.12	.18	.16	.11	.07	.04	.02	.03	.01	8667
1966	7091	.07	.04	.04	.06	.08	.09	.12	.10	.09	.08	.16	.07	8232
								45-54						
1957	4604	.10	.07	.10	.13	.17	.14	.10	.06	.04	.02	.04	.02	7017
1966	6500	.07	.05	.05	.07	.10	.10	.12	.11	.09	.06	.12	.05	6195
							Full Coverage Group							
								25-34						
1957	3842	.07	.13	.16	.17	.20	.13	.07	.03	.02	.008	.01	.002	6460
1966	7308	.02	.02	.03	.06	.09	.09	.14	.13	.12	.09	.16	.05	6460
								35-44						
1957	5032	.03	.04	.09	.12	.19	.19	.13	.08	.05	.02	.04	.01	6166
1966	7545	.02	.02	.03	.05	.07	.09	.13	.12	.11	.09	.18	.08	6166
								45-54						
1957	4973	.04	.05	.08	.13	.19	.16	.13	.07	.05	.02	.05	.03	4608
1966	6812	.03	.04	.04	.06	.09	.11	.13	.12	.10	.07	.14	.06	4608

Nonwhite Males

Reporting Group

25-34

Year														
1957	1879	.28	.26	.22	.12	.07	.03	.01	.001	.001	0	.001	0	1136[c]
1966	3981	.12	.09	.13	.16	.14	.12	.10	.06	.03	.02	.02	.004	1138

35-44

1957	2668	.20	.18	.20	.16	.14	.08	.03	.004	.007	.004	.003	0	1099
1966	4022	.15	.10	.12	.13	.12	.11	.09	.07	.04	.03	.03	.04	1060

45-54

1957	2572	.19	.19	.20	.16	.14	.06	.03	.009	.004	.002	.005	0	879
1966	3539	.15	.10	.16	.15	.11	.11	.08	.05	.04	.02	.02	.005	773

Full Coverage Group

25-34

1957	2173	.19	.26	.25	.15	.09	.04	.01	.003	.001	0	.001	0	737
1966	4510	.06	.06	.13	.17	.15	.15	.11	.07	.04	.03	.02	.003	737

35-44

1957	3106	.10	.17	.21	.18	.17	.09	.05	.007	.01	.004	.006	0	721
1966	4961	.07	.06	.10	.13	.14	.13	.11	.10	.05	.05	.04	.004	721

45-54

1957	3082	.10	.17	.22	.19	.17	.09	.03	.01	.006	.004	.007	0	542
1966	4272	.08	.06	.17	.15	.14	.13	.10	.06	.06	.03	.02	.004	542

[a]See Note a, Table 4-1 for earning categories.

[b]The number of observations in the less than 25 age group increased from 4971 in 1957 to 16,525 in 1966.

[c]The number of observations in the less than 25 age group increased from 602 in 1957 to 2419 in 1966.

Table 4.5
Female Income Distributions by Race and Age, 1957-68

White
Reporting Group

	Median	1[a]	2	3	4	5	6	7	8	9	10	11	12	Number of Observations
							25-34							
1957	1634	.36	.21	.20	.16	.06	.008	.001	.001	.001	0	.001	0	4186[b]
1966	2340	.29	.17	.15	.14	.12	.07	.04	.01	.007	.004	.003	.001	4423[c]
							35-44							
1957	1883	.33	.20	.21	.15	.08	.02	.007	.002	.001	.001	.002	0	4171
1966	2791	.21	.16	.16	.17	.13	.08	.045	.022	.01	.004	.005	.001	5327
							45-54							
1957	2151	.27	.20	.23	.16	.09	.03	.008	.006	.003	.001	.002	.001	3822
1966	2937	.18	.15	.18	.17	.13	.08	.06	.02	.01	.006	.008	.002	2958

Full Coverage Group

	Median	1[a]	2	3	4	5	6	7	8	9	10	11	12	Number of Observations
							25-34							
1957	2407	.21	.20	.25	.23	.10	.01	.001	.001	.001	0	.003	0	1366
1966	4042	.10	.09	.13	.17	.20	.14	.11	.03	.02	.01	.006	.002	1366
							35-44							
1957	2414	.19	.20	.25	.21	.11	.03	.01	.002	.001	.001	.002	0	2220
1966	3868	.07	.10	.15	.21	.19	.14	.08	.04	.02	.006	.009	.003	2220
							45-54							
1957	2600	.16	.18	.27	.20	.13	.03	.01	.007	.004	.001	.003	.001	2234
1966	3741	.08	.10	.17	.20	.18	.11	.08	.03	.01	.01	.01	.005	2234

Nonwhite
Reporting Group

25-34												
1957	895	.54	.25	.15	.06	.006	0	0	0	0	0	0	645[d]
1966	1724	.34	.20	.17	.12	.08	.02	.007	.004	.001	.004	0	842
35-44												
1957	1062	.48	.28	.15	.07	.01	.005	0	0	0	.001	0	611
1966	1606	.34	.22	.19	.11	.06	.01	.005	.008	.004	.004	0	750
45-54												
1957	1105	.46	.28	.17	.06	.03	0	.004	0	0	0	0	498
1966	1472	.38	.22	.14	.14	.05	.02	.004	.004	.002	.002	0	511

Nonwhite
Full Coverage Group

25-34												
1957	1560	.32	.31	.25	.11	.01	0	0	0	0	0	0	232
1966	3025	.13	.15	.20	.20	.14	.06	.01	.009	.004	.009	0	232
35-44												
1957	1621	.28	.34	.24	.10	.02	.007	0	0	0	.003	0	290
1966	2744	.14	.20	.26	.18	.09	.03	.007	.02	.01	.003	0	290
45-54												
1957	1629	.32	.31	.22	.09	.04	0	.008	0	0	0	0	258
1966	2563	.18	.21	.19	.22	.08	.03	.008	.004	.004	.004	0	258

[a]See Note a, Table 4-1 for earning categories.

[b]The number of observations in the less than 25 age group increased from 3421 in 1957 to 9966 in 1966.

[c]Note that the number of females in the 25-54 age group increased from 1957 to 1966, whereas number of males in this age group declined. This was true for both whites and nonwhites.

[d]The number of observations in the less than 25 age group increased from 289 in 1957 to 1632 in 1966.

Table 4-6
Theil Coefficients for Males by Race and Age, 1966

	White		Nonwhite	
	Reporting	Full Coverage	Reporting	Full Coverage
25-34	.19	.15	.22	.16
35-44	.23	.18	.26	.17
45-54	.26	.21	.24	.17
55-64	.44	.35	.43	.30

(1953), Cramer (1971), Cramer (1957), Mandelbrot (1960), and Mincer (1970). For the most part, these theories are not sufficiently powerful to justify the a priori choice of one skew family of distributions over any other skew family. The main reason for the popularity of the Pareto and lognormal families is that they are mathematically convenient and sometimes provide approximations that are "good enough" for the purpose at hand.

The lognormal distribution has the following density function

$$f(y) = \frac{1}{\sqrt{2\pi}\,\sigma} \exp\left(-(y-\mu)^2 \Big/ 2\sigma^2\right) ,$$

where $y = \log x$ and μ and σ^2 are the mean and variance of the log of income. Under these conditions, x is said to have a lognormal distribution.

The density function for the Pareto distribution is given by

$$f(x) = \frac{\alpha x_0^{\alpha}}{x^{\alpha+1}}$$

where α is the Pareto constant and x_0 is the point such that below x_0 the Pareto distribution does not apply. In estimating the Pareto, several different values of x_0 were tried.

All individuals who had covered earnings in the given year were used to estimate the lognormal and Pareto distributions for each year and for each of the four subgroups male white, male nonwhite, female white, and female nonwhite. The actual distributions were then compared with theoretical distributions possessing parameter values that were estimated from the data. Both χ-square and Kolmogorov-Smirnov goodness of fit tests were applied.[9] For all of the forty distributions tested, the lognormal *always* provided a substantially better fit than the Pareto. This was true for both the χ-square and Kolmogorov-Smirnov criteria. These results are shown in Table 4-16 for selected years when x_0,

Table 4-7
Total Median Relative Earnings Distribution

						Reporting Group									Number of
	Median	1[a]	2	3	4	5	6	7	8	9	10	11	12	13	Observations
1957	2570	.190	.121	.097	.093	.092	.080	.084	.063	.086	.044	.022	.009	.020	62822
1966	3423	.190	.122	.093	.095	.084	.077	.076	.060	.090	.050	.027	.013	.024	68411
							Full Coverage Group								
1957	3375	.121	.124	.125	.130	.140	.113	.091	.061	.058	.021	.009	.004	.005	34029
1966	5752	.089	.101	.150	.162	.164	.129	.088	.049	.042	.014	.007	.003	.005	34029

aThe relative earnings (total earnings ÷ median earnings) categories are: 1. 0-.25, 2. .26-.50, 3. .51-.75, 4. .76-1.00, 5. 1.01-1.25, 6. 1.26-1.50, 7. 1.51-1.75, 8. 1.76-2.00, 9. 2.01-2.50, 10. 2.51-3.00, 11. 3.01-3.50, 12. 3.51-4.00, 13. > 4.00.

Table 4-8
White Median Relative Earnings Distribution for 1957 and 1966

						Reporting Group									
1957	2734	.186	.120	.096	.098	.093	.087	.086	.065	.084	.039	.019	.009	.019	55982
1966	3665	.188	.120	.094	.098	.089	.081	.081	.061	.088	.044	.025	.010	.022	60572
							Full Coverage								
1957	3564	.118	.120	.127	.134	.149	.119	.088	.060	.053	.016	.008	.004	.004	30459
1966	6036	.087	.096	.151	.166	.176	.136	.079	.044	.039	.013	.006	.003	.004	30459

Table 4-9
Nonwhite Median Relative Earnings Distribution for 1957 and 1966

	Median	1[a]	2	3	4	5	6	7	8	9	10	11	12	13	Number of Observations
							Reporting Group								
1957	1483	.186	.121	.104	.090	.075	.077	.065	.055	.078	.065	.041	.021	.024	6840
1966	2166	.189	.126	.106	.080	.080	.078	.065	.050	.076	.062	.037	.023	.029	7839
							Full Coverage								
1957	2134	.129	.119	.128	.124	.124	.093	.068	.069	.086	.036	.013	.006	.005	3570
1966	3776	.101	.108	.129	.162	.132	.111	.092	.062	.071	.021	.007	.003	.002	3570

Table 4-10
Female Median Relative Earnings Distribution for 1957 and 1966

	Median	1[a]	2	3	4	5	6	7	8	9	10	11	12	13	Number of Observations
							Reporting Group								
1957	1487	.202	.122	.096	.080	.075	.076	.075	.067	.101	.065	.023	.008	.010	21492
1966	2019	.200	.123	.099	.078	.080	.080	.072	.061	.099	.061	.024	.010	.013	24620
							Full Coverage								
1957	2241	.130	.118	.115	.137	.145	.121	.097	.072	.045	.012	.044	.002	.002	8545
1966	3594	.099	.115	.120	.166	.165	.140	.085	.057	.036	.009	.003	.002	.002	8545

aSee Note a, Table 4-7 for earnings categories.

Table 4-11
Male Median Relative Earnings Distribution for 1957 and 1966

	Median	1[a]	2	3	4	5	6	7	8	9	10	11	12	13	Number of Observations
							Reporting Group								
1957	3746	.168	.123	.100	.109	.130	.114	.089	.059	.059	.021	.010	.005	.013	41330
1966	4880	.173	.121	.102	.104	.116	.107	.089	.063	.067	.026	.010	.007	.015	43791
						Full Coverage									
1957	4000	.115	.125	.123	.138	.171	.135	.086	.047	.040	.013	.005	.002	.003	25484
1966	6627	.073	.084	.144	.199	.198	.139	.074	.035	.033	.011	.005	.002	.003	25484

Table 4-12
White Male Relative Earnings Distribution for 1957 and 1966

	Median	1	2	3	4	5	6	7	8	9	10	11	12	13	Number of Observations
							Reporting Group								
1957	3710	.165	.120	.102	.114	.142	.120	.088	.056	.052	.017	.009	.005	.013	36901
1966	5236	.175	.112	.104	.109	.130	.117	.086	.058	.059	.020	.010	.006	.014	38917
						Full Coverage									
1957	4182	.113	.117	.121	.149	.182	.133	.085	.041	.037	.012	.005	.002	.002	22886
1966	6889	.068	.076	.146	.211	.207	.138	.070	.040	.029	.011	.005	.002	.004	22886

aSee Note a, Table 4-7 for earnings categories.

Table 4-13
Nonwhite Male Relative Earnings Distribution for 1957 and 1966

	Median	Reporting Group													Number of Observations
		1[a]	2	3	4	5	6	7	8	9	10	11	12	13	
1957	2001	.175	.117	.110	.099	.098	.093	.064	.065	.101	.046	.022	.005	.008	4429
1966	2932	.180	.111	.103	.106	.098	.084	.065	.059	.092	.055	.025	.014	.009	4874
								Full Coverage							
1957	2455	.119	.116	.129	.136	.120	.097	.094	.071	.078	.026	.009	.002	.003	2598
1966	4317	.088	.094	.152	.166	.145	.122	.101	.056	.057	.013	.005	.001	.002	2598

Table 4-14
White Female Relative Earnings Distribution for 1957 and 1966

	Median	Reporting Group													Number of Observations
		1[a]	2	3	4	5	6	7	8	9	10	11	12	13	
1957	1604	.203	.120	.096	.080	.080	.083	.082	.070	.009	.055	.016	.007	.008	19081
1966	2165	.203	.118	.100	.080	.085	.089	.075	.065	.104	.047	.019	.006	.011	21655
								Full Coverage							
1957	2363	.126	.116	.112	.146	.154	.129	.098	.066	.038	.009	.003	.002	.002	7573
1966	3718	.095	.109	.125	.172	.172	.145	.084	.053	.031	.008	.003	.002	.002	7573

Table 4-15
Nonwhite Female Relative Earnings Distribution for 1957 and 1966

	Median	1[a]	2	3	4	5	6	7	8	9	10	11	12	13	Number of Observations
								Reporting Group							
1957	872	.172	.138	.103	.088	.076	.070	.051	.047	.094	.064	.037	.024	.038	2411
1966	1335	.172	.131	.104	.093	.072	.054	.052	.053	.085	.059	.041	.029	.055	2965
							Full Coverage								
1957	1460	.120	.132	.125	.125	.114	.109	.096	.051	.069	.042	.007	.004	.006	972
1966	2686	.106	.154	.111	.129	.153	.106	.082	.047	.070	.020	.014	.004	.003	972

[a]See Note a, Table 4-7 for earnings categories.

Table 4-16
Goodness of Fit Tests for Lognormal and Pareto Distributions, 1957, 1962, 1966, by Race and Sex (x_O = \$300)

Year	Group	χ^2 Normal/χ^2 Pareto	Kolmogorov-Smirnov Normal	Kilmogorov-Smirnov Pareto
1957	Male White (1)	.0365	.1009	.3070
1957	Female White (2)	.0189	.0830	.2516
1957	Male Nonwhite (3)	.0160	.0635	.2739
1957	Female Nonwhite (4)	.0043	.0376	.1756
1962	1	.0393	.1068	.3096
1962	2	.0207	.0769	.2555
1962	3	.0134	.0519	.2846
1962	4	.0061	.0444	.1899
1966	1	.0473	.1139	.3064
1966	2	.0247	.0836	.2542
1966	3	.0255	.0775	.2687
1966	4	.0092	.0480	.2101

the truncation point for the Pareto distribution, was set equal to \$300. The truncation point was varied from \$100 to \$1000 without altering the superiority of the lognormal. Nevertheless, even though the fit was much improved when a lognormal was applied instead of a Pareto, the hypothesis of lognormality was always rejected at very high significance levels. This result was not unexpected because of the large sample sizes used in all these fits. Given these sample sizes, no standard distribution could survive either of these goodness of fit tests.

Table 4-17 shows the relation between the actual and theoretical earnings distributions when a lognormal form was applied to male-white earnings for 1957. The fit is not too bad for low earnings, but does poorly in the higher earnings ranges. This poor performance is a consequence of the method used by the Social Security Administration in estimating annual earnings. Regardless of total annual earnings, this method never permits an observation to exceed a fairly conservative minimum.[10] Furthermore, estimated income is based only on covered earnings and therefore constantly underestimates total annual earnings. Accordingly, the upper tail of the observed earning distribution is much thinner than it should be.

If the distribution is lognormal, T, the entropy measure of inequality used by Theil reduces to

$$T = \sigma^2 \Big/ 2 \, ,$$

Table 4-17
Comparison between Actual and Theoretical Distribution for a Lognormal
Approximation, Male Whites, 1957

Interval	Observed Frequency	Theoretical Frequency
< 500	.107	.102
1000	.068	.134
1500	.076	.109
2000	.054	.087
2500	.053	.074
3000	.061	.058
3500	.059	.047
4000	.067	.040
4500	.083	.034
5000	.069	.029
5500	.063	.025
6000	.054	.022
6500	.041	.019
7000	.032	.017
7500	.025	.015
8000	.018	.014
8500	.037	.012
9000	.012	.011
9500	.007	.009
10000	.006	.009
12500	.016	.034
15000	.007	.023
20000	.011	.028
> 20000	.011	.048

where σ^2 is the variance of log earnings. For most of the distributions examined,
this theoretical result was closely approximated.

Mobility within the Income Distribution

Measures of inequality for a cross section of incomes are inadequate to measure
income mobility within a particular society. In two societies identical with
respect to these cross-section measures, the first might have individuals persistently earning the same annual incomes over time, whereas the second might
have individuals randomly assigned to income classes from year to year. The
greater income mobility that is evident in the second society could be detected

only by a longitudinal analysis, that is, an investigation of individual income behavior over time. The longitudinal data of the Social Security file permit such an investigation.

In this study of income mobility, special emphasis is placed on racial differences. It will be shown that the earnings of nonwhite males who made movements across low-income thresholds are more responsive to changes in GNP than their white counterparts. On the other hand, nonwhite males are more likely to remain in low-income categories than demographically similar whites. Of course, white and nonwhite income mobility are quite different in that the average income of whites is substantially greater than that of nonwhites. The question addressed here is whether or not there are differences in income mobility in addition to these mean differences.

Two measures will be used to assess mobility differentials between whites and nonwhites. The first simply looks at the variance of log income for each individual over the ten years. These are averaged over all whites and then over all nonwhites in the sample, and the magnitudes of both are compared. The second is a calculation of the stayer proportions across the entire income distribution. These calculations include all classes of the income distribution. Finally, the ten-step Markov transition matrix is calculated. This assigns a probability to each of the 144 entries in the 12x12 matrix that relates a transition from income class i in 1957 to income class j in 1966, where i and j run over all 12 of the income classes. A matrix like this has been calculated for 12 different demographic groups.

Variance Method

The total variation of individual income about the average income for the ten years, S, was decomposed into S_1, the variation caused by individuals deviating from their own ten-year averages; and S_2, the variation produced by deviations of individual means from the average income for the ten years, the grand mean.[11] The estimated variance associated with S_1, s_1^2, is a crude measure of the mobility of individual incomes over the ten years. If $S_1 = 0$, the initial distribution of income would be invariant over time and the situation could be said to characterize perfect immobility. The inequality associated with the initial distribution would persist over time. A convenient measure of income inequality over the ten-year period is s_2^2, the estimated variance calculated from S_2. Note that s_2^2 measures the variation of average individual incomes over the ten years about the grand mean. It therefore represents a better measure of income inequality than the variances calculated for any one year.[12] If $S_2 = 0$, average incomes would be equal over time and changes in annual income for individuals could occur only through positive values of S_1. In fact neither S_1 nor S_2 is close to zero. A simple one-way analysis of variance shows that average individual incomes (over the ten years) are significantly different from one another. This was true for all four race and sex combinations.[13]

Table 4-18 presents the calculated values of s_1^2 and s_2^2 by race and sex for both the reporting group and the fully covered group. These results suggest that for the reporting group male-white incomes possess more inequality than nonwhite male incomes, whereas the opposite is true for the full coverage group. However, for both groups there is greater mobility among nonwhite males. This is consistent with the findings of the poverty dynamics model (see Chapter 5 and Appendix A). The inequality and mobility measures are very similar for white and nonwhite women.

If it was impossible to identify individual ten-year income patterns, it would be impossible to decompose S into S_1 and S_2. The total sample could be partitioned by race and sex, all observations being viewed as a single cross section, and S could be estimated by s^2. The results of this longitudinal blindness are presented in Table 4-19. The overall variability of income is greater (less) for white males than for nonwhites in the reporting (full coverage) group. There is little difference between white and nonwhite females.

Table 4-18
Calculated Values of s_1^2 and s_2^2 by Race and Sex, 1957-66

Reporting Group			Full Coverage Group	
s_1^2	s_2^2		s_1^2	s_2^2
.119	2.00	White Males	.059	.804
.152	1.45	Nonwhite Males	.079	.856
.165	1.11	White Females	.064	.873
.153	1.09	Nonwhite Females	.067	.878

Table 4-19
Calculated Values of s^2 by Race and Sex, 1957-1966

Reporting Group		Full Coverage Group
.385	White Males	.134
.345	Nonwhite Males	.156
.341	White Females	.145
.335	Nonwhite Females	.148

Stayer Proportions

The probability of remaining in a particular income class for the entire ten-year period, given occupancy in that class in 1957, is the definition of a stayer proportion. A concept like this is useful in interpreting income mobility over time. Table 4-20 presents the stayer proportions as functions of the eleven different partition points along the income distribution. The proportion who remained covered is also noted.[14] In Table 4-20 four age groups are distinguished: 25-34, 35-44, 45-54, and 55-64.

In a comparison of white and nonwhite males, the nonwhite stayer proportion is less than the white for the under $1000 income class. However, the modest income levels—$3000, $4000, and $5000—there is a much higher probability for nonwhites to remain below these levels than whites. For example, the probability of a nonwhite in the 35-44 age group staying below $5000 is .33; the corresponding probability for whites is .16. The covered proportions are lower for nonwhites than whites.

The Ten-Step Transition Matrix

As a final indicator of differences in income mobility among various demographic groups, the ten-step Markov transition matrix was calculated. For an individual with given demographic characteristics, this ten-step matrix tells the probability of being in income class j in 1966 given occupancy in income class i in 1957. Let P^9 denote the ten-step transition matrix; then $p^{(0)}$, the initial (1957) marginal income distribution is related to $p^{(9)}$, the final (1966) marginal distribution by

$$p^{(9)} = p^{(0)} P^9$$

where P^9 is the product of the nine year-to-year one-step Markov transition matrixes. If the underlying stochastic process were stationary over time, the rows of P^n would converge to the steady-state distribution of the process, as n went to infinity. The process is, however, nonstationary, so this nice convergence does not take place here. Nevertheless, the ten-step Markov matrix does provide insight into the structure of income mobility during 1957-66. Tables 4-21 and 4-22 are respectively displays of the white and nonwhite male Markov matrixes for the 35-44 age group; Tables 4-23 through 4-26 present Markov matrixes for the 25-34 and 45-54 age groups; Tables 4-27 through 4-32 report similar matrixes for females.

If a male white in this age group begins with a 1957 income between $3000 and $3999, the probability of his moving to an income greater than $4000 by 1966 is .79, the probability of his moving to an income less than $3000 is .13,

Table 4-20
Stayer Proportions for Different Income Levels, 1957-66

	<1000	<2000	<3000	<4000	<5000	<6000	<7000	<8000	<9000	<10,000	<15,000	Covered
Male white												
25-34	.008	.021	.035	.084	.147	.207	.289	.387	.482	.556	.698	.745
35-44	.020	.047	.070	.108	.158	.210	.290	.370	.456	.524	.675	.747
45-54	.031	.065	.097	.146	.201	.267	.338	.417	.486	.543	.651	.700
55-64	.023	.043	.083	.128	.169	.209	.253	.303	.337	.363	.414	.437
Male nonwhite												
25-34	.003	.041	.114	.241	.344	.430	.504	.564	.597	.622	.648	.651
35-44	.020	.077	.170	.250	.327	.398	.455	.526	.576	.618	.659	.662
45-54	.018	.065	.211	.304	.352	.429	.487	.525	.565	.590	.617	.621
55-64	.050	.107	.187	.248	.288	.309	.336	.372	.392	.411	.417	.419
Female white												
25-34	.007	.031	.077	.134	.209	.261	.298	.311	.317	.321	.327	.327
35-44	.015	.060	.144	.252	.353	.440	.486	.510	.522	.528	.536	.538
45-54	.042	.113	.204	.313	.415	.482	.532	.554	.563	.574	.589	.593
55-64	.036	.108	.179	.254	.306	.349	.372	.380	.386	.389	.398	.400
Female nonwhite												
25-34	.006	.055	.139	.220	.276	.326	.349	.357	.360	.361	.364	.364
35-44	.041	.129	.255	.351	.400	.440	.454	.457	.466	.472	.478	.478
45-54	.097	.214	.301	.420	.462	.490	.514	.522	.524	.526	.532	.532
55-64	.120	.198	.269	.318	.331	.340	.348	.348	.350	.350	.358	.358

Table 4-21
Ten-Step Markov Matrix for Male Whites in the 35-44 Age Group, 1957-66

1957 \ 1966	<1000	1-1999	2-2999	3-3999	4-4999	5-5999	6-6999	7-7999	8-8999	9-9999	10-15000	>15000	1957 Total #
<1000	.2610	.1312	.1251	.1103	.0815	.0832	.0541	.0332	.0253	.0312	.0352	.0277	479
1-1999	.1794	.1092	.1192	.1513	.1269	.0920	.0622	.0498	.0274	.0348	.0423	.0149	402
2-2999	.0648	.0602	.0708	.1446	.2424	.1446	.1190	.0437	.0301	.0301	.0406	.0090	664
3-3999	.0522	.0355	.0433	.0832	.1653	.1921	.2009	.0721	.0610	.0377	.0477	.0089	901
4-4999	.0253	.0261	.0283	.0395	.0633	.1363	.2427	.1794	.1050	.0678	.0722	.0141	1343
5-5999	.0171	.0108	.0217	.0202	.0326	.0575	.1401	.2016	.2093	.1221	.1464	.0195	1285
6-6999	.0168	.0090	.0101	.0090	.0236	.0224	.0719	.1213	.1658	.1628	.3285	.0562	889
7-7999	.0074	.0056	.0056	.0149	.0056	.0205	.0372	.1043	.1043	.1434	.4548	.0915	536
8-8999	.0126	.0031	.0126	.0159	.0126	.0159	.0411	.0343	.0639	.0912	.4922	.1991	316
9-9999	.0062	0	.0062	.0306	0	.0185	.0185	.0185	.0246	.0368	.4789	.3612	163
10-15000	.0072	0	.0109	.0182	.0072	.0109	.0361	.0182	.0295	.0255	.2293	.6016	274
>15000	0	.0229	.0114	0	0	.0114	.0344	0	.0114	.0114	.1369	.7575	87
1966 Total #	369	242	281	395	557	646	930	813	645	597	1238	530	

Table 4-22
Ten-Step Markov Matrix for Male Nonwhites in the 35-44 Age Group, 1957-66

1957 \ 1966	<1000	1-1999	2-2999	3-3999	4-4999	5-5999	6-6999	7-7999	8-8999	9-9999	10-15000	>15000	1957 Total #
<1000	.3071	.1811	.1741	.1671	.0901	.0350	.0139	.0069	.0069	0	.0139	0	143
1-1999	.1893	.1681	.2434	.1490	.0871	.0678	.0337	.0337	.0203	.0068	0	0	148
2-2999	.0891	.0736	.1362	.2307	.2192	.1204	.0527	.0361	.0105	.0210	.0053	.0053	191
3-3999	.0472	.0472	.0678	.1015	.2434	.2434	.1219	.0608	.0337	.0135	.0203	0	148
4-4999	.0226	.0300	.0150	.0375	.0452	.1355	.2711	.2408	.0903	.0753	.0226	.0075	133
5-5999	.0273	0	.0273	.0546	.0546	.0821	.1759	.1913	.1913	.0821	.1094	0	73
6-6999	0	.0542	0	.0542	.0542	.1084	.0271	.1897	.0542	.2168	.2168	.0271	37
7-7999	.2000	0	0	0	0	0	0	.2000	.2000	0	.4000	0	5
8-8999	0	0	0	0	.1250	0	.1250	0	.1250	.1250	.5000	0	8
9-9999	0	0	0	0	0	0	.3333	0	0	.3333	.3333	0	3
10-15000	.2500	0	0	0	0	.2500	.2500	0	0	0	.2500	0	4
>15000	0	0	0	0	0	0	0	0	0	0	0	0	0
1966 Total #	103	78	101	116	117	103	89	76	41	33	33	4	

Table 4-23
Ten-Step Markov Matrix for White Males in the 25-34 Age Group

			<1000	1-1999	2-2999	3-3999	4-4999	5-5999	6-6999	7-7999	8-8999	9-9999	10-15000	>15000	UNCOV
M	W	25-34	<1000	0.10	0.09	0.07	0.07	0.07	0.05	0.05	0.05	0.06	0.03	0.06	0.01	0.29
M	W	25-34	1-1999	0.06	0.05	0.06	0.09	0.11	0.07	0.11	0.08	0.07	0.04	0.08	0.02	0.16
M	W	25-34	2-2999	0.04	0.03	0.05	0.10	0.18	0.13	0.10	0.08	0.05	0.04	0.06	0.01	0.13
M	W	25-34	3-3999	0.03	0.02	0.02	0.06	0.09	0.13	0.16	0.12	0.10	0.06	0.07	0.02	0.11
M	W	25-34	4-4999	0.02	0.02	0.02	0.03	0.04	0.07	0.18	0.16	0.14	0.10	0.12	0.02	0.08
M	W	25-34	5-5999	0.01	0.01	0.01	0.02	0.02	0.04	0.09	0.14	0.16	0.13	0.21	0.05	0.10
M	W	25-34	6-6999	0.02	0.00	0.01	0.01	0.02	0.02	0.06	0.09	0.13	0.15	0.33	0.07	0.08
M	W	25-34	7-7999	0.0	0.01	0.01	0.01	0.00	0.01	0.03	0.04	0.07	0.13	0.48	0.14	0.07
M	W	25-34	8-8999	0.03	0.01	0.01	0.03	0.03	0.0	0.06	0.07	0.03	0.09	0.35	0.23	0.07
M	W	25-34	9-9999	0.0	0.0	0.0	0.02	0.02	0.0	0.04	0.07	0.04	0.02	0.33	0.43	0.04
M	W	25-34	10-15000	0.01	0.0	0.03	0.0	0.0	0.0	0.07	0.07	0.04	0.01	0.32	0.38	0.07
M	W	25-34	>15000	0.14	0.0	0.0	0.0	0.0	0.0	0.0	0.0	0.07	0.0	0.07	0.71	0.0
M	W	25-34	UNCOV	0.10	0.07	0.07	0.07	0.06	0.05	0.07	0.04	0.04	0.03	0.08	0.03	0.30

Table 4-24

Ten-Step Markov Matrix for Nonwhite Males in the 25-34 Age Group

	<1000	1-1999	2-2999	3-3999	4-4999	5-5999	6-6999	7-7999	8-8999	9-9999	10-15000	>15000	UNCOV
M NW 25-34 <1000	0.13	0.13	0.12	0.15	0.09	0.06	0.03	0.02	0.02	0.01	0.01	0.01	0.22
M NW 25-34 1-1999	0.07	0.09	0.16	0.16	0.12	0.08	0.07	0.03	0.01	0.02	0.01	0.0	0.17
M NW 25-34 2-2999	0.08	0.04	0.11	0.21	0.19	0.13	0.07	0.04	0.01	0.02	0.00	0.0	0.11
M NW 25-34 3-3999	0.05	0.04	0.04	0.10	0.11	0.18	0.18	0.09	0.02	0.03	0.01	0.0	0.13
M NW 25-34 4-4999	0.04	0.01	0.01	0.04	0.11	0.16	0.27	0.13	0.11	0.05	0.04	0.0	0.05
M NW 25-34 5-5999	0.0	0.0	0.0	0.03	0.11	0.21	0.05	0.18	0.18	0.0	0.08	0.03	0.13
M NW 25-34 6-6999	0.0	0.0	0.0	0.0	0.0	0.09	0.0	0.27	0.09	0.09	0.27	0.0	0.18
M NW 25-34 7-7999	0.0	0.0	0.0	0.0	0.0	0.0	0.0	0.0	0.0	0.50	0.50	0.0	0.0
M NW 25-34 8-8999	0.0	0.0	0.0	0.0	0.0	0.0	0.0	0.0	0.0	0.0	1.00	0.0	0.0
M NW 25-34 9-9999	0.0	0.0	0.0	0.0	0.0	0.0	0.0	0.0	0.0	0.0	0.0	0.0	0.0
M NW 25-34 10-15000	0.0	0.0	0.0	0.0	1.00	0.0	0.0	0.0	0.0	0.0	0.0	0.0	0.0
M NW 25-34 >15000	0.0	0.0	0.0	0.0	0.0	0.0	0.0	0.0	0.0	0.0	0.0	0.0	0.0
M NW 25-34 UNCOV	0.16	0.07	0.12	0.09	0.10	0.06	0.06	0.02	0.01	0.00	0.02	0.00	0.28

Table 4-25
Ten-Step Markov Matrix for White Males in the 45-54 Age Group

M	W	45-54	<1000	0.15	0.08	0.06	0.04	0.05	0.03	0.02	0.01	0.00	0.01	0.01	0.00	0.52
M	W	45-54	1-1999	0.07	0.11	0.12	0.07	0.07	0.08	0.04	0.02	0.01	0.01	0.01	0.01	0.37
M	W	45-54	2-2999	0.05	0.07	0.07	0.15	0.15	0.09	0.05	0.04	0.01	0.01	0.02	0.00	0.28
M	W	45-54	3-3999	0.03	0.03	0.04	0.10	0.18	0.17	0.10	0.07	0.03	0.01	0.02	0.01	0.21
M	W	45-54	4-4999	0.02	0.03	0.02	0.04	0.08	0.16	0.20	0.13	0.08	0.03	0.04	0.01	0.16
M	W	45-54	5-5999	0.02	0.02	0.01	0.03	0.05	0.07	0.16	0.18	0.17	0.07	0.06	0.01	0.15
M	W	45-54	6-6999	0.02	0.01	0.02	0.02	0.03	0.04	0.09	0.15	0.17	0.14	0.18	0.02	0.11
M	W	45-54	7-7999	0.01	0.02	0.01	0.02	0.02	0.03	0.05	0.08	0.11	0.15	0.31	0.05	0.13
M	W	45-54	8-8999	0.01	0.00	0.01	0.01	0.03	0.01	0.05	0.05	0.06	0.09	0.47	0.07	0.13
M	W	45-54	9-9999	0.01	0.01	0.03	0.01	0.01	0.04	0.04	0.04	0.06	0.10	0.41	0.17	0.07
M	W	45-54	10-15000	0.00	0.00	0.01	0.02	0.01	0.02	0.03	0.03	0.04	0.03	0.31	0.37	0.11
M	W	45-54	>15000	0.03	0.02	0.01	0.0	0.0	0.01	0.02	0.03	0.01	0.01	0.09	0.67	0.10
M	W	45-54	UNCOV	0.13	0.07	0.06	0.06	0.07	0.05	0.06	0.03	0.03	0.01	0.04	0.02	0.39

Table 4-26
Ten-Step Markov Matrix for Nonwhite Males in the 45-54 Age Group

M NW 45-54	<1000	0.21	0.11	0.16	0.04	0.04	0.02	0.01	0.01	0.0	0.01	0.0	0.0	0.39
M NW 45-54	1-1999	0.12	0.11	0.22	0.17	0.05	0.02	0.01	0.01	0.0	0.0	0.0	0.0	0.29
M NW 45-54	2-2999	0.09	0.08	0.18	0.21	0.14	0.06	0.03	0.01	0.01	0.0	0.01	0.0	0.19
M NW 45-54	3-3999	0.03	0.01	0.08	0.12	0.22	0.24	0.09	0.01	0.02	0.01	0.0	0.0	0.16
M NW 45-54	4-4999	0.03	0.01	0.02	0.11	0.07	0.17	0.20	0.07	0.09	0.09	0.04	0.0	0.20
M NW 45-54	5-5999	0.05	0.0	0.04	0.04	0.04	0.07	0.18	0.22	0.18	0.11	0.04	0.0	0.05
M NW 45-54	6-6999	0.0	0.0	0.04	0.04	0.04	0.0	0.07	0.18	0.11	0.13	0.14	0.04	0.32
M NW 45-54	7-7999	0.0	0.0	0.0	0.0	0.0	0.0	0.0	0.13	0.13	0.13	0.25	0.0	0.13
M NW 45-54	8-8999	0.0	0.0	0.0	0.0	0.0	0.25	0.0	0.0	0.25	0.25	0.25	0.25	0.0
M NW 45-54	9-9999	0.0	0.0	0.0	0.0	0.0	0.0	0.0	0.50	0.0	0.0	0.50	0.0	0.0
M NW 45-54	10-15000	0.0	0.0	0.0	0.0	0.0	0.0	0.50	0.0	0.0	0.0	0.25	0.25	0.0
M NW 45-54	>15000	0.0	0.0	0.0	0.0	0.0	0.0	0.0	0.0	0.0	0.0	0.0	0.0	0.0
M NW 45-54	UNCOV	0.19	0.12	0.07	0.07	0.03	0.06	0.03	0.02	0.01	0.01	0.01	0.01	0.39

Table 4-27
Ten-Step Markov Matrix for White Females in the 35-44 Age Group

			<1000	1-1999	2-2999	3-3999	4-4999	5-5999	6-6999	7-7999	8-8999	9-9999	10-15000	>15000	UNCOV
F	W	35-44	<1000	0.17	0.12	0.12	0.10	0.05	0.03	0.01	0.00	0.00	0.0	0.00	0.0	0.38
F	W	35-44	1-1999	0.10	0.12	0.17	0.18	0.08	0.05	0.02	0.00	0.00	0.0	0.00	0.00	0.28
F	W	35-44	2-2999	0.08	0.06	0.11	0.25	0.18	0.07	0.03	0.01	0.00	0.00	0.00	0.0	0.21
F	W	35-44	3-3999	0.04	0.04	0.05	0.11	0.23	0.24	0.08	0.02	0.01	0.01	0.00	0.0	0.18
F	W	35-44	4-4999	0.03	0.05	0.04	0.03	0.10	0.19	0.20	0.14	0.03	0.06	0.02	0.00	0.16
F	W	35-44	5-5999	0.02	0.02	0.05	0.01	0.02	0.06	0.12	0.23	0.16	0.04	0.05	0.0	0.17
F	W	35-44	6-6999	0.0	0.07	0.07	0.04	0.07	0.0	0.11	0.07	0.19	0.0	0.19	0.0	0.15
F	W	35-44	7-7999	0.14	0.0	0.0	0.0	0.14	0.0	0.14	0.0	0.0	0.33	0.29	0.0	0.29
F	W	35-44	8-8999	0.0	0.0	0.0	0.0	0.0	0.0	0.0	0.0	0.0	0.0	0.0	0.33	0.33
F	W	35-44	9-9999	0.0	0.0	0.0	0.0	0.20	0.0	0.0	0.20	0.0	0.0	0.0	0.20	0.40
F	W	35-44	10-15000	0.0	0.0	0.0	0.0	0.0	0.14	0.14	0.0	0.0	0.0	0.0	0.29	0.43
F	W	35-44	>15000	0.0	0.0	0.0	0.0	0.0	0.0	0.0	0.0	1.00	0.0	0.0	0.0	0.0
F	W	35-44	UNCOV	0.21	0.14	0.12	0.09	0.06	0.03	0.01	0.01	0.00	0.00	0.00	0.0	0.32

Table 4-28
Ten-Step Markov Matrix for Nonwhite Females in the 35-44 Age Group

F NW 35-44	<1000	0.25	0.20	0.13	0.05	0.02	0.00	0.0	0.0	0.0	0.0	0.0	0.0	0.34
F NW 35-44	1-1999	0.14	0.15	0.27	0.14	0.04	0.03	0.0	0.01	0.01	0.0	0.0	0.0	0.22
F NW 35-44	2-2999	0.05	0.12	0.21	0.22	0.15	0.09	0.01	0.0	0.01	0.01	0.01	0.0	0.12
F NW 35-44	3-3999	0.05	0.05	0.05	0.10	0.14	0.19	0.10	0.02	0.02	0.02	0.0	0.0	0.26
F NW 35-44	4-4999	0.0	0.0	0.0	0.0	0.14	0.0	0.57	0.0	0.14	0.0	0.0	0.0	0.14
F NW 35-44	5-5999	0.0	0.0	0.0	0.0	0.0	0.0	0.0	0.0	0.50	0.0	0.50	0.0	0.0
F NW 35-44	6-6999	0.0	0.0	0.33	0.0	0.0	0.0	0.0	0.0	0.0	0.33	0.0	0.33	0.33
F NW 35-44	7-7999	0.0	0.0	0.0	0.0	0.0	0.0	0.0	0.0	0.0	0.0	0.0	0.0	0.0
F NW 35-44	8-8999	0.0	0.0	0.0	0.0	0.0	0.0	0.0	0.0	0.0	0.0	0.0	0.0	0.0
F NW 35-44	9-9999	0.0	0.0	0.0	0.0	0.0	0.0	0.0	0.0	0.0	0.0	0.0	0.0	0.0
F NW 35-44	10-15000	0.0	0.0	0.0	0.0	0.0	0.0	0.0	0.0	0.0	0.0	0.0	0.0	0.0
F NW 35-44	>15000	0.0	0.0	0.0	0.0	0.0	0.0	0.0	0.0	0.0	0.0	0.0	0.0	0.0
F NW 35-44	UNCOV	0.33	0.16	0.08	0.04	0.03	0.02	0.00	0.00	0.0	0.0	0.00	0.0	0.33

Table 4-29
Ten-Step Markov Matrix for White Females in the 25-34 Age Group

F	W	25-34	<1000	0.18	0.09	0.09	0.07	0.05	0.02	0.01	0.00	0.00	0.0	0.00	0.0	0.48
F	W	25-34	1-1999	0.12	0.10	0.12	0.11	0.08	0.03	0.02	0.00	0.00	0.0	0.00	0.00	0.42
F	W	25-34	2-2999	0.10	0.05	0.08	0.12	0.13	0.06	0.03	0.01	0.01	0.0	0.00	0.0	0.42
F	W	25-34	3-3999	0.06	0.04	0.05	0.05	0.16	0.12	0.08	0.02	0.00	0.01	0.00	0.00	0.40
F	W	25-34	4-4999	0.03	0.02	0.07	0.04	0.05	0.10	0.22	0.04	0.05	0.02	0.00	0.0	0.34
F	W	25-34	5-5999	0.03	0.06	0.03	0.06	0.0	0.06	0.15	0.06	0.0	0.09	0.03	0.0	0.42
F	W	25-34	6-6999	0.0	0.0	0.25	0.0	0.0	0.0	0.0	0.0	0.0	0.0	0.0	0.0	0.75
F	W	25-34	7-7999	0.0	0.0	0.0	0.0	0.0	0.25	0.0	0.0	0.0	0.0	0.50	0.0	0.25
F	W	25-34	8-8999	0.0	0.0	0.0	0.0	0.0	0.0	0.0	0.0	0.0	0.0	0.0	0.50	0.50
F	W	25-34	9-9999	0.0	0.0	0.0	0.0	0.0	0.0	0.0	0.0	0.0	0.0	0.0	0.0	0.0
F	W	25-34	10-15000	0.0	0.0	0.0	0.25	0.0	0.0	0.0	0.50	0.0	0.0	0.25	0.0	0.0
F	W	25-34	>15000	0.0	0.0	0.0	0.0	0.0	0.0	0.0	0.0	0.0	0.0	0.0	0.0	0.0
F	W	25-34	UNCOV	0.24	0.14	0.10	0.08	0.05	0.03	0.01	0.00	0.00	0.00	0.00	0.0	0.36

Table 4-30
Ten-Step Markov Matrix for Nonwhite Females in the 25-34 Age Group

	<1000	1-1999	2-2999	3-3999	4-4999	5-5999	6-6999	7-7999	8-8999	9-9999	10-15000	>15000	UNCOV
F NW 25-34 <1000	0.22	0.17	0.12	0.07	0.02	0.01	0.01	0.0	0.0	0.0	0.0	0.0	0.37
F NW 25-34 1-1999	0.19	0.10	0.20	0.13	0.07	0.05	0.01	0.0	0.0	0.0	0.01	0.0	0.24
F NW 25-34 2-2999	0.06	0.16	0.14	0.18	0.16	0.07	0.05	0.02	0.0	0.0	0.0	0.0	0.16
F NW 25-34 3-3999	0.08	0.05	0.03	0.13	0.18	0.05	0.16	0.05	0.05	0.03	0.0	0.0	0.18
F NW 25-34 4-4999	0.25	0.0	0.0	0.0	0.25	0.0	0.0	0.0	0.0	0.0	0.25	0.0	0.25
F NW 25-34 5-5999	0.0	0.0	0.0	0.0	0.0	0.0	0.0	0.0	0.0	0.0	0.0	0.0	0.0
F NW 25-34 6-6999	0.0	0.0	0.0	0.0	0.0	0.0	0.0	0.0	0.0	0.0	0.0	0.0	0.0
F NW 25-34 7-7999	0.0	0.0	0.0	0.0	0.0	0.0	0.0	0.0	0.0	0.0	0.0	0.0	0.0
F NW 25-34 8-8999	0.0	0.0	0.0	0.0	0.0	0.0	0.0	0.0	0.0	0.0	0.0	0.0	0.0
F NW 25-34 9-9999	0.0	0.0	0.0	0.0	0.0	0.0	0.0	0.0	0.0	0.0	0.0	0.0	0.0
F NW 25-34 10-15000	0.0	0.0	0.0	0.0	0.0	0.0	0.0	0.0	0.0	0.0	0.0	0.0	0.0
F NW 25-34 >15000	0.0	0.0	0.0	0.0	0.0	0.0	0.0	0.0	0.0	0.0	0.0	0.0	0.0
F NW 25-34 UNCOV	0.29	0.13	0.10	0.06	0.04	0.02	0.01	0.00	0.00	0.0	0.00	0.0	0.34

Table 4-31
Ten-Step Markov Matrix for White Females in the 45-54 Age Group

			<1000	1-1999	2-2999	3-3999	4-4999	5-5999	6-6999	7-7999	8-8999	9-9999	10-15000	>15000	UNCOV
F	W	45-54	<1000	0.18	0.13	0.12	0.06	0.04	0.02	0.00	0.00	0.00	0.00	0.00	0.0	0.44
F	W	45-54	1-1999	0.13	0.14	0.21	0.14	0.06	0.02	0.01	0.01	0.00	0.0	0.00	0.0	0.28
F	W	45-54	2-2999	0.05	0.06	0.16	0.25	0.17	0.05	0.01	0.00	0.00	0.0	0.0	0.0	0.23
F	W	45-54	3-3999	0.05	0.03	0.06	0.14	0.26	0.20	0.08	0.01	0.00	0.0	0.00	0.0	0.17
F	W	45-54	4-4999	0.03	0.02	0.04	0.05	0.09	0.18	0.25	0.11	0.03	0.01	0.03	0.01	0.14
F	W	45-54	5-5999	0.01	0.03	0.06	0.04	0.05	0.06	0.22	0.18	0.09	0.03	0.04	0.03	0.15
F	W	45-54	6-6999	0.06	0.0	0.0	0.06	0.03	0.03	0.03	0.13	0.13	0.22	0.13	0.0	0.19
F	W	45-54	7-7999	0.0	0.0	0.04	0.04	0.08	0.0	0.08	0.13	0.04	0.21	0.04	0.08	0.29
F	W	45-54	8-8999	0.08	0.0	0.08	0.15	0.08	0.0	0.15	0.08	0.15	0.0	0.08	0.0	0.15
F	W	45-54	9-9999	0.0	0.0	0.0	0.33	0.0	0.0	0.0	0.0	0.0	0.33	0.33	0.0	0.0
F	W	45-54	10-15000	0.0	0.11	0.0	0.11	0.0	0.11	0.22	0.0	0.0	0.11	0.11	0.0	0.22
F	W	45-54	>15000	0.0	0.0	0.0	0.0	0.0	0.0	0.0	0.0	0.0	0.0	0.0	0.67	0.33
F	W	45-54	UNCOV	0.18	0.13	0.13	0.09	0.04	0.02	0.01	0.00	0.00	0.00	0.00	0.00	0.38

Table 4-32
Ten-Step Markov Matrix for Nonwhite Females in the 45-54 Age Group

		<1000	1-1999	2-2999	3-3999	4-4999	5-5999	6-6999	7-7999	8-8999	9-9999	10-15000	>15000	UNCOV
F NW 45-54	<1000	0.29	0.18	0.04	0.04	0.03	0.00	0.00	0.0	0.0	0.0	0.0	0.0	0.41
F NW 45-54	1-1999	0.10	0.20	0.19	0.17	0.01	0.01	0.0	0.01	0.0	0.0	0.0	0.0	0.31
F NW 45-54	2-2999	0.08	0.05	0.20	0.29	0.13	0.04	0.0	0.0	0.0	0.0	0.0	0.0	0.20
F NW 45-54	3-3999	0.03	0.0	0.10	0.17	0.17	0.24	0.17	0.07	0.0	0.07	0.0	0.0	0.10
F NW 45-54	4-4999	0.0	0.0	0.0	0.0	0.07	0.36	0.21	0.0	1.00	0.0	0.0	0.0	0.21
F NW 45-54	5-5999	0.0	0.0	0.0	0.0	0.0	0.0	0.0	0.0	0.0	0.0	0.0	0.0	0.0
F NW 45-54	6-6999	0.0	0.0	0.0	0.50	0.0	0.0	0.0	0.0	0.0	0.0	0.0	0.0	0.0
F NW 45-54	7-7999	0.0	0.0	0.0	0.0	0.0	0.0	0.0	0.0	0.0	0.0	0.50	0.0	0.0
F NW 45-54	8-8999	0.0	0.0	0.0	0.0	0.0	0.0	0.0	0.0	0.0	0.0	0.0	0.0	0.0
F NW 45-54	9-9999	0.0	0.0	0.0	0.0	0.0	0.0	0.0	0.0	0.0	0.0	0.0	0.0	0.0
F NW 45-54	10-15000	0.0	0.0	0.0	0.0	0.0	0.0	0.0	0.0	0.0	0.0	0.0	0.0	0.0
F NW 45-54	>15000	0.0	0.0	0.0	0.0	0.0	0.0	0.0	0.0	0.0	0.0	0.0	0.0	0.0
F NW 45-54	UNCOV	0.37	0.13	0.05	0.03	0.01	0.02	0.00	0.0	0.00	0.0	0.0	0.0	0.37

and the probability of his staying in the $3000-$3999 interval is .08. Similar probabilities for the male nonwhite are, respectively, .74, .16, and .10. Differences become more pronounced for larger income changes. For this same beginning income, the probability of a white earning more than $7000 in 1966 is .23; the same probability for a nonwhite is .12. These matrixes can be used to calculate the expected income in 1966 conditional on the beginning 1957 income. These conditional expected incomes are shown for whites and non-whites respectively in Tables 4-33 and 4-34. The differences in these conditional expected values clearly demonstrate that whites did substantially better than nonwhites in this time interval *even when their initial positions are equated.*

**Relation between Income Inequality and
Inflation, Growth, and Unemployment**

In his recent paper Schultz (1969) constructed an empirical model to explain the behavior of the Gini coefficient over time. This model was applied to both the United States and the Netherlands. Here attention is restricted to his U.S. analysis, which was based on the Current Population Surveys 1947-65. The regression model had the following form:

$$G_t = \beta_1 + \beta_2 \dot{P}_t + \beta_3 \dot{y}_t + \beta_4 u_t + \beta_5 T_t + e_t,$$

Table 4-33
Expected Income in 1966 as a Function of 1957 Income, White Males, 35-44

1957 Income[a]	Expected Value of 1966 Income
< 1000	4011.95
1-1999	4355.95
2-2999	5031.42
3-3999	5794.50
4-4999	6967.65
5-5999	8233.30
6-6999	9983.70
7-7999	11187.10
8-8999	12708.90
9-9999	14977.80
10-15000	17152.50
> 15000	18930.60

[a] < 1000 = 500
> 15000 = 22,000

Table 4-34
Expected Income in 1966 as a Function of 1957 Income, Nonwhite Males, 35-44

1957 Income[a]	
< 1000	2417.75
1-1999	2950.60
2-2999	4036.40
3-3999	4969.95
4-4999	6672.25
5-5999	7321.85
6-6999	8536.50
7-7999	8300.00[b]
8-8999	9875.00[b]
9-9999	9499.05[b]
10-15000	6250.00[b]
> 15000	N.A.

[a]$< 1000=500$
> 15000 - no observations (sample sizes for other categories)
[b]These estimates should not be taken too seriously since only twenty nonwhites in this sample had 1957 incomes greater than $7000.

where

G_t is the Gini coefficient in year t;
$\dot{P}_t$ is the rate of change in wholesale prices in year t;
$\dot{y}_t$ is the rate of change in real output in year t;
u_t is the unemployment rate in year t;
T_t is a linear time trend equal to the number of years elapsed since 1943 at year t;
e_t is the classical error term.

Schultz hypothesized that β_3 and β_4 should both be positive. The argument for $\beta_4 > 0$ is that high labor turnover costs cause employers to stockpile employees during a downturn while firing marginal workers. The argument for a positive β_3 is less convincing and must be mollified by the strong negative relation between u_t and $\dot{y}_t$. The sign of β_2 cannot be specified a priori, and β_5 will be positive if income inequality has a positive trend component.

The estimated regression line for the United States in 1944-65 was:

$$G_t = .475 - .0003\dot{P}_t + .006\dot{y}_t + .0015u_t + .0014T_t, R^2 = .54.$$
$$ (.005) \quad (.008) \quad (.0025) \quad (.0006)$$

where the standard errors of the estimates are in parentheses. Only the estimate of β_5 is significant.

Application of the same empirical model to the reporting group of the total Social Security sample, 1957-66 yields the following sample regression:

$$G_t = .439 + .0004\dot{P}_t - .00005\dot{y}_t + .001u_t + .002T_t, R^2 = .97.$$
$$(.005) \ (.0005) \qquad (.0003) \qquad (.0009) \quad (.0002)$$

Only the time-trend coefficient and the intercept have t-statistics exceeding two.

The reporting group sample was reclassified by sex, and two separate regressions were run. The estimates for males and females, respectively, were,

$$G_t^M = .39 + .0009\dot{P}_t + .0004\dot{y}_t + .004u_t + .001T_t, R^2 = .896.$$
$$(.007) \ (.0006) \qquad (.0004) \qquad (.001) \qquad (.0002)$$

and

$$G_t^F = .42 - .001\dot{P}_t - .0002\dot{y}_t - .0009u_t + .0025T_t, R^2 = .99.$$
$$(.002) \ (.0002) \qquad (.0001) \qquad (.0003)$$

The intercept and trend coefficient remain significant with the same sign as before. However, the unemployment coefficient is significantly positive for males and significantly negative for females. The positive sign for males confirms the specific human-capital hypothesis. The income inequality of females does not conform to this hypothesis. The average level of specific human capital is much less in females than in males. Accordingly, there is less tendency for wage disparities to increase as unemployment rises. Also, the composition of females in the labor force probably changes with the unemployment rate. Note also that the estimate of β_1 is significantly negative for females.

The reporting group sample was then reclassified by race, and regressions were calculated for both whites and nonwhites. The sample regressions for whites and nonwhites, respectively, were:

$$G_t^W = .43 + .0007\dot{P}_t + .00004\dot{y}_t + .0011u_t + .002T_t, R^2 = .97$$
$$(.004) \ (.0005) \qquad (.0003) \qquad (.0008) \qquad (.0002)$$

and

$$G_t^N = .45 - .0016\dot{P}_t + .0003\dot{y}_t - .0026u_t + .0026T_t, R^2 = .99.$$
$$(.006) \ (.0005) \qquad (.0003) \qquad (.0009) \qquad (.0002)$$

The same phenomenon that occured between males and females is, to a lesser extent, also exhibited between whites and nonwhites. The unemployment coefficient is significantly negative for nonwhites and positive, but not as significant, for whites. These results are consistent with human-capital theory.

After a period of unemployment, nonwhites in the labor force are much more homogeneous than whites. During loose labor markets, nonwhites with marginal training are fired. This tends to reduce inequality of income among those *remaining* in the labor force. As the labor market tightens, more marginal nonwhites are hired, thereby increasing inequality. For whites, large numbers possess substantial amounts of specific human capital, and their wages are inflexible during loose labor markets. Marginal whites are also fired, but many low paid whites remain in the labor force. Consequently, inequality increases. As the labor market tightens, high human-capital wages are relatively sticky, while low human-capital wages are very responsive. This causes inequality to decline.[15] Note also that the estimate of β_1 is also significantly negative for nonwhites.

Alternative Measures of Inequality

In a recent paper Atkinson (1970) has shown that normative interpretations of conventional measures of income inequality are hampered by serious theoretical flaws. The social welfare assumptions underlying the normative implications of these measures are almost never specified; indeed, the unwary may conclude that such inequality measures as the Gini coefficient and the variance of log income are independent of the form of the social welfare function. The Gini coefficient is consistent with a social welfare function that places more weight on income transfers affecting the middle of the distribution than those affecting the tails. The variance of log income places more weight on transfers affecting the lower tail of the income distribution. The coefficient of variation weights all transfers independently of their location on the income distribution.[16]

It is important that differences among social welfare functions be explicitly considered when the corresponding inequality measures are applied. For this purpose Atkinson has proposed the following inequality measure

$$I = 1 - \frac{Y_{EDE}}{\mu}, \tag{4.1}$$

where Y_{EDE} is the "equally distributed equivalent level of income" or the level of income per person such that, if it were equally distributed, it would yield the same level of social welfare as the current distribution; μ is the mean of the current distribution.

Given this definition I is forced to lie in the unit interval, with $I = 0$ ($Y_{EDE} = \mu$) and $I = 1$ representing perfect equality and perfect inequality, respectively. In order to insure that I is invariant to proportional changes in the income distribution, the social welfare function must be of the form:

$$U(y) = \begin{cases} A + B \dfrac{y^{1-\epsilon}}{1-\epsilon} , & \epsilon \neq 1 \\[2em] \log (y) , & \epsilon \neq 1 \end{cases} \tag{4.2}$$

with $\epsilon \geqslant o$ to insure concavity.[17] The inequality measure implied by the discrete form of (4.2) is

$$I = 1 - \left[\sum_i \left(\frac{y_i}{\mu} \right)^{1-\epsilon} f(y_i) \right]^{1/{1-\epsilon}} .$$

The parameter ϵ measures the degree of inequality aversion that characterizes this society.

With this index, inequality of the income distribution for the total sample was calculated for $\epsilon = 1$, 1.5, and 2 for both the reporting group and the full coverage group. The results are presented in Tables 4-35 through 4-39. The inequality measure is an increasing function of ϵ, the degree of inequality aversion in the society. Note that inequality increases over time for the full coverage group. Finally, *if this social welfare function is taken seriously* and $\epsilon = 1$, then in 1966 the same welfare could have been achieved for the full coverage group with only 74 percent of the actual income, provided the 74 percent was equally distributed.

Table 4-35
Atkinson Measure for the Total Earnings Distribution, 1957-66

Year	Reporting Group			Full Coverage Group		
	$\epsilon = 1$	$\epsilon = 1.5$	$\epsilon = 2$	$\epsilon = 1$	$\epsilon = 1.5$	$\epsilon = 2$
1957	.4347	.7065	.8980	.3013	.5238	.7856
1958	.4414	.7154	.9034	.2810	.4852	.7474
1959	.4405	.7150	.9053	.2424	.4161	.6641
1960	.4425	.7144	.9023	.2294	.3960	.6636
1961	.4433	.7128	.8991	.2285	.3989	.6792
1962	.4533	.7193	.9020	.2329	.3907	.6365
1963	.4562	.7234	.9048	.2301	.3880	.6393
1964	.4550	.7229	.9075	.2306	.3937	.6728
1965	.4581	.7265	.9090	.2317	.3989	.6633
1966	.4596	.7267	.9087	.2581	.4643	.7697

Table 4-36
Atkinson Measure for the White Male Earnings Distribution

	Reporting Group			Full Coverage Group		
Year	$\epsilon = 1$	$\epsilon = 1.5$	$\epsilon = 2$	$\epsilon = 1$	$\epsilon = 1.5$	$\epsilon = 2$
1957	.372	.654	.883	.271	.495	.780
1958	.385	.667	.890	.258	.462	.737
1959	.379	.665	.897	.214	.379	.642
1960	.380	.663	.891	.199	.352	.617
1961	.384	.667	.890	.198	.363	.677
1962	.395	.670	.888	.201	.346	.608
1963	.398	.674	.890	.197	.344	.617
1964	.391	.665	.892	.196	.346	.658
1965	.397	.677	.898	.195	.344	.622
1966	.397	.676	.898	.214	.407	.752

Table 4-37
Atkinson Measure for the Nonwhite Male Earnings Distribution

	Reporting Group			Full Coverage Group		
Year	$\epsilon = 1$	$\epsilon = 1.5$	$\epsilon = 2$	$\epsilon = 1$	$\epsilon = 1.5$	$\epsilon = 2$
1957	.391	.657	.871	.283	.495	.758
1958	.411	.679	.877	.275	.475	.702
1959	.413	.698	.909	.227	.386	.589
1960	.415	.690	.890	.229	.427	.770
1961	.409	.682	.889	.230	.416	.696
1962	.414	.686	.883	.221	.406	.684
1963	.401	.667	.875	.203	.347	.539
1964	.420	.696	.896	.219	.397	.667
1965	.417	.695	.898	.206	.392	.692
1966	.402	.668	.877	.228	.416	.675

Distribution of Total Ten-Year Earnings

One of the defects of conventional income distribution measures is that they are calculated for annual rather than lifetime income. This difficulty is obviated to some extent here because I calculate the distribution of ten-year earnings for individuals who reported earnings in each of the ten years and for those who reported earnings in at least one of the ten years. In any one year, chance factors will cause some individuals to have earnings in excess of their normal earnings,

Table 4-38
Atkinson Measure for the White Female Earnings Distribution

	Reporting Group			Full Coverage Group		
Year	$\epsilon = 1$	$\epsilon = 1.5$	$\epsilon = 2.0$	$\epsilon = 1$	$\epsilon = 1.5$	$\epsilon =$
1957	.431	.699	.885	.273	.488	.74
1958	.439	.713	.896	.239	.442	.73
1959	.436	.705	.886	.209	.383	.64
1960	.435	.702	.887	.192	.350	.59
1961	.435	.700	.882	.193	.348	.60
1962	.433	.702	.888	.190	.338	.57
1963	.438	.710	.893	.191	.349	.60
1964	.439	.709	.892	.193	.350	.61
1965	.438	.709	.894	.201	.369	.63
1966	.439	.709	.893	.239	.450	.75

Table 4-39
Atkinson Measure for the Nonwhite Female Earnings Distribution

	Reporting Group			Full Coverage Group		
Year	$\epsilon = 1$	$\epsilon = 1.5$	$\epsilon = 2$	$\epsilon = 1$	$\epsilon = 1.5$	ϵ
1957	.436	.679	.863	.296	.502	.7
1958	.421	.662	.855	.248	.403	.5
1959	.431	.667	.847	.239	.403	.6
1960	.439	.678	.857	.237	.400	.6
1961	.435	.665	.840	.221	.360	.5
1962	.441	.676	.857	.231	.372	.5
1963	.451	.691	.862	.245	.405	.0
1964	.451	.696	.876	.225	.361	.5
1965	.450	.682	.852	.240	.384	.5
1966	.452	.692	.868	.281	.479	.

and others will report earnings considerably below normal. Over the ten-period, the law of large numbers will begin to operate, reducing the influenc chance factors. Consequently, measures of earnings inequality should be les the ten-year total compared with any single year. In addition, the central l theorem should cause the total earnings over the ten years to be more clc approximated by a normal (symmetric) distribution than the earnings of single year.

Table 4-40 presents several measures of earnings inequality for the e sample. These measures are reported for both the full coverage and the repo groups. The numbers in parentheses refer to the corresponding inequ

Table 4-40

Inequality Measures for the Distribution of Total Ten-Year Earnings for all Demographic Groups Combined, 1957-66

	Reporting Group	Full Coverage Group
Mean Income	23369	51046
Coefficient of Variation	1.27 (1.01)[a]	0.67 (.77)
Theil Measure	0.2780 (.40)	0.0793 (.24)
Atkinson (ϵ = 1.50)	0.9039 (.72)	0.2693 (.44)
Atkinson (ϵ = 2.00)	0.9801 (.90)	0.3802 (.72)

[a]Numbers in parentheses refer to corresponding measures for the 1966 earnings distribution.

Table 4-41

Inequality Measures for the Distribution of Total Ten-Year Earnings for Whites, 1957-66

	Reporting Group	Full Coverage
Mean Income	24668	53211
Coefficient of Variation	1.25 (1.00)[a]	0.65 (.76)
Theil Measure	0.2724 (.39)	0.0759 (.23)
Atkinson (ϵ = 1.50)	0.9033 (.72)	0.2575 (.44)
Atkinson (ϵ = 2.00)	0.9805 (.90)	0.3684 (.72)

[a]Numbers in parentheses refer to corresponding measures for the 1966 earnings distribution.

Table 4-42

Inequality Measures for the Distribution of Total Ten-Year Earnings for Nonwhites, 1957-66

	Reporting Group	Full Coverage Group
Mean Income	13880	32147
Coefficient of Variation	1.22 (.92)[a]	0.57 (.67)
Theil Measure	0.2724 (.39)	0.0685 (.21)
Atkinson (ϵ = 1.50)	0.8907 (.70)	0.2549 (.45)
Atkinson (ϵ = 2.00)	0.9729 (.89)	0.3489 (.70)

[a] Numbers in parentheses refer to corresponding measure for the 1966 earnings distribution.

measures for the single year 1966. For the full coverage group the law of large numbers does operate to cancel out the fortuitous events associated with a particular year, thereby reducing inequality. The coefficient of variation declined from .77 for 1966 to .66 for the ten years. The corresponding changes for the Theil measure and for the Atkinson measure (ϵ = 1.5 and ϵ = 2.0) were,

Table 4-43

Inequality Measures for the Distribution of Total Ten-Year Earnings for Males, 1957-66

	Reporting Group	Full Coverage Group
Mean Income	32155	57512
Coefficient of Variation	1.08 (.90)[a]	0.62 (.71)
Theil Measure	0.2205 (.34)	0.0689 (.22)
Atkinson (ϵ = 1.50)	0.8783 (.68)	0.2361 (.42)
Atkinson (ϵ = 2.00)	0.9773 (.90)	0.3462 (.71)

[a]Numbers in parentheses refer to corresponding measure for the 1966 earnings distribution.

Table 4-44

Inequality Measures for the Distribution of Total Ten-Year Earnings for Females, 1957-66

	Reporting Group	Full Coverage Group
Mean Income	11409	31322
Coefficient of Variation	1.25 (.87)[a]	0.54 (.63)
Theil Measure	0.2783 (.36)	0.0593 (.19)
Atkinson (ϵ = 1.50)	0.8887 (.71)	0.2254 (.41)
Atkinson (ϵ = 2.00)	0.9727 (.89)	0.3193 (.67)

[a]Numbers in parentheses refer to corresponding measure for the 1966 earnings distribution.

Table 4-45

Inequality Measures for the Distribution of Total Ten-Year Earnings for White Males, 1957-66

	Reporting Group	Full Coverage Group
Mean Income	33971	59910
Coefficient of Variation	1.06 (.88)[a]	0.61 (.72)
Theil Measure	0.2141 (.33)	0.0654 (.21)
Atkinson (ϵ = 1.50)	0.8759 (.67)	0.2235 (.41)
Atkinson (ϵ = 2.00)	0.9774 (.89)	0.3349 (.70)

[a]Numbers in parentheses refer to corresponding measure for the 1966 earnings distribution.

respectively, .24 to .08, .44 to .27 and .72 to .38. For the reporting group, the great variability of participation rates over the ten years produced increases in the inequality measures (except for the Theil measure) compared with the corresponding 1966 measures.

Remarkably similar changes in earnings inequality occurred for different demographic subgroups. These results are reported in Tables 4-41 through 4-48.

Table 4-46
Inequality Measures for the Distribution of Total Ten-Year Earnings for Nonwhite Males, 1957-66

	Reporting Group	Full Coverage Group
Mean Income	18502	35676
Coefficient of Variation	1.04 (.84)[a]	0.52 (.64)
Theil Measure	0.2196 (.33)	0.0585 (.18)
Atkinson (ϵ = 1.50)	0.8697 (.68)	0.2201 (.43)
Atkinson (ϵ = 2.00)	0.9708 (.89)	0.3033 (.70)

[a]Numbers in parentheses refer to corresponding measure for the 1966 earning distribution.

Table 4-47
Inequality Measures for the Distribution of Total Ten-Year Earnings for White Females, 1957-66

	Reporting Group	Full Coverage Group
Mean Income	11902	32419
Coefficient of Variation	1.23	0.53
Theil Measure	0.2728	0.0557
Atkinson (ϵ = 1.50)	0.8884 (.71)[a]	0.2117 (.40)
Atkinson (ϵ = 2.00)	0.9733 (.89)	0.3024 (.67)

[a]Numbers in parentheses refer to corresponding measure for the 1966 earnings distribution.

Table 4-48
Inequality Measures for the Distribution of Total Ten-Year Earnings for Nonwhite Females, 1957-66

	Reporting Group	Full Coverage Group
Mean Income	7942	22839
Coefficient of Variation	1.33	0.60
Theil Measure	0.2992	0.0720
Atkinson (ϵ = 1.50)	0.8808 (.68)[a]	0.2600 (.42)
Atkinson (ϵ = 2.00)	0.9660 (.86)	0.3529 (.64)

[a]Numbers in parentheses refer to corresponding measure for the 1966 earnings distribution.

The central limit theorem did cause the ten-year distributions (for the fully covered) to be more symmetric than the single-year distributions. However, χ^2 tests rejected the hypothesis of normality for each of the different demographic subgroups. The distributions are reported in Table 4-49.

Table 4-49
Distribution of Total Ten-Year Earnings for Different Demographic Groups, 1957-66

	1[a]	2	3	4	5	6	7	8	9	10	11	12	13
All Groups													
Reporting	.340	.122	.149	.101	.074	.060	.050	.038	.025	.014	.009	.013	.007
Fully Covered	.007	.021	.093	.150	.158	.150	.135	.110	.076	.040	.024	.031	.006
Whites													
Reporting	.328	.118	.146	.100	.075	.063	.053	.041	.027	.016	.010	.015	.007
Fully Covered	.007	.017	.078	.138	.156	.153	.141	.117	.082	.044	.027	.034	.006
Nonwhites													
Reporting	.428	.147	.169	.107	.061	.038	.025	.014	.007	.002	.001	.001	.000
Fully Covered	.016	.057	.212	.254	.177	.122	.078	.053	.020	.005	.003	.002	0
Males													
Reporting	.243	.097	.134	.105	.088	.082	.076	.061	.041	.024	.015	.023	.011
Fully Covered	.005	.012	.058	.109	.137	.152	.158	.139	.097	.052	.032	.041	.008
Females													
Reporting	.471	.155	.170	.094	.054	.031	.014	.005	.003	.001	.001	.001	.000
Fully Covered	.016	.046	.195	.270	.222	.141	.064	.024	.012	.003	.002	.003	0
White Males													
Reporting	.233	.092	.127	.101	.088	.085	.080	.066	.045	.027	.017	.026	.013
Fully Covered	.005	.010	.046	.095	.130	.153	.165	.147	.105	.057	.035	.045	.008
Nonwhite Males													
Reporting	.319	.132	.186	.136	.086	.058	.042	.024	.011	.004	.001	.002	.000
Fully Covered	.007	.036	.164	.238	.200	.145	.098	.073	.025	.007	.005	.003	0

White Females

	1	2	3	4	5	6	7	8	9	10	11	12	13
Reporting	.458	.154	.174	.097	.058	.034	.016.	.006	.003	.001	.001	.001	.000
Fully Covered	.013	.038	.177	.267	.236	.152	.069	.027	.013	.003	.002	.003	0
Nonwhite Females													
Reporting	.568	.165	.147	.071	.030	.013	.004	.001	.001	.000	.000	.000	.000
Fully Covered	.040	.111	.335	.296	.119	.062	.028	.002	.008	0	0	0	0

[a]Earnings categories are: 1. < 5000; 2. 5000-10,000; 3. 10,001-20,000; 4. 20,001-30,000; 5. 30,001-40,000; 6. 40,001-50,000; 7. 50,001-60,000; 8. 60,001-70,000; 9. 70,001-80,000; 10. 80,001-90,000; 11. 90,001-100,000; 12. 100,001-150,000; 13. > 150,000.

5

An Empirical Study of
Poverty Dynamics:
First Application of the
Stayer-Mover Model

Introduction

The modified Markov model (the stayer-mover model) described earlier will
be applied to Social Security data for the period 1962-65, a period of
sustained economic growth. A more detailed application will be presented
later when I analyze Social Security data for the period 1957-66. These
analyses measure income mobility with special emphasis on two groups:
those whose earnings remained below a poverty threshold for the entire
period and those whose earnings moved across a particular poverty threshold
sometime during the period. The data for the 1962-65 period include information on race, age, sex, and estimated annual earnings for approximately
840,000 individuals.

Given the limitations of the Social Security data (see Chapter 3), the use of
the word *poverty* in the context of this study would refer only to covered
earnings (earnings that are reported to Social Security) of employees and is
irrespective of family size. Consequently, there is no one-to-one corre-
spondence between those who would be designated poor here and those who
are poor according to the "official" definition of poverty. This study distinguishes between individuals who have a low-earning status (L) for the year
under investigation and those who do *not* have a low-earning status (N). These
two sets are obviously mutually exclusive; and, when combined with the set
of individuals who were not covered by Social Security for the particular year,
the uncovered (U) constitute the entire continuous work history sample for
that year. Whenever reference is made to poverty or nonpoverty it will be
with regard to the rather arbitrary definitions of low earnings and earnings that
are not low, respectively. The reader is urged to keep these definitions in mind
whenever policy implications are considered.

Three different definitions of low earnings are considered here—$1,500,
$3,000, and $4,500—mainly to measure the sensitivity of the empirical findings
to changes in earning levels. A subsidiary reason is the presence of several
poverty standards in use—for example, the Orshansky definition and that of the
family security plan.[1] Although there is considerable difference between the
definition of low earnings and these poverty definitions, they are certainly
positively related.

The data presented here suggest that some groups are unaffected by economic
growth. For this rather short time series, the probability of membership in the

hard-core poor was higher for nonwhites than for whites. For example, using a $3,000 poverty line, the probability of a nonwhite male between the ages of 25 and 34 remaining in poverty for the entire four-year period was .20; the same probability for a white male in the same age group was .05. Similar probabilities for females were .27 and .16, respectively. In general, the male stayer proportion was significantly greater for nonwhites than for whites. Stayer proportions were very similar for nonwhite males and white females, while nonwhite females had the highest stayer proportions. The probability of being a stayer in nonpoverty tended to be higher for whites than for nonwhites. For example, using a $3,000 poverty line, the probability of a nonwhite male between the ages of 25 and 34 remaining in nonpoverty for the four-year period 1962-65 was .29; the same probability for a white male in the same age group was .60. Similar probabilities for nonwhite and white females were .07 and .14, respectively.

The first of these findings was true for all age groups studied here. The three age groups were 25-34, 35-44, and 45-54, where membership in each group was determined by the individual's age as of 1962. The first finding was also true for each of the three definitions of poverty considered here. These poverty thresholds were the $1,500, $3,000, and $4,500 earning levels defined earlier. The second finding was true for all males of all age groups and for all poverty lines. However, for some age groups and poverty lines the probability of being a stayer in nonpoverty was higher for nonwhite women than for white women. The differences between white and nonwhite stayer probabilities did vary by age, sex, and poverty line.

An individual who stayed neither in poverty nor in nonpoverty for all four years was called a mover.[2] The probability of being a mover depended on race, age, sex, and poverty level. For example, with a $3,000 poverty line, the probability of being a mover for white males between the ages of 25 and 34 was .35; the same probability for nonwhites was .51. The most striking result regarding the male movers was that nonwhite movers tended to improve their economic position relative to white movers over this four-year period. The percentage changes in money GNP for the three periods 1962-63, 1963-64, and 1964-65 were, respectively, 5.3, 6.9, and 7.9. The price level was relatively constant over this four-year period. The male unemployment rate dropped from 5.2 percent in 1962 to 4.0 percent in 1965. By 1966 it had decreased to 3.3 percent. The comparable female unemployment rates were 6.2, 5.5, and 4.8. The relative improvement of nonwhites was most conspicuous for prime age males 25-54 and for each of the three poverty levels. Economic improvement was measured by the effect of growth on the transition probabilities into and out of poverty (see pp. 107-111 for a more lengthy discussion of this measure). For now, it is sufficient to note that the one-stage transition probability of moving from poverty to nonpoverty ($3,000 poverty line) was .28 in 1962-63 and .41 in 1964-65 for nonwhite males in the 25-34 age group. For whites in the same age group, the same transition probability increased from .36 in 1962-63 to .41 in 1964-65.

Some very tentative conclusions may be drawn from these preliminary empirical results. The first is that a significant proportion of individuals were in poverty (even using a $1,500 poverty line) throughout these four years of substantial growth, tending to substantiate the backwash thesis and suggesting that in addition to full employment and high growth, other policies must be adopted in order to alleviate poverty. For each age category, the proportions of stayers in poverty and nonpoverty were significantly greater and less, respectively, for nonwhite males than for white males. This is another indicator of the economic plight of black males.[3] Nevertheless, although the backwash thesis could not be rejected and disproportionate numbers of nonwhites were stayers in poverty, the effects of growth on nonwhite movers were substantial. Indeed, the nonwhite movers gained relatively more during these four years of growth than their white counterparts. This relative gain was much more pronounced for nonwhite males than for nonwhite females. The major tentative conclusion of this analysis, then, is that although growth of GNP may not be sufficient to eradicate all poverty, it does have a powerful influence on those who are subject to movements into and out of poverty, and this influence is stronger for nonwhites than for whites.

This tentative conclusion is consistent with the empirical results of A. Wohlstetter and S. Coleman (1972) who have found that during periods of growth, the gains of nonwhites relative to whites have been greatest at the lower end of the income distribution. Also, Kosters and Welch in some recent work (1972) have found that the nonwhite employment rate increases more rapidly than the white rate during periods of growth.

Empirical Findings for Males

The focus here will be on males in the prime working age group (25-54). Within this group, three age groups and three poverty levels are distinguished: ages 25-34, 35-44, and 45-54; and $1,500, $3,000, and $4,500.

For each poverty level, an individual may occupy one of three states: poverty, nonpoverty, and uncovered. Movements among these states are assumed to be governed by the stayer-mover probability process described above. With three income classes, three age categories, two sex categories, and two race categories, there is a total of thirty-six states. The single 36x36 transition matrix decomposes into twelve different 3x3 income matrixes, one for each of the twelve nonincome categories. Transition matrixes like these are calculated for each of the successive periods 1962-63, 1963-64, and 1964-65 and for each of the three poverty definitions. Those individuals who remained in poverty or nonpoverty for the four periods are withdrawn from these transition matrixes, giving rise to the mover matrixes. Comparisons between nonwhite and white males will be the primary concern here. Similar comparisons between sexes and between nonwhite and white females are presented below.

Two kinds of stayer proportions or probabilities will be calculated. The first is the conditional probability of remaining in poverty (nonpoverty) over the whole time period, given that a person was in poverty (nonpoverty) in 1962. This stayer proportion is estimated for each of the six male nonincome categories by dividing the total number in poverty (nonpoverty) for all four periods by the number in poverty (nonpoverty) in the first period. These proportions are displayed in Table 5-1 for each of the three poverty lines. The proportion of male white stayers in poverty is significantly less (at .001) than the proportion of male nonwhite stayers in poverty for each of the three age categories.[4] Similar statistically significant relations hold for the stayers in nonpoverty with the inequality reversed.[5] The proportion of stayers in poverty is positively related to age for both whites and nonwhites and for all three definitions of poverty. This is not surprising, since younger workers may invest in job skills in the first few years and then make a transit to nonpoverty in the third or fourth year. And, perhaps more important, the younger worker is more mobile and, in general, more adaptable to improving economic conditions. The proportion of stayers in nonpoverty was greatest for the 35-44 age group. This was true for both whites and nonwhites and for all three definitions of poverty.

The second stayer probability is the unconditional probability of remaining in poverty (nonpoverty) for the four periods. This probability is obtained by dividing the total number of stayers in poverty (nonpoverty) by the total number in the specific demographic category, for example, male, white, 25-34.[6]

Table 5-1
Male Stayer Proportions, 1962-65

Age Group	Poverty		Nonpoverty	
	Nonwhite	White	Nonwhite	White
		$1,500		
25-34	.17[a]	.13	.79	.88
35-44	.23	.18	.83	.89
45-54	.25	.19	.82	.88
		$3,000		
25-34	.40	.24	.77	.86
35-44	.43	.29	.81	.88
45-54	.47	.32	.80	.87
		$4,500		
25-34	.58	.36	.72	.84
35-44	.59	.41	.80	.86
45-54	.62	.45	.78	.84

[a]All the poverty stayer proportions are significantly different from zero at the .001 level.

These stayer probabilities are reported in Table 5-2 for white and nonwhite males, for each age group, and for each poverty definition. Within each demographic category, the proportion of movers is obtained by subtracting the proportion of stayers in poverty plus the proportion of stayers in nonpoverty from one. The proportion of movers in each demographic category is also recorded in Table 5-2. It is important to keep these mover proportions in mind when discussing differences in various mover matrixes. The relations between the male white and male nonwhite unconditional proportions are the same as those for the conditional stayer proportions. The probability of staying in poverty (nonpoverty) is an increasing (decreasing) function of age for both whites and nonwhites and for all three poverty lines. The proportion of movers is greater for nonwhites than for whites. This is true for all age groups and for all poverty lines.

Deleting the stayers from the transition matrixes gives the mover matrixes discussed earlier. Mover matrixes are shown in Table 5-3 for white and nonwhite males between the ages of 35 and 44 for each of the transition periods, 1962-63, 1963-64, and 1964-65, when a $3,000 poverty line is used. The steady-state distributions associated with two of the mover matrixes are presented in Table 5-3. These distributions show the proportion of individuals in each category at any point in time, *assuming* that the particular transition matrix persists indefinitely. More specifically, let π_i be the steady-state proportion in state i. Then the vector $\pi = (\pi_1, \pi_2, \pi_3)$ denotes the steady-state distribution. Letting M denote the mover matrix, π can be calculated from: $\pi = \pi M$, and $\Sigma \pi = 1$.

Casual observation of the transition matrixes reveals their nonstationarity;

Table 5-2

Stayers and Movers as Proportions of Each Age-Race Category (Males)

Age Group	Nonwhite Stayers in Poverty	Nonpoverty	Nonwhite Movers	White Stayers in Poverty	Nonpoverty	White Movers
			$1,500			
25-34	.05	.48	.47	.02	.70	.28
35-44	.06	.52	.42	.02	.73	.25
45-54	.06	.52	.42	.02	.72	.26
			$3,000			
25-34	.21	.29	.51	.05	.60	.35
35-44	.19	.36	.45	.05	.65	.30
45-54	.21	.35	.44	.06	.63	.31
			$4,500			
25-34	.39	.15	.46	.13	.46	.41
35-44	.36	.21	.43	.12	.54	.34
45-54	.39	.20	.41	.15	.51	.34

Table 5-3
Mover Matrixes for Males, 35-44 ($3,000 Poverty Line)

		White			Nonwhite	
	P	NP	U	P	NP	U
			1962-63			
P	.42	.32	.26	.52	.27	.21
NP	.35	.55	.10	.49	.49	.02
U	.37	.09	.54	.45	.03	.52
			1963-64			
P	.39	.34	.28	.48	.29	.23
NP	.30	.62	.08	.33	.64	.03
U	.32	.09	.59	.43	.03	.54
			1964-65			
P	.37	.34	.29	.41	.34	.25
NP	.25	.67	.08	.24	.73	.03
U	.31	.10	.59	.42	.04	.54

Steady-State Distributions for 1962-63 and 1964-65 Matrixes of A

	White	Nonwhite
	1962-63	
P	.38	.50
NP	.33	.28
U	.29	.23
	1964-65	
P	.30	.34
NP	.40	.45
U	.29	.22

P = poverty; NP = nonpoverty; U = uncovered.

that is, the transition probabilities are not constant over time.[7] For example, the probability of a nonwhite transiting from poverty to poverty in 1962-63 is .52, in 1963-64 is .48, and in 1964-65 is .41. Given the sustained growth throughout this period, the existence of stationarity would be as remarkable as it was discouraging. One would hope and anticipate that the persistence of high growth rates would affect the poverty to nonpoverty transition matrix. In particular, it would be expected that for the movers, as GNP increased, the probabilities of transits from poverty to poverty and from nonpoverty to poverty would decline, whereas the probabilities of transits from poverty to nonpoverty and from nonpoverty to nonpoverty would increase.[8] This in fact did occur. Tables 5-4

Table 5-4
Changes in Poverty to Nonpoverty Transition Probabilities, 1962-65 (Males)

Year	Male Whites 25-34	Male Whites 35-44	Male Whites 45-54	Male Nonwhites 25-34	Male Nonwhites 35-44	Male Nonwhites 45-54
			$1,500			
1962-63	.41	.36	.34	.38	.36	.34
1963-64	.38	.34	.31	.38	.34	.28
1964-65	.40	.35	.32	.43	.38	.32
Change (1962-65)	.01	−.01	−.02	+.05	+.02	−.02
			$3,000			
1962-63	.36	.32	.29	.28	.27	.22
1963-64	.38	.34	.30	.33	.29	.26
1964-65	.41	.34	.32	.41	.34	.29
Change (1962-65)	.05	.02	.03	.13	.07	.07
			$4,500			
1962-63	.33	.30	.26	.20	.22	.18
1963-64	.38	.34	.31	.27	.25	.23
1964-65	.45	.37	.34	.36	.29	.25
Change (1962-65)	.12	.07	.08	.16	.07	.07

Note: These transition probabilities are only for the mover matrixes. Hence a significant number of each population has been excluded, namely, stayers in poverty and stayers in nonpoverty (see Table 5-2).

through 5-7 show the manner in which these transition probabilities changed over the four-year period for each of the poverty lines and for both male whites and male nonwhites in the three prime working age categories. Table 5-4 displays the changes in the conditional probability of movements from poverty to nonpoverty. Table 5-5 shows changes in the conditional probability of movements from nonpoverty to nonpoverty. Table 5-6 shows changes in the conditional probability of movements from poverty to poverty. Finally, Table 5-7 displays changes in the conditional probability of transiting to poverty in one year, given current presence in nonpoverty. In all four tables, improvements in the transition probabilities over the four-year interval were positively related to the poverty line. As the poverty line increases (over the range considered here), people who are more likely to benefit from economic growth are classified as movers.

These tables also reveal that the sustained growth that occurred during 1962-65 did, for the most part, have the hypothesized effect on the four transition probabilities; that is, poverty to nonpoverty and nonpoverty to

Table 5-5
Changes in Nonpoverty to Nonpoverty Transition Probabilities, 1962-65 (Males)

| Year | Group and Age | | | | | |
| | Male Whites | | | Male Nonwhites | | |
	25-34	35-44	45-54	25-34	35-44	45-54
	$1,500					
1962-63	.57	.57	.59	.52	.54	.56
1963-64	.64	.62	.61	.62	.62	.60
1964-65	.69	.64	.60	.72	.68	.65
Change (1962-65)	.12	.07	.01	.20	.14	.09
	$3,000					
1962-63	.54	.55	.57	.50	.49	.52
1963-64	.66	.62	.61	.64	.64	.62
1964-65	.72	.67	.63	.76	.73	.69
Change (1962-65)	.18	.12	.06	.26	.24	.17
	$4,500					
1962-63	.53	.54	.56	.50	.50	.48
1963-64	.68	.64	.61	.67	.68	.64
1964-65	.77	.70	.67	.78	.74	.71
Change (1962-65)	.24	.16	.11	.28	.24	.23

nonpoverty probabilities both increased, and nonpoverty to poverty and poverty to poverty probabilities both declined. The most interesting feature of these tables is the relative improvement of nonwhite males compared with white males, where improvement is measured in terms of changes in transition probabilities. For example, consider the $3,000 poverty level and the age group 35-44. Over the period 1962-65, the white and nonwhite nonpoverty to poverty probabilities declined by .10 and .25, respectively; the white and nonwhite poverty to poverty probabilities declined by .05 and .11, respectively; the white and nonwhite nonpoverty to nonpoverty probabilities increased by .12 and .24, respectively; and, finally, the white and nonwhite poverty to nonpoverty probabilities increased by .02 and .07 respectively. Indeed, the probability of transiting from nonpoverty to poverty in 1964-65 was less for the nonwhites in this category than for whites; the probability of transiting from nonpoverty to nonpoverty in 1964-65 was greater for nonwhites; the probability of transiting from poverty to nonpoverty in 1964-65 was the same for whites and nonwhites. Only the probability of remaining in poverty from 1964 to 1965 was less for whites than for nonwhites. Even here the difference between the two probabilities decreased from .10 in 1962-63 to .04 in 1964-65.

Table 5-6

Changes in Poverty to Poverty Transition Probabilities, 1962-65 (Males)

	Group and Age					
	Male Whites			Male Nonwhites		
Year	25-34	35-44	45-54	25-34	35-44	45-54
			$1,500			
1962-63	.33	.33	.32	.40	.40	.38
1963-64	.33	.34	.33	.38	.40	.41
1964-65	.31	.33	.31	.35	.35	.37
Change (1962-65)	−.02	0	−.01	−.05	−.05	−.01
			$3,000			
1962-63	.43	.42	.42	.53	.52	.53
1963-64	.39	.39	.40	.46	.48	.47
1964-65	.34	.37	.36	.39	.41	.41
Change (1962-65)	−.09	−.05	−.06	−.14	−.11	−.12
			$4,500			
1962-63	.51	.48	.49	.60	.56	.57
1963-64	.44	.43	.44	.52	.50	.49
1964-65	.34	.38	.38	.43	.45	.43
Change (1962-65)	−.17	−.10	−.11	−.17	−.11	−.14

Similar results tend to hold for all age groups and for all three definitions of poverty. This differential effect of growth on nonwhites compared with whites has, as have all empirical results, many explanations and in fact probably has multiple causes. Note, however, that it is consistent with the income mobility theory of Chapter 2.

Tables 5-8, 5-9, and 5-10 indicate movements into and out of the uncovered category. The improvements that have already been noted in the four transition probabilities, poverty to poverty, poverty to nonpoverty, and so on, could have been offset by changes in the five poverty-uncovered-nonpoverty transition probabilities. For example, there could have been large increases in the transition probabilities of poverty to uncovered or great discrepancies between the behavior of white and nonwhite transition probabilities. These were not observed. The actual movements do not appear to affect the findings of Tables 5-4 through 5-7.

In some cases the transition matrixes for white and nonwhite males appeared somewhat similar for the 1964-65 transition period.[9] Contrary to appearances, the matrixes were significantly different for all age groups and all poverty lines.

Table 5-7
Changes in Nonpoverty to Poverty Transition Probabilities, 1962-65 (Males)

	Group and Age					
	Male Whites			Male Nonwhites		
Year	25-34	35-44	45-54	25-34	35-44	45-54
	$1,500					
1962-63	.29	.26	.24	.40	.39	.35
1963-64	.23	.23	.23	.32	.29	.30
1964-65	.19	.20	.23	.21	.25	.26
Change (1962-65)	−.10	−.06	−.01	−.19	−.14	−.09
	$3,000					
1962-63	.38	.35	.34	.47	.49	.45
1963-64	.28	.30	.30	.33	.33	.34
1964-65	.22	.25	.28	.22	.24	.28
Change (1962-65)	−.16	−.10	−.06	−.25	−.25	−.17
	$4,500					
1962-63	.44	.41	.39	.48	.49	.50
1963-64	.29	.32	.34	.31	.31	.35
1964-65	.21	.26	.29	.21	.25	.27
Change (1962-65)	−.23	−.15	−.10	−.27	−.24	−.23

Empirical Findings for Females

The empirical findings presented here emphasize comparisons between the economic performances of white and nonwhite females. Differences among age categories (25-34, 35-44, 45-54) are also noted for both whites and nonwhites.

A cursory examination of the differences between males and females clearly illustrates that the economic performance of males is, in general, superior to that of females.[10] The most obvious explanation is job market discrimination.[11] Furthermore, because of the female role in our society, many of the utility-producing services they perform either are not or cannot be converted into their income equivalents. By the same token, female participation in the labor force lacks the stability of the male participation. Employers are therefore less willing to invest in female human capital, which lowers female productivity and wages.

With respect to females whose poverty or nonpoverty status is affected by sustained growth (the so-called movers), both whites and nonwhites exhibited substantial improvements, with nonwhites benefiting slightly more than whites. These differences in white and nonwhite performance are not nearly as great, however, as those discovered in the case of nonwhite and white male movers. These relative improvements were again measured by changes in the transition

Table 5-8

Behavior of Movements into and out of the Uncovered State, 1962-65, $1,500 Poverty Line (Males)

Age Group and Year	Male Whites					Male Nonwhites				
	PU	NPU	UU	UP	UNP	PU	NPU	UU	UP	UNP
25-34:										
1962-63	.26[a]	.15[b]	.53[c]	.29[d]	.19[e]	.22	.08	.53	.36	.11
1963-64	.29	.13	.57	.26	.17	.24	.07	.50	.38	.12
1964-65	.29	.13	.59	.23	.17	.22	.07	.48	.37	.15
Change	.03	−.02	+.06	−.06	−.02	0	−.01	−.05	+.01	+.04
35-44:										
1962-63	.31	.17	.54	.29	.17	.25	.08	.52	.37	.11
1963-64	.33	.15	.59	.25	.16	.27	.09	.53	.36	.11
1964-65	.33	.15	.60	.24	.16	.27	.07	.54	.34	.12
Change	.02	−.02	.06	−.05	−.01	.02	−.01	.02	−.03	.01
45-54:										
1962-63	.33	.17	.55	.29	.16	.28	.09	.55	.37	.09
1963-64	.36	.16	.63	.24	.13	.31	.10	.54	.38	.09
1964-65	.37	.17	.65	.22	.13	.31	.10	.60	.32	.09
Change	.04	0	.10	−.07	−.03	.03	.01	.05	−.05	0

[a]Probability of going from poverty to uncovered.

[b]Probability of going from nonpoverty to uncovered.

[c]Probability of going from uncovered to uncovered.

[d]Probability of going from uncovered to poverty.

[e]Probability of going from uncovered to nonpoverty.

probabilities of the mover matrix. For both white and nonwhite females, the probabilities of moving from poverty to nonpoverty and from nonpoverty to nonpoverty increased, and the probabilities of moving from nonpoverty to poverty and from poverty to poverty declined. In general, the improvements were slightly better for nonwhites than for whites. This positive response to economic growth is especially important for nonwhite females, since they are more likely to be heads of households than are white females.[12]

The proportion of females who remained in nonpoverty through 1965, given their presence in nonpoverty in 1962, was approximately the same for whites and nonwhites for all three definitions of poverty. The corresponding conditional probability of remaining in poverty was higher for nonwhites than for whites. This was again independent of the definition of poverty and corresponds to the finding for nonwhite males relative to white males. The probabilities of staying in poverty were very similar for white females and nonwhite males.

Table 5-9

Behavior of Movements into and out of the Uncovered State, 1962-65, $3,000 Poverty Line (Males)

Age Group and Year	Male Whites					Male Nonwhites				
	PU	NPU	UU	UP	UNP	PU	NPU	UU	UP	UNP
25-34:										
1962-63	.21	.08	.53	.38	.09	.19	.03	.53	.44	.03
1963-64	.23	.07	.57	.34	.09	.20	.02	.50	.46	.03
1964-65	.25	.06	.59	.31	.09	.20	.03	.48	.47	.05
Change	.04	−.02	.06	−.07	0	.01	0	−.05	.03	.02
35-44:										
1962-63	.27	.09	.54	.37	.09	.21	.03	.52	.45	.03
1963-64	.28	.08	.59	.32	.09	.23	.03	.53	.43	.03
1964-65	.28	.08	.60	.31	.10	.25	.03	.54	.42	.04
Change	+.01	−.01	.06	−.06	.01	.04	0	.02	−.03	.01
45-54										
1962-63	.29	.09	.55	.37	.08	.25	.04	.55	.43	.03
1963-64	.30	.09	.63	.30	.06	.27	.04	.54	.44	.02
1964-65	.32	.09	.65	.28	.07	.30	.03	.60	.38	.02
Change	.03	0	.10	−.09	−.01	.05	−.01	.05	−.05	−.01

Movements among the states of poverty, nonpoverty, and uncovered were assumed to be governed by the stayer-mover probability process. With three income classes, three age categories, two sex categories, and two race categories, there are thirty-six states. The single 36x36 transition matrix decomposes into twelve different 3x3 income matrixes, one for each of the twelve nonincome categories. Transition matrixes such as these are calculated for each of the successive periods 1962-63, 1963-64, and 1964-65 and for each of the three poverty definitions. Those individuals who remained in poverty or nonpoverty for the four periods are withdrawn from these transition matrixes, giving rise to stayer proportions for both poverty and nonpoverty and also to revised transition matrixes, the mover matrixes. Comparisons between nonwhite and white females will be the primary concern here.

Two kinds of stayer proportions or probabilities will again be calculated. The first is the conditional probability of remaining in poverty (nonpoverty) over the whole time period, given that a person was in poverty (nonpoverty) in 1962. These proportions are displayed in Table 5-11 for each of the three poverty lines. Note that for each poverty definition the conditional probability of staying in poverty is an increasing function of age for both whites and nonwhites. This was also true for males. Differences between conditional

Table 5-10

Behavior of Movements Into and Out of the Uncovered State, 1962-65, $4,500 Poverty Line

Age Group and Year	Male Whites					Male Nonwhites				
	PU	NPU	UU	UP	UNP	PU	NPU	UU	UP	UNP
25-34:										
1962-63	.16	.04	.53	.43	.05	.20	.01	.53	.46	.01
1963-64	.18	.03	.57	.39	.04	.21	.01	.50	.48	.02
1964-65	.21	.03	.59	.36	.05	.22	.01	.48	.50	.02
Change	.05	−.01	.06	−.07	0	.02	0	−.05	.04	.01
35-44:										
1962-63	.22	.05	.54	.41	.05	.22	.01	.52	.47	.01
1963-64	.23	.04	.59	.36	.05	.24	.01	.53	.45	.01
1964-65	.25	.04	.60	.35	.05	.26	.01	.54	.45	.01
Change	.03	−.01	.06	−.06	0	.04	0	.02	−.02	0
45-54:										
1962-63	.25	.05	.55	.41	.04	.25	.02	.55	.45	.01
1963-64	.26	.05	.63	.33	.03	.29	.01	.54	.46	.00
1964-65	.29	.04	.65	.31	.04	.32	.01	.60	.39	.01
Change	.04	−.01	.10	−.10	0	.07	−.01	.05	−.06	0

Table 5-11

Female Stayer Proportions, 1962-65

Age Group	Poverty		Nonpoverty	
	Nonwhite	White	Nonwhite	White
		$1,500		
25-34	.25	.16	.66	.62
35-44	.36	.21	.73	.76
45-54	.45	.26	.76	.80
		$3,000		
25-34	.49	.33	.62	.59
35-44	.57	.44	.72	.75
45-54	.62	.50	.77	.79
		$4,500		
25-34	.60	.49	.63	.58
35-44	.68	.61	.74	.74
45-54	.71	.66	.80	.78

probabilities of remaining in nonpoverty for all four periods (Table 5-11) are not as great as they were for males. In fact, for some categories they are higher for nonwhite than for white females. It is also interesting to note that the probabilities of staying in poverty were very similar for nonwhite males and white females (see Table 5-1).

The second stayer probability is the unconditional probability of remaining in poverty (nonpoverty) for the four periods. These stayer probabilities are reported in Table 5-12 for white and nonwhite females, for each age group, and for each poverty definition. Probabilities of staying in poverty are similar for nonwhite males and white females (see Table 5-2). Within each nonincome category the proportion of movers is obtained by subtracting the proportion of stayers in nonpoverty from one. The proportion of movers in each nonincome category is also recorded in Table 5-12. It is important to keep these mover proportions in mind when discussing differences in various mover matrixes. In Table 5-12, note that the proportion of movers is roughly the same for whites and nonwhites for each of the age categories and poverty definitions. This was not the case for males. Indeed, all the differences between white and nonwhite females are much less than the corresponding differences for males.[13]

Deleting the stayers from the transition matrixes gives the mover matrixes discussed earlier. Mover matrixes are shown in Table 5-13 for white and nonwhite females between the ages of 35 and 44 for each of the transition periods, 1962-63, 1963-64, and 1964-65 when a $1,500 poverty line is used.

Tables 5-14 through 5-17 show the manner in which the transition probabilities of the mover matrixes changed over the four-year period. This is again done

Table 5-12
Stayers and Movers as Proportions of Each Age-Race Category (Female)

Age Group	Nonwhite Stayers In		Nonwhite Movers	White Stayers In		White Movers
	Poverty	Nonpoverty		Poverty	Nonpoverty	
			$1,500			
25-34	.09	.20	.71	.05	.26	.69
35-44	.14	.26	.60	.06	.37	.57
45-54	.20	.28	.52	.07	.46	.47
			$3,000			
25-34	.27	.07	.66	.16	.14	.70
35-44	.34	.10	.56	.21	.21	.58
45-54	.41	.10	.49	.25	.27	.48
			$4,500			
25-34	.39	.02	.59	.31	.05	.64
35-44	.48	.03	.49	.42	.09	.49
45-54	.24	.01	.75	.24	.06	.70

Table 5-13
Mover Matrixes for Females, 35-44 ($1,500 Poverty Line)

	White			Nonwhite		
	P	NP	U	P	NP	U
1962-63						
P	.40	.29	.31	.46	.22	.32
NP	.35	.53	.12	.41	.51	.08
U	.34	.06	.60	.37	.04	.59
1963-64						
P	.40	.30	.30	.46	.23	.31
NP	.29	.62	.09	.33	.60	.07
U	.36	.07	.57	.38	.05	.57
1964-65						
P	.38	.32	.30	.44	.25	.31
NP	.23	.69	.08	.26	.68	.06
U	.40	.08	.52	.46	.07	.47

Table 5-14
Changes in Poverty to Nonpoverty Transition Probabilities, 1962-65 (Females)

	Group and Age					
	Female Whites			Female Nonwhites		
Year	25-34	35-44	45-54	25-34	35-44	45-54
$1,500						
1962-63	.24	.29	.27	.23	.22	.18
1963-64	.27	.30	.28	.26	.23	.20
1964-65	.27	.32	.30	.28	.25	.21
Change (1962-65)	.03	.03	.03	.05	.03	.03
$3,000						
1962-63	.16	.19	.19	.14	.13	.10
1963-64	.19	.22	.22	.14	.15	.12
1964-65	.20	.24	.24	.17	.17	.14
Change (1962-65)	.04	.05	.05	.03	.04	.04
$4,500						
1962-63	.09	.12	.13	.07	.07	.05
1963-64	.11	.15	.16	.08	.08	.06
1964-65	.13	.15	.17	.09	.08	.06
Change (1962-65)	.04	.03	.04	.02	.01	.01

Table 5-15
Changes in Nonpoverty to Nonpoverty Transition Probabilities, 1962-65

Year	Female Whites			Female Nonwhites		
	25-34	35-44	45-54	25-34	35-44	45-54
			$1,500			
1962-63	.52	.53	.55	.51	.51	.54
1963-64	.55	.62	.62	.59	.60	.61
1964-65	.62	.69	.64	.69	.68	.62
Change (1962-1965)	.10	.16	.09	.18	.17	.08
			$3,000			
1962-63	.50	.52	.54	.50	.52	.46
1963-64	.56	.64	.65	.64	.60	.71
1964-65	.65	.72	.69	.68	.71	.70
Change (1962-1965)	.15	.20	.15	.18	.19	.24
			$4,500			
1962-63	.49	.52	.53	.37	.50	.41
1963-64	.61	.66	.68	.66	.76	.77
1964-65	.70	.75	.74	.78	.73	.76
Change (1962-1965)	.21	.23	.21	.41	.23	.35

for each of the poverty lines and for both female whites and nonwhites in the three age categories. Table 5-14 displays the changes in the conditional probability of movements from poverty to nonpoverty. For this very important type of transition, young nonwhite females are more like young white females than are other nonwhite age groups like their white counterparts. Table 5-15 shows changes in the conditional probability of movements from nonpoverty to nonpoverty, Table 5-16 those from poverty to poverty. Table 5-17 displays changes in the conditional probability of transiting to poverty in one year given current presence in nonpoverty. These tables reveal that the sustained growth that occurred during 1962-1965 did, for the most part, have the hypothesized effect on the four transition probabilities; that is, poverty to nonpoverty and nonpoverty to nonpoverty probabilities both increased, and nonpoverty to poverty and poverty to poverty probabilities both declined. Furthermore, on the basis of these measures, nonwhites (movers) appear to have benefited more from growth than did whites. This appearance is not as strong as it was for males.

In Tables 5-18, 5-19, and 5-20, movements into and out of the uncovered category are displayed. An interesting feature of these tables is the decline in the probability of moving from uncovered to uncovered and the almost equal increase in the probability of moving from uncovered to poverty for females in

Table 5-16
Changes in Poverty to Poverty Transition Probabilities, 1962-65

| | Group and Age | | | | | |
| | Female Whites | | | Female Nonwhites | | |
Year	25-34	35-44	45-54	25-34	35-44	45-54
	$1,500					
1962-63	.38	.40	.41	.47	.46	.50
1963-64	.37	.40	.40	.43	.46	.44
1964-65	.39	.38	.38	.39	.44	.46
Change (1962-65)	+.01	−.02	−.03	−.08	−.02	−.04
	$3,000					
1962-63	.48	.52	.53	.54	.54	.59
1963-64	.47	.50	.49	.53	.54	.52
1964-65	.47	.48	.45	.51	.52	.52
Change (1962-65)	−.01	−.04	−.08	−.03	−.02	−.07
	$4,500					
1962-63	.53	.57	.57	.57	.55	.59
1963-64	.52	.55	.53	.55	.57	.53
1964-65	.53	.55	.49	.57	.57	.56
Change (1962-65)	0	−.02	−.08	0	+.02	−.03

the 25-44 age category. The changes are more pronounced for nonwhites and seem to be independent of the poverty definition. Apparently, women who were previously unable to obtain covered employment could now work at least part time and supplement the family income.

Summary

The analysis of the Social Security data was based on a fairly simple Markov model. Year-to-year transition matrixes were calculated for all those who stayed in neither poverty nor nonpoverty for the entire four years. The Markov transition matrixes for the period 1962-63, 1963-64, and 1964-65 were nonstationary; that is, the transition probabilities associated with these matrixes changes with time. The behavior of the transition probabilities was consistent with the hypothesis that changes in the level of economic activity were the primary cause of the observed nonstationarity. During this period of persistent economic growth, the poverty to poverty and nonpoverty to nonpoverty probabilities declined. Furthermore, the relative changes in these transition probabilities were greater for nonwhites than for whites. This was especially true

Table 5-17
Changes in Nonpoverty to Poverty Transition Probabilities, 1962-65

	Group and Age					
	Female Whites			Female Nonwhites		
Year	25-34	35-44	45-54	25-34	35-44	45-54
			$1,500			
1962-63	.32	.35	.35	.41	.41	.40
1963-64	.30	.29	.28	.32	.33	.31
1964-65	.26	.23	.27	.25	.26	.30
Change (1962-65)	−.06	−.12	−.08	−.16	−.15	−.10
			$3,000			
1962-63	.43	.43	.42	.48	.45	.53
1963-64	.38	.33	.31	.34	.38	.27
1964-65	.30	.25	.28	.30	.27	.29
Change (1962-65)	−.13	−.18	−.14	−.18	−.18	−.24
			$4,500			
1962-63	.49	.46	.44	.63	.49	.60
1963-64	.37	.32	.31	.32	.24	.21
1964-65	.28	.24	.25	.22	.26	.24
Change (1962-65)	−.21	−.22	−.19	−.41	−.23	−.36

for males. This result held for three different poverty lines ($1,500, $3,000, $4,500), and was also true for all three age groups studied (25-34, 35-44, and 45-54). These findings suggest that nonwhite males who are close to the poverty line benefit more from economic growth than their white counterparts.

On the other hand, a significant proportion of individuals stayed in poverty for the entire four-year period. This finding was consistent with the "backwash thesis," which maintains that certain groups in our society are unaffected by economic growth. The male stayer proportion was significantly greater for nonwhites than for whites. The stayer proportions were very similar for nonwhite males and white females. Nonwhite females had the highest stayer proportions. These results were also independent of poverty line and age.

Table 5-18
Behavior of Movements into and out of the Uncovered State, 1962-65 (Females)
$1,500 Poverty Line

Age Group and Year	Female Whites					Female Nonwhites				
	PU	NPU	UU	UP	UNP	PU	NPU	UU	UP	UNP
25-34:										
1962-63	.38	.16	.60	.34	.06	.30	.08	.59	.37	.04
1963-64	.36	.15	.60	.34	.07	.32	.08	.54	.41	.05
1964-65	.34	.12	.57	.36	.07	.32	.06	.43	.50	.07
Change	−.04	−.04	−.03	+.02	+.01	+.02	−.02	−.16	+.13	+.03
35-44:										
1962-63	.31	.12	.60	.34	.06	.32	.07	.59	.37	.04
1963-64	.30	.09	.57	.36	.07	.31	.06	.57	.38	.05
1964-65	.30	.08	.52	.40	.08	.31	.06	.48	.46	.07
Change	+.01	−.04	−.08	+.06	+.02	−.01	−.01	−.11	+.09	+.03
45-54:										
1962-63	.32	.09	.58	.36	.06	.32	.05	.58	.39	.04
1963-64	.32	.09	.60	.33	.07	.36	.08	.56	.40	.04
1964-65	.33	.09	.60	.33	.06	.33	.08	.58	.39	.03
Change	+.01	0	+.02	−.03	0	+.01	+.03	0	0	−.01

Table 5-19
Behavior of Movements into and out of the Uncovered State, 1962-65 (Females)
$3,000 Poverty Line

Age Group and Year	Female Whites					Female Nonwhites				
	PU	NPU	UU	UP	UNP	PU	NPU	UU	UP	UNP
25-34:										
1962-63	.36	.07	.60	.39	.01	.32	.01	.59	.40	.01
1963-64	.34	.07	.60	.39	.01	.33	.03	.54	.45	.01
1964-65	.32	.06	.57	.42	.02	.32	.02	.44	.55	.01
Change	−.04	−.01	−.03	+.03	+.01	0	+.01	−.15	+.15	0
35-44:										
1962-63	.29	.05	.60	.39	.01	.32	.03	.59	.40	.01
1963-64	.28	.03	.57	.41	.01	.31	.02	.57	.42	.01
1964-65	.28	.03	.52	.47	.02	.31	.02	.48	.51	.01
Change	−.01	−.02	−.08	+.08	+.01	−.01	−.01	−.11	+.11	0
45-54:										
1962-63	.28	.04	.58	.40	.01	.31	.02	.58	.42	.00
1963-64	.29	.04	.60	.38	.02	.36	.03	.56	.44	.00
1964-65	.30	.03	.60	.38	.02	.34	.02	.58	.41	.00
Change	+.02	−.01	+.02	−.02	+.01	+.03	0	0	−.01	0

Table 5-20

Behavior of Movements into and out of the Uncovered State, 1962-65, $4,500 Poverty Line (Females)

Age Group and Year	Female Whites					Female Whites				
	PU	NPU	UU	UP	UNP	PU	NPU	UU	UP	UNP
25-34:										
1962-63	.38	.03	.60	.40	.00	.36	0	.59	.41	.00
1963-64	.37	.03	.60	.40	.00	.36	.01	.54	.46	.00
1964-65	.34	.02	.57	.43	.00	.34	.01	.43	.56	.00
Change	−.04	−.01	−.03	+.03	0	−.02	+.01	−.16	+.15	0
35-44:										
1962-63	.32	.03	.60	.40	.00	.38	.01	.59	.41	.00
1963-64	.30	.02	.57	.42	.00	.36	0	.57	.42	.00
1964-65	.30	.01	.51	.48	.00	.35	.01	.48	.52	.00
Change	−.02	−.02	−.09	+.08	0	−.03	0	−.11	+.11	0
45-54:										
1962-63	.30	.03	.58	.41	.00	.36	0	.58	.42	0
1963-64	.31	.02	.60	.39	.01	.41	.02	.56	.44	0
1964-65	.33	.01	.60	.39	.01	.38	0	.58	.42	0
Change	+.03	−.02	+.02	−.02	+.01	+.02	0	0	0	0

Appendixes

Introduction

Methods similar to those applied to the 1962-65 Social Security data above are now used to analyze income mobility during the ten-year period 1957-66. A difference of some importance is that age is now defined in two different ways. In the first, the age of each individual is his age as of 1960. The analysis based on this definition follows each individual over the ten-year period continuously assigning him his 1960 age. The second definition records the actual age of the individual and analyzes the behavior of this changing group over the ten-year period. The 1960 definition analyzes the same people while letting their ages change; the current age group definition holds age fixed and analyzes different individuals over time.

The proportion of male stayers in a low earnings status (L) is significantly different from zero for the three earning levels $1500, $3000, and $4500, and the three age groups 25-34, 35-44, 45-54. Many who made movements only between L and uncovered during the ten years were actually stayers in L, although they are here designated as movers; and many of the stayers in uncovered were really stayers in L. These three facts are verification of the "backwash thesis." The non-low earnings (N) and uncovered stayers proportions were also significantly different from zero for all age groups and all earning levels. These results justify the use of the stayer-mover model instead of a simple Markov chain model.

The proportion of stayers in L was significantly higher for nonwhite than for white males. Also, the proportion of stayers in N was significantly higher for whites than for nonwhites. These findings were true for all age groups and all definitions of L. From this one can conclude that the backwash population has disproportionately more nonwhites, whereas the population of persistently non-low earners has disproportionately more whites.

Year-by-year transition matrixes were calculated for the male movers, and the behavior of these nine matrixes over this period of economic growth was analyzed. The L to L and N to L transition probabilities declined, and L to N and N to N transition probabilities increased. These changes were greater for nonwhite than whites. Once again these results were true for all age groups and all earning levels. For example, for a $3000 earning level and the 35-44 age group, the white L to L and N to L transition probabilities declined, respectively, from .62 and .28 in 1957-58 to .52 and .10 in 1965-66. Similar probabilities for nonwhites declined from .74 and .40 in 1957-58 to .59 and .12 in 1965-66. On the other hand, the white L to N and N to N transition probabilities increased, respectively, from .23 and .69 in 1957-58 to .27 and .87 in 1965-66. The corresponding changes in the nonwhite probabilities were from .13 to .58 in 1957-58 to .26 and .86 in 1965-66. All changes were highly significant.

As anticipated, the male transition probabilities were very highly correlated with percentage changes in GNP. For example, a simple least squares regression of the L to L transition probabilities, p_{11}, on percentage change in GNP, g, gave the following sample estimators for whites and nonwhites,[1] respectively:

$$p_{11}^w = .63 - 1.1 g$$

with an r^2 of .94 and a t-statistic for the slope of -11, and

$$p_{11}^n = .71 - 1.5 g,$$

with an r^2 of .72 and a t-statistic for the slope of -4. Note that the absolute value of the g coefficient was larger for nonwhites than for whites. This tended to be true for all such regressions, again indicating the greater sensitivity of nonwhites to changes in economic growth.[2]

Similar regression results were obtained for the estimated relationships between the other transition probabilities and percentage change in GNP. Although the significance levels varied, they were high for all age groups and all earning levels.

These empirical results suggest that economic growth and the concomitant tight labor markets have a very strong positive influence on the mover population. More interesting, the effect of growth is stronger and more beneficial for nonwhite movers than for white movers. Of course, these results also imply that if the effects of growth are symmetric, then a decline in economic growth would be detrimental for both white and nonwhite movers with nonwhites harmed more.

Another measure of the influence of growth on the male mover population is the sensitivity of the steady-state distribution to percentage changes in GNP. This distribution is obtained by substituting the estimated linear regressions for the transition probabilities in the mover matrix and then solving for the steady-state distribution—that is, the long-run proportion in each of the three categories L, N, and U. The steady-state proportions for both whites and nonwhites are very sensitive to changes in economic growth. For example, using a $3000 earning level, male whites in the 35-44 (constant) age group have the following steady-state distribution as a function of g:

Steady State Male Proportion in

g (percent)	L	N	U
−5	.53	.23	.24
−1	.44	.31	.26
0	.41	.33	.26
1	.39	.35	.26
5	.29	.45	.26
10	.19	.58	.23

The same relationship for the corresponding nonwhite group is:

−5	.68	.07	.25
−1	.60	.13	.26
0	.58	.15	.26
1	.56	.18	.26
5	.44	.33	.23
10	.26	.60	.14

Steady-state distributions like these were sensitive to growth rates for all age groups and all earning levels, with nonwhites being more growth sensitive than whites. Note that the labor participation rates for nonwhites (as measured by proportion in U) is much more sensitive to g than the corresponding measure for whites.[3]

The Markovian analysis of the Social Security data produced the following results for females in the 25-55 age group.

The proportion of female stayers in L was significantly higher for nonwhites than for whites. With the exception of the youngest age group, the proportion of female stayers in N was significantly greater for whites than for nonwhites. All stayer proportions were significantly different from zero. These results justify the use of the stayer-mover model for females.

Year-by-year transition matrixes were also calculated for the female movers. Both whites and nonwhites benefitted from economic growth. The relationships between the four L-N transition probabilities and g were not nearly as strong as those for males. For example, a simple least squares regression of the L to L transition probability p_{11} on a g gave the following sample estimates for whites and nonwhites respectively:[4]

$$p_{11}^{w} = .58 - .63g$$

with an r^2 of .79 and a t-statistic of −5, and

$$p_{11}^n = .64 - 1.5\,g,$$

with an r^2 of .16 and a t-statistic of -1.1. The transition probabilities from uncovered to L and uncovered to N were more closely associated with g than the corresponding male probabilities. Using the same age group and earning level as before, the following least squares estimates were obtained for whites and nonwhites, respectively:[5]

$$p_{32}^w = .03 + .19\,g$$

with an r^2 of .57 and a t-statistic of 3, and

$$p_{32}^n = .02 + .21\,g$$

with identical r^2 and t-statistic. These relations suggest that female labor participation rates are strongly affected by growth.

The steady-state proportions for both white and nonwhite females are quite sensitive to changes in economic growth. For example, using a \$1500 earning level, female whites in the 35-44 age group[6] have the following steady-state distribution as a function of g:

Steady-State Female Proportion in

g (percent)	L	N	U
−5	.37	.18	.44
−1	.34	.25	.40
0	.33	.27	.39
1	.33	.29.	.38
5	.29	.39	.33
10	.23	.52	.25

The same relationship for the corresponding nonwhite group is:

−5	.40	.13	.47
−1	.40	.18	.42
0	.39	.20	.41
1	.39	.22	.39
5	.37	.30	.33
10	.32	.43	.25

Steady-state distributions such as these were sensitive to growth rates for all age groups and all earning levels. Note that the steady-state proportion in uncovered for both white and nonwhite females is very responsive to g.

Empirical Findings for Prime Working Age Males

This section presents empirical results for the 1957-66 Continuous Work History Sample. The focus will be on males in the prime working age group (25-54). Within this group, three subgroups are distinguished: 25-34, 35-44, and 45-54; and three earning levels are discussed, $1500, $3000, and $4500.

Table A-1 reports the male stayer proportions by race, age, and earnings level. The stayer proportions are all significantly different from zero.[7] This validates the use of the stayer-mover model. The fact that the proportion of stayers in L exceeded zero tends to substantiate the backwash thesis. There are groups in our society who were relatively immune to the economic growth that occurred in the 1957-66 period.[8] Furthermore, the probability of staying in L for the remaining nine years, given poverty in 1957, is an increasing function of age. This probability is, of course, also an increasing function of the earning level. The difference in these probabilities across race agree with the hypotheses mentioned above that the probability of staying in L was significantly greater for nonwhites than for whites[9] and the probability of staying in N was significantly greater for whites than for nonwhites.[10] These results were true for all age groups and all earnings lines.

The proportion of stayers in L is positively related to age for both whites and nonwhites and for all three definitions of low earnings. The proportion of

Table A-1
Male Stayer Proportions, 1957-66 (Age as of 1960)

Low Earnings			Non-Low Earnings	
Nonwhite	White		Nonwhite	White
		Age Group		
		$1500 Earning Level		
.03	.02	25-34	.53	.69
.05	.04	35-44	.57	.73
.06	.05	45-54	.55	.70
		$3000 Earning Level		
.14	.05	25-34	.48	.64
.17	.08	35-44	.53	.69
.19	.10	45-54	.52	.65
		$4500 Earning Level		
.28	.10	25-34	.34	.57
.31	.14	35-44	.40	.62
.32	.17	45-54	.39	.58

stayers in N was greatest for the 35-44 age group. This was true for both whites and nonwhites and for all three definitions of L.

The second stayer probability is the unconditional probability of remaining in L or N for the ten periods. This probability is obtained by dividing the total number of stayers in L or N by the total number in the specific nonincome category; for example, male, white, 25-34.[11] These stayer probabilities are reported in Table A-2 for white and nonwhite males, for each age group, and for each low-earnings definition. Within each nonincome category, the proportion of movers is obtained by subtracting the proportion of stayers in L plus the proportion of stayers in N from one. The proportion of movers in each nonincome category is also recorded in Table A-2. It is important to keep these mover proportions in mind when discussing differences in various mover matrixes. The relations between the male white and male nonwhite unconditional proportions are the same as those for the conditional stayer proportions.

The proportion of movers is greater for nonwhites than for whites. This is true for all age groups and for all poverty lines.

Table A-2
Male Stayers and Movers as Proportions of Each Age-Race Category

| | | | | Nonwhite Stayers In | | White Stayers In | | |
L	N	U	Nonwhite Movers	Age Group[a]	L	N	U	White Movers
				$1500				
.008	.25	.05	.69	25-34	.003	.49	.03	.48
.011	.32	.05	.62	35-44	.004	.54	.04	.41
.015	.32	.06	.61	45-54	.005	.50	.05	.44
				$3000				
.07	.11	.05	.77	25-34	.01	.36	.03	.59
.08	.18	.05	.69	35-44	.02	.45	.04	.50
.09	.18	.06	.68	45-54	.02	.41	.05	.52
				$4500				
.20	.03	.05	.73	25-34	.05	.18	.03	.74
.20	.06	.05	.69	35-44	.05	.29	.04	.62
.21	.06	.06	.68	45-54	.07	.26	.05	.63

[a]In the 25-34 age group, there were 12,760 nonwhites, 84,447 whites.
In the 35-44 age group, there were 12,757 nonwhites, 94,802 whites.
In the 45-54 age group, there were 10,316 nonwhites, 80,370 whites.

Analysis of the Male Mover Matrixes
for the 1960 Age Group

The male mover matrixes are first analyzed for the 1960 age groups; that is, an individual is placed in one of the three age groups based on his age as of 1960. The behavior of each individual is then analyzed for the ten years. In the following subsection, the behavior of age groups is analyzed where the composition of each age group varies over time.

Deleting the stayers from the transition matrixes gives the mover matrixes discussed earlier. Mover matrixes are shown in Table A-3 for white and nonwhite males between the ages of 35 and 44 (age as of 1960) for each of the transition periods (1957-58, 1960-61, and 1965-66, when a $3000 earnings line is used). The steady-state distributions associated with the 1957-58 and 1965-66 mover matrixes are also presented in Table A-4. Table A-5 shows the corresponding population (stayers and movers) steady-state distribution. These distributions show the proportion of individuals in each category at any point in time

Table A-3
Mover Matrixes for Males (35-44) $3000 Earning Level[a] (1960 Age Group)

		White			Nonwhite		
		L	N	U	L	N	U
			1957-58				
	L	.62	.23	.15	.74	.13	.14
	N	.28	.69	.03	.40	.58	.02
	U	.22	.06	.72	.28	.02	.70
			1961-62				
	L	.56	.26	.19	.68	.17	.14
	N	.13	.83	.03	.17	.81	.01
	U	.21	.05	.74	.28	.02	.70
			1965-66				
	L	.52	.27	.21	.59	.26	.16
	N	.10	.87	.03	.13	.86	.01
	U	.13	.04	.83	.19	.02	.78

[a]This group includes 94,802 whites and 12,757 nonwhites. Almost 50 percent of the whites are movers, whereas 69 percent of nonwhites are movers. Approximately 45 percent of whites were stayers in N; only 18 percent of nonwhites were in this category. Almost 8 percent of nonwhites stayed in L while 1.6 percent of whites were similarly affected. The percentage who stayed in uncovered were about the same for the two groups: 4 percent for whites and 5 percent for nonwhites.

Table A-4
Steady-State Distributions for the 1957-58 and 1965-66 Matrixes of Table A-3

		White	Nonwhite
		1957-58	
L	.40		.56
N	.35		.18
U	.24		.26
		1965-66	
L	.19		.26
N	.49		.51
U	.32		.23

Table A-5
Population Steady-State Distributions for the 1957-58 and 1965-66 Matrixes of Table A-3

		White	Nonwhite
		1957-58	
L	.22		.47
N	.63		.30
U	.16		.23
		1965-66	
L	.12		.26
N	.70		.53
U	.20		.21

assuming that the particular transition matrix persists indefinitely. More specifically, let π_i be the steady-state proportion in state i. Then the vector $\pi = (\pi_1, \pi_2, \pi_3)$ denotes the steady-state distribution. Letting M denote the mover matrix, π can be calculated from the following equations:[12]

$$\pi = \pi M \text{ and}$$

$$\Sigma \pi_i = 1.$$

Casual observation of the transition matrixes reveals their nonstationarity, that is, the transition probabilities are not constant over time.[13] For example, the probability of a nonwhite transiting from L to L in 1957-58 is .74, in 1960-61 is .68, and in 1965-66 is .59. As previously hypothesized, one would anticipate that the persistence of high growth rates would affect the mover transition matrix. In particular, it would be expected that for the movers, as GNP increased the probabilities of transits from L to L and from N to L would decline, while the probabilities of L to N and from N to N would increase.[14] This in fact did occur. Tables A-6 to A-8 show the manner in which these transition probabilities changed over the ten-year period for each of the earning levels and for both male whites and male nonwhites in the three prime working age categories. Table A-6 displays the changes in the conditional probabilities for the 25-34 age class. Table A-7 for the 35-44 age class, and Table A-8 for the 45-54 age class. In all three tables, improvements in the transition probabilities over the ten-year interval tended to be positively related to the earning level. As the earning level increased (over the range considered here), people who are more likely to benefit from economic growth are classified as movers.

These tables also reveal that the growth that occurred over 1957-66 did for the most part have the hypothesized effect on the four transition probabilities; that is, L to N and N to N probabilities both increased, and N to L and L to L probabilities both declined. The most interesting feature of these tables is the relative improvement of nonwhite males compared with white males, where improvement is measured in terms of changes in transition probabilities. For example, consider the $3000 earning level and the age group 35-44. Over the period 1957-66 the white and nonwhite N to L probabilities declined by .18 and .28, respectively; the white and nonwhite L to L probabilities declined by .10 and .15, respectively; the white and nonwhite N to N probabilities increased by .18 and .28, respectively; and, finally, the white and nonwhite L to N probabilities increased by .04 and .13, respectively.

To gain additional insight, the hypotheses of the relation between the transition probabilities and growth were tested by regressing each of the four male transition probabilities, L to L, p_{11}, L to N, p_{12}, N to L, p_{21}, and N to N, p_{22}, on, g, percentage change in GNP. Since the dependent variable is a probability and must be in the interval (0, 1), a logit regression is more appropriate than the simple linear regressions. The logit regression proceeds in two stages in estimating the regression

$$ln\left(\frac{p}{1-p}\right) = \alpha + \beta g$$

where p is a transition probability.[15] For a discussion of this procedure, see Zellner and Lee (1965).

For the 35-44 age group and a $3000 earning level, the following simple linear regressions were obtained:[16]

Table A-6

Behavior of Male Transition Probabilities, 1957-66 for 25-34 Age Category (1960 Age Group)

	White					Nonwhite		
L-L	L-N	N-L	N-N	Year	L-L	L-N	N-L	N-N
				$1500 Earning Level				
.50	.30	.25	.70	1957-58	.56	.24	.35	.59
.42	.40	.14	.80	1958-59	.52	.33	.20	.76
.44	.34	.13	.82	1959-60	.55	.28	.20	.77
.46	.29	.13	.81	1960-61	.57	.23	.21	.75
.44	.33	.10	.84	1961-62	.51	.32	.15	.82
.44	.31	.09	.85	1962-63	.52	.28	.14	.83
.43	.32	.09	.86	1963-64	.51	.30	.13	.84
.43	.33	.07	.88	1964-65	.48	.35	.10	.87
.42	.33	.07	.88	1965-66	.47	.34	.09	.87
−.08	+.03	−.18	+.18		−.09	+.10	−.26	+.28
				$3000 Earning Level				
.63	.24	.35	.63	1957-58	.75	.11	.49	.48
.54	.33	.17	.80	1958-59	.70	.19	.22	.76
.57	.28	.16	.82	1959-60	.73	.15	.22	.77
.59	.24	.15	.82	1960-61	.73	.14	.21	.78
.55	.29	.11	.86	1961-62	.68	.20	.16	.82
.55	.26	.11	.87	1962-63	.66	.20	.15	.84
.5	.28	.09	.88	1963-64	.64	.21	.13	.86
.52	.29	.08	.89	1964-65	.60	.27	.11	.88
.50	.31	.08	.90	1965-66	.56	.29	.11	.88
−.13	+.06	−.27	+.27		−.19	+.18	−.38	+.40
				$4500 Earning Level				
.74	.18	.45	.54	1957-58	.81	.05	.61	.38
.64	.28	.21	.78	1958-59	.77	.12	.26	.74
.66	.24	.16	.83	1959-60	.78	.11	.23	.77
.67	.20	.15	.84	1960-61	.78	.09	.21	.79
.63	.25	.10	.87	1961-62	.75	.13	.13	.86
.63	.24	.10	.89	1962-63	.74	.13	.13	.87
.60	.26	.09	.90	1963-64	.71	.16	.12	.88
.57	.28	.07	.92	1964-65	.68	.19	.10	.89
.53	.31	.08	.91	1965-66	.63	.23	.10	.89
−.21	+.13	−.37	+.37		−.18	+.18	−.51	+.51

Table A-7

Behavior of Male Transition Probabilities, 1957-66, for 35-44 Age Category (1960 Age Group)

White					Non White			
L-L	L-N	N-L	N-N	Year	L-L	L-N	N-L	N-N
				$1500 Earning Level				
.51	.26	.19	.76	1957-58	.59	.21	.31	.64
.45	.33	.13	.81	1958-59	.53	.29	.20	.76
.48	.27	.12	.82	1959-60	.56	.24	.19	.77
.50	.23	.13	.79	1960-61	.59	.19	.20	.75
.46	.29	.11	.82	1961-62	.53	.27	.16	.80
.47	.26	.11	.82	1962-63	.54	.25	.16	.81
.46	.27	.10	.83	1963-64	.54	.25	.14	.82
.46	.28	.09	.84	1964-65	.51	.29	.12	.85
.46	.29	.09	.84	1965-66	.49	.31	.11	.85
−.05	+.03	−.10	+.08		−.10	+.10	−.20	+.21
				$3000 Earning Level				
.62	.23	.28	.69	1957-58	.74	.13	.40	.58
.54	.30	.17	.80	1958-59	.68	.18	.22	.77
.58	.24	.16	.81	1959-60	.71	.15	.22	.77
.60	.20	.16	.80	1960-61	.71	.13	.24	.74
.56	.26	.13	.83	1961-62	.68	.17	.17	.81
.56	.23	.12	.84	1962-63	.68	.17	.17	.82
.54	.25	.11	.86	1963-64	.64	.20	.14	.85
.54	.25	.10	.87	1964-65	.63	.22	.11	.87
.52	.27	.10	.87	1965-66	.59	.26	.12	.86
−.10	+.04	−.18	+.18		−.15	+.13	−.28	+.28
				$4500 Earning Level				
.71	.20	.39	.60	1957-58	.80	.08	.56	.43
.60	.29	.21	.78	1958-59	.72	.16	.27	.72
.65	.23	.16	.82	1959-60	.76	.12	.20	.79
.67	.18	.16	.82	1960-61	.76	.09	.20	.79
.63	.23	.12	.86	1961-62	.73	.14	.15	.85
.63	.21	.11	.87	1962-63	.73	.13	.13	.87
.61	.23	.10	.89	1963-64	.70	.16	.11	.89
.59	.24	.09	.90	1964-65	.67	.16	.10	.89
.55	.28	.09	.89	1965-66	.65	.20	.12	.88
−.16	+.08	−.30	+.29		−.15	+.12	−.44	+.45

Table A-8

Behavior of Male Transition Probabilities, 1957-66, for 45-54 Age Category (1960 Age Group)

	White					Nonwhite		
L-L	L-N	N-L	N-N	Year	L-L	L-N	N-L	N-N
				$1500 Earning Level				
.54	.25	.17	.79	1957-58	.61	.21	.26	.71
.46	.29	.11	.82	1958-59	.55	.23	.18	.78
.49	.25	.12	.83	1959-60	.58	.22	.19	.77
.49	.22	.14	.79	1960-61	.57	.19	.20	.76
.46	.27	.12	.82	1961-62	.54	.23	.16	.78
.47	.23	.11	.81	1962-63	.54	.21	.15	.81
.45	.25	.11	.81	1963-64	.55	.22	.15	.80
.45	.26	.11	.81	1964-65	.53	.24	.13	.82
.43	.28	.11	.80	1965-66	.48	.27	.15	.80
−.11	+.03	−.06	+.01		−.13	+.06	−.11	+.09
				$3000 Earning Level				
.66	.21	.26	.72	1957-58	.77	.10	.38	.60
.56	.27	.15	.82	1958-59	.70	.16	.22	.77
.61	.21	.16	.82	1959-60	.73	.13	.22	.76
.61	.18	.17	.80	1960-61	.73	.10	.22	.77
.58	.22	.14	.83	1961-62	.69	.14	.15	.83
.57	.20	.14	.83	1962-63	.68	.14	.17	.81
.56	.22	.13	.84	1963-64	.66	.17	.14	.84
.54	.23	.12	.85	1964-65	.63	.18	.14	.84
.51	.26	.13	.83	1965-66	.58	.22	.14	.85
−.15	+.05	−.13	+.11		−.19	+.12	−.24	+.25
				$4500 Earning Level				
.74	.17	.36	.63	1957-58	.82	.07	.56	.44
.63	.25	.20	.78	1958-59	.73	.14	.27	.72
.66	.20	.17	.82	1959-60	.77	.10	.21	.78
.69	.16	.17	.82	1960-61	.77	.08	.20	.79
.65	.20	.14	.85	1961-62	.73	.11	.13	.80
.65	.18	.13	.85	1962-63	.73	.11	.15	.84
.62	.21	.12	.87	1963-64	.70	.13	.13	.8
.61	.21	.11	.87	1964-65	.68	.14	.12	.8
.56	.25	.12	.86	1965-66	.64	.17	.13	.8
−.18	+.07	−.24	+.23		−.18	+.10	−.43	+.4

								Durbin-Watson Statistic[17]

(1) p_{11}^w = .63 − 1.1g, r^2 = .94, t_b = −11   2.1

(2) p_{11}^n = .76 − 1.5g, r^2 = .72, t_b = −4   1.4

(3) p_{12}^w = .20 + .74g, r^2 = .53, t_b = 2.8   1.0

(4) p_{12}^n = .09 + 1.4g, r^2 = .80, t_b = 5.3   1.3

(5) p_{21}^w = .25 − 1.7g, r^2 = .63, t_b = 3.4   1.1

(6) p_{21}^n = .36 − 2.7g, r^2 = .70, t_b = −4   1.2

(7) p_{22}^w = .72 + 1.7g, r^2 = .63, t_b = 3.5   1.2

(8) p_{22}^n = .62 + 2.8g, r^2 = .71, t_b = 4.1   1.2

These regressions tend to verify the growth hypotheses. Note first that for both whites (w) and nonwhites (n), the coefficients of g have the right sign. Furthermore, the values of these coefficients are highly significant as revealed by the size of the t-ratios, t_b. Finally, in all four cases the absolute size of the g coefficient is larger for nonwhites than for whites. This is consistent with the hypotheses that nonwhite movers are more sensitive to growth than their white counterparts. Results like these held for all age groups and all earning levels. The results of the simple linear regressions are virtually identical to both the weighted and unweighted logit regressions. For this reason the logit results are not presented.

From the relations between the nine transition probabilities and g, one can obtain the relation between the steady-state distribution and growth.[18] This steady-state relation is another way of measuring the influence of percentage change in GNP on the mover population. Table A-10 shows this relation for both whites and nonwhites in the 35-44 age group when a $3000 earning level is used. Although the exact proportions should not be taken too seriously, the effect of growth on this mover group is too powerful to be dismissed. For example, as GNP increases from 0 to 10 percent, the proportion of whites (nonwhites) in L declines from .41 (.58 to .20 (.27). It is also interesting to note that the proportion of nonwhites in N, which was .05 when $g = -10$ percent, increases to .56 when $g = 10$ percent. This is higher than the corresponding white proportion (.54) at the growth rate. Similar results hold for the other age groups and for different poverty lines.

Elimination of the Uncovered Category

The uncovered category can be removed by the following method. Let $\lambda = P_{31}/(P_{31} + P_{32})$ represent the fraction of individuals moving (between years) from uncovered to L who were previously in L; it also represents the fraction of individuals moving (between years) from L to uncovered who stayed in L; finally, it represents the fraction of those who stayed in uncovered (for two consecutive years) who also remained in L. The fraction $(1 - \lambda)$ has a similar interpretation for the $\overline{L}$ category. A λ was calculated for each of the nine mover matrixes. Several of the condensed mover matrixes are presented in the first part of Table A-9.[19] The associated steady-state proportions are displayed in the second part of Table A-9 for the movers, and in the third part of A-9 for both movers and stayers. For the 35-44 group and a $3000 earning level, the simple regressions of the revised transition probabilities on g were (all statistically significant):

	Probability	r^2	Durbin-Watson Statistic
$p_{11}{}^{w}$	$= .78 - .61g,$	.52	.89
$p_{12}{}^{w}$	$= .32 - 1.3g,$	.54	1.7
$p_{11}{}^{N}$	$= .91 - 1.0g,$	.73	2.0
$p_{12}{}^{N}$	$= .41 - 2.6g,$	.64	1.8

Comparing both these regressions with those previously obtained and Tables A-3 through A-5 with Table A-9 demonstrates invariant conclusions. Both white and nonwhite movers benefit from increases in g, with nonwhites benefiting more.

Analysis of the Male Mover Matrixes for
the Current Age Group

In the analysis of the mover matrixes for the current age group, the age intervals 25-34, 35-44, and 45-54 are held fixed over time while membership changes. The 1960 age grouping confounds the effects of aging and of transitions as of a fixed age. The current age-group analysis is better designed to hold the effects of age constant. The difference between the two analyses measures the effect of aging.

These modified mover matrixes are displayed in Table A-11 for white and nonwhite males between the ages of 35 and 44 (constant age group) for each of the transition periods 1957-58, 1960-61, and 1965-66 when a $3000 earning level is used. The steady-state distribution associated with the 1957-58 and 1965-66 mover matrixes are presented in Table A-12. These matrixes possess approximately the same characteristics as those for the 1960 age group. Both the L to L and N to L transition probabilities declined over time, while the L to N and N to N probabilities increased. Tables A-13 to A-15 show the manner in which these transition probabilities changed over the ten-year period for each of

Table A-9
Matrix Analysis for Males (35-44), $3,000 Earning Level[a]

Year and Category	White		Nonwhite	
	L	L	L	L
		Mover Matrixes		
1957-58				
L	.75	.25	.88	.12
L	.36	.64	.45	.55
1961-62				
L	.74	.26	.85	.15
L	.22	.78	.23	.77
1965-66				
L	.72	.28	.79	.21
L	.20	.80	.18	.82
		Steady-State Distributions		
1957-58	.59	.41	.79	.21
1965-66	.43	.57	.46	.53
		Total Steady-State Distributions		
1957-58	.34	.66	.69	.31
1965-66	.26	.74	.44	.56

[a]Uncovered category removed.

the poverty lines and for both white and nonwhite males in the three age categories. Table A-13 presents the changes in these transition probabilities for the 25-34 age class; Table A-14 shows the behavior for the 35-44 age class; Table A-15 shows the changes for the 45-54 age class. These changes were somewhat smaller but similar in every other respect to the 1960 age group data. For example, improvements in the transition probabilities tended to be positively related to the earning level, and changes in the nonwhite probabilities were superior to those of the whites.

As before, regressions were calculated between each of the four male transition probabilities and g, percentage change in GNP. Ordinary least squares and logit regressions were both calculated and for all practical purposes were identical. For the 35-44 age group and a $3000 earning level, the following simple linear regressions were obtained:

Table A-10
Male Mover Steady-State Proportions as a Function of g, Percentage Change in GNP, 35-44 Age Group, \$3000 (Age as of 1960)

	Whites Proportion in		g		Nonwhites Proportion in	
L	N	U	(Percentage)	L	N	U
.62	.20	.17	−10	.76	.05	.20
.60	.21	.18	− 9	.74	.05	.21
.59	.22	.19	− 8	.73	.06	.21
.57	.24	.20	− 7	.71	.06	.22
.54	.25	.21	− 6	.70	.07	.23
.52	.27	.21	− 5	.68	.08	.24
.50	.28	.22	− 4	.66	.10	.24
.48	.30	.23	− 3	.64	.11	.25
.45	.31	.23	− 2	.62	.14	.25
. 8	.33	.24	− 1	.60	.14	.25
.41	.35	.25	0	.58	.16	.26
.38	.36	.25	1	.55	.19	.26
.36	.38	.26	2	.53	.22	.25
.34	.40	.26	3	.50	.25	.25
.31	.42	.26	4	.47	.29	.24
.29	.44	.27	5	.44	.33	.24
.27	.46	.27	6	.41	.37	.23
.25	.48	.27	7	.37	.42	.21
.23	.50	.27	8	.34	.46	.20
.21	.52	.27	9	.30	.51	.18
.20	.54	.26	10	.27	.56	.17

		Durbin-Watson Statistics
(1) p_{11}^{w} = .64 − 1.2g, r^2 = .92, t_b = −9		2.1
(2) p_{11}^{n} = .77 − 1.67g, r^2 = .69, t_b = −4		1.5
(3) p_{12}^{w} = .19 + .99g, r^2 = .79, t_b = 5.1		1.2
(4) p_{12}^{n} = .09 + 1.6g, r^2 = .77, t_b = 4.9		1.6
(5) p = .18 − 1.0g, r^2 = .72, t_b = −4.3		1.9
(6) p = 1.8 − 1.8g, r^2 = .65, t_b = −3.6		1.6
(7) p = .76 + .96g, r^2 = .72, t_b = 4.2		2.0
(8) p = .67 + 1.97g, r^2 = .65, t_b = 3.6		1.7

Table A-11
Mover Matrixes for Males (35-44) $3000 Earning Level (Current Age Group)

		White				Nonwhite	
	L	N	U		L	N	U
				1957-58			
L	.56	.20	.14		.68	.11	.13
N	.26	.63	.02		.36	.53	.02
U	.20	.06	.65		.25	.02	.64
				1961-62			
L	.50	.24	.16		.62	.17	.13
N	.12	.76	.03		.16	.74	.01
U	.19	.05	.67		.27	.02	.63
				1965-66			
L	.46	.26	.18		.51	.24	.15
N	.08	.80	.02		.10	.81	.01
U	.12	.04	.73		.19	.03	.68

Table A-12
Steady-State Distributions for the 1957-58 and 1965-66 Matrixes of Table A-11

	White		Nonwhite
		1957-58	
L	.40		.56
N	.35		.18
U	.25		.27
		1965-66	
L	.18		.24
N	.55		.57
U	.27		.19

Again the results are very similar to those obtained for the 1960 age group. The slopes of the nonwhite regressions are larger (absolutely) than the slopes of the whites; the t-ratios are all highly significant. However, the Durbin-Watson statistic was uniformly higher for the constant age regressions and six of the eight coefficients of determination were higher.

The relation between the steady-state proportions and growth were again calculated and are reported in Table A-16. In moving from a growth rate of 0 to 10 percent the white steady-state proportions in N and L changed respectively from .33 to .58 and .41 to .19. The corresponding changes in the nonwhite steady-state proportions were .15 to .60 and .58 to .26.

Table A-13
Behavior of Male Transition Probabilities, 1957-66, for 25-34 Age Category (Current Age Group)

	White					Nonwhite		
L-L	L-N	N-L	N-N	Year	L-L	L-N	N-L	N-N
				$1500 Earning Level				
.45	.27	.20	.65	1957-1958	.51	.21	.31	.55
.38	.36	.12	.72	1958-1959	.46	.30	.17	.68
.40	.31	.11	.74	1959-1960	.50	.25	.17	.70
.41	.26	.12	.73	1960-1961	.51	.21	.19	.69
.38	.31	.09	.77	1961-1962	.46	.29	.14	.75
.39	.29	.08	.78	1962-1963	.47	.27	.13	.75
.38	.30	.07	.79	1963-1964	.45	.29	.11	.77
.36	.32	.06	.82	1964-1965	.44	.32	.08	.80
.35	.34	.05	.83	1965-1966	.41	.35	.08	.81
−.10	+.07	−.15	+.18		−.10	+.14	−.23	+.26
				$3000 Earning Level				
.56	.23	.29	.59	1957-1958	.67	.11	.43	.45
.49	.30	.15	.72	1958-1959	.62	.18	.19	.67
.51	.26	.14	.74	1959-1960	.66	.14	.20	.69
.53	.22	.14	.75	1960-1961	.66	.12	.19	.71
.49	.26	.10	.78	1961-1962	.62	.18	.14	.74
.50	.25	.09	.79	1962-1963	.61	.18	.14	.76
.	.27	.07	.81	1963-1964	.59	.20	.12	.76
.4	.28	.06	.82	1964-1965	.56	.24	.09	.79
.43	.31	.06	.83	1965-1966	.53	.28	.09	.80
−.13	+.08	−.23	+.24		−.14	+.17	−.34	+.35
				$4500 Earning Level				
.66	.18	.38	.50	1957-1958	.73	.06	.50	.37
.57	.27	.18	.70	1958-1959	.67	.12	.23	.63
.60	.22	.14	.74	1959-1960	.70	.10	.20	.67
.61	.19	.13	.76	1960-1961	.70	.08	.18	.68
.57	.23	.09	.79	1961-1962	.69	.11	.12	.75
.57	.21	.09	.80	1962-1963	.69	.10	.12	.76
.54	.24	.07	.80	1963-1964	.67	.13	.12	.74
.52	.26	.06	.81	1964-1965	.64	.16	.09	.76
.48	.30	.06	.80	1965-1966	.61	.21	.10	.76
−.18	+.12	−.22	+.30		−.12	+.16	−.40	+.39

Table A-14

Behavior of Male Transition Probabilities, 1957-66, for 35-44 Age Category (Current Age Group)

White				Year	Nonwhite			
L-L	L-N	N-L	N-N		L-L	L-N	N-L	N-N
				$1500 Earning Level				
.47	.23	.17	.69	1957-1958	.53	.19	.27	.59
.41	.29	.11	.73	1958-1959	.49	.25	.19	.68
.44	.24	.11	.74	1959-1960	.52	.21	.18	.71
.45	.21	.13	.72	1960-1961	.54	.18	.18	.68
.42	.27	.10	.75	1961-1962	.49	.25	.15	.74
.42	.24	.09	.75	1962-1963	.49	.24	.14	.75
.41	.26	.09	.77	1963-1964	.46	.25	.12	.76
.41	.28	.08	.77	1964-1965	.44	.29	.11	.78
.39	.28	.08	.78	1965-1966	.43	.28	.09	.79
−.08	+.05	−.09	+.09		−.10	+.09	−.18	+.20
				$3000 Earning Level				
.56	.20	.26	.63	1957-1958	.68	.11	.36	.53
.49	.26	.15	.72	1958-1959	.62	.16	.20	.70
.53	.22	.14	.74	1959-1960	.65	.14	.20	.70
.54	.19	.15	.73	1960-1961	.65	.12	.22	.68
.50	.24	.12	.76	1961-1962	.62	.17	.16	.74
.	.21	.11	.77	1962-1963	.61	.17	.15	.75
.49	.24	.10	.79	1963-1964	.59	.18	.12	.79
.49	.24	.08	.80	1964-1965	.56	.21	.10	.80
.46	.26	.08	.80	1965-1966	.51	.24	.10	.81
−.08	+.06	−.18	+.17		−.17	+.13	−.26	+.28
				$4500 Earning Level				
.65	.18	.34	.55	1957-1958	.72	.07	.52	.39
.55	.26	.19	.70	1958-1959	.66	.14	.23	.67
.59	.21	.15	.75	1959-1960	.70	.10	.18	.73
.61	.16	.15	.75	1960-1961	.70	.08	.18	.72
.57	.21	.11	.79	1961-1962	.67	.12	.14	.78
.57	.19	.10	.80	1962-1963	.67	.12	.12	.79
.55	.22	.09	.82	1963-1964	.64	.15	.10	.80
.53	.24	.07	.82	1964-1965	.63	.16	.09	.82
.49	.27	.08	.82	1965-1966	.58	.20	.10	.81
−.16	+.09	−.26	+.27		−.14	+.13	−.42	+.42

Table A-15

Behavior of Male Transition Probabilities, 1957-66, for 45-54 Age Category (Current Age Group)

	White				Nonwhite		
L-L	L-N	N-L	N-N	Year	L-L	L-N	N-L	N-N
				$1500 Earning Level				
.51	.23	.15	.72	1957-1958	.58	.18	.23	.66
.42	.26	.10	.74	1958-1959	.51	.20	.16	.72
.44	.23	.10	.75	1959-1960	.54	.20	.17	.71
.45	.20	.12	.72	1960-1961	.52	.17	.19	.70
.42	.25	.10	.74	1961-1962	.50	.22	.14	.73
.42	.22	.10	.73	1962-1963	.50	.20	.14	.75
.42	.24	.10	.74	1963-1964	.51	.21	.13	.74
.41	.24	.09	.75	1964-1965	.48	.22	.11	.76
.41	.26	.09	.76	1965-1966	.45	.28	.12	.77
				$3000 Earning Level				
.62	.18	.22	.66	1957-1958	.72	.09	.33	.58
.51	.24	.13	.74	1958-1959	.65	.14	.19	.70
.55	.19	.14	.74	1959-1960	.67	.11	.20	.70
.55	.17	.15	.72	1960-1961	.67	.10	.21	.70
.52	.21	.13	.75	1961-1962	.64	.14	.14	.76
.	.19	.12	.75	1962-1963	.64	.13	.16	.76
.	.21	.11	.77	1963-1964	.60	.17	.13	.78
.49	.22	.10	.78	1964-1965	.57	.17	.11	.80
.47	.24	.10	.78	1965-1966	.54	.22	.12	.79
				$4500 Earning Level				
.69	.15	.31	.59	1957-1958	.77	.06	.48	.44
.58	.22	.18	.71	1958-1959	.68	.12	.24	.66
.62	.18	.16	.74	1959-1960	.71	.10	.20	.72
.63	.15	.15	.75	1960-1961	.71	.07	.19	.72
.58	.19	.13	.78	1961-1962	.67	.10	.12	.80
.59	.17	.11	.78	1962-1963	.67	.10	.14	.78
.56	.20	.10	.80	1963-1964	.65	.13	.11	.80
.54	.20	.09	.81	1964-1965	.62	.13	.10	.82
.50	.25	.09	.81	1965-1966	.60	.18	.11	.80

Table A-16

Male Mover Steady-State Proportions as a Function of g, Percentage Change in GNP, 35-44 Age Group, $3,000 Poverty Line (Current Age Group)

| | Whites Proportion in | | | | Nonwhites Proportion in | |
L	N	U	g (Percentage)	L	N	U
.63	.16	.20	−10	.75	.04	.22
.61	.17	.21	− 9	.73	.04	.22
.59	.19	.22	− 8	.72	.05	.23
.57	.20	.22	− 7	.71	.05	.24
.55	.22	.23	− 6	.69	.06	.25
.53	.23	.24	− 5	.68	.07	.25
.51	.25	.24	− 4	.66	.08	.26
.48	.27	.25	− 3	.64	.10	.26
.46	.29	.25	− 2	.62	.11	.26
.44	.31	.26	− 1	.60	.13	.26
.41	.33	.26	0	.58	.15	.26
.39	.35	.26	1	.56	.18	.26
.36	.38	26	2	.53	.21	.26
.34	.40	.26	3	.50	.25	.25
.32	.42	.26	4	.47	.29	.24
.29	.45	.26	5	.44	.33	.23
.27	.48	.26	6	.40	.38	.22
.25	.50	.25	7	.37	.43	.20
.23	.53	.25	8	.33	.49	.18
.21	.55	.24	9	.29	.54	.16
.19	.58	.23	10	.26	.60	.14

A Finer Partition of the Earnings Distribution

The dichotomous partition of the earnings distribution is momentarily replaced by the following finer partition: < 2000, 2000-3999, 4000-5999, > 6000. The stayer proportions for this decomposition of the income distribution are reported in Table A-17. All of these proportions are significantly greater than zero. The nonwhite stayer proportions for the two lowest income categories are significantly greater than those of whites. On the other hand, the white stayer proportions in the highest income category were significantly greater than those of nonwhites. These results were true of all age groups. In the $4000-5999 income group, the relation between white and nonwhite stayer proportions depended on age.

The steady-state distributions for this finer partition are presented in Table

Table A-17
Male Stayer Proportions, 1957-66[a]

Earnings	Age Group as of 1960	Whites	Nonwhites
	25-34	.037	.063
< 2000	35-44	.088	.118
	45-54	.119	.100
	25-34	.027	.071
2000-3999	35-44	.048	.075
	45-54	.089	.146
	25-34	.020	.045
4000-5999	35-44	.038	.025
	45-54	.064	.073
	25-34	.636	.375
> 6000	35-44	.660	.448
	45-54	.611	.458

[a]These proportions may be interpreted as the probability of remaining in an earnings class all ten years given occupancy in that earnings class in 1957.

A-18 along with the associated mover matrixes. The improvements in the mover matrixes and steady-state distributions over this ten-year period are impressive. Furthermore, the relative comparisons between white and nonwhite movers demonstrate the same superiority of nonwhite as before.

Empirical Findings for Females

The effect of improved economic conditions on female labor participation rates could in theory be either positive or negative (see Cain, 1966, and Mincer, 1962). The rise in family income accompanying growth could cause a wife to reduce her labor-force participation. On the other hand, occupations previously closed to women would in periods of sustained growth demand their services. These improved job opportunities could cause female labor participation to increase. Unfortunately, the results of the analysis here are inconclusive on this point since the unit of measure is the individual and not the family. Nevertheless, they do suggest that, for both whites and nonwhites, the female labor participation rate is positively related to economic growth.

With respect to females whose low-earning (L) or non-low-earning (N) status is affected by sustained growth (the so-called movers), both whites and nonwhites exhibited substantial improvements, with nonwhites benefiting slightly more than whites. These differences in white and nonwhite performance are not nearly as great, however, as those discovered in the case of nonwhite and

Table A-18

Matrix Analysis for Males (35-44) When the Earnings Distribution is Partitioned into Four Categories (1960 Age Group)

Mover Matrixes

Year and Category	White					Nonwhite				
	$2000	$2000-3999	$4000-5999	$6000	U	$2000	$2000-3999	$4000-5999	$6000	U
1957-58										
$2000	.57	.22	.05	.01	.14	.66	.17	.01	.00	.15
$2000-3999	.20	.52	.24	.02	.02	.23	.64	.09	.01	.04
$4000-5999	.05	.15	.65	.15	.01	.06	.21	.66	.08	.00
$6000	.06	.12	.33	.48	.01	.02	.07	.56	.36	.00
U	.26	.06	.02	.01	.65	.26	.07	.00	.00	.67
1965-66										
$2000	.50	.19	.06	.03	.22	.51	.26	.04	.01	.19
$2000-3999	.13	.38	.30	.11	.08	.15	.55	.26	.02	.02
$4000-5999	.04	.07	.49	.38	.01	.03	.10	.63	.23	.01
$6000	.01	.03	.05	.90	.01	.02	.03	.08	.85	.02
U	.10	.03	.01	.01	.84	.18	.03	.00	.00	.80
Steady-State Distributions										
1957-58	.19	.22	.32	.15	.13	.38	.31	.13	.02	.19
1965-66	.08	.08	.12	.57	.18	.14	.16	.20	.35	.18
Total Steady-State Distributions[a]										
1957-58	.17	.19	.26	.24	.18	.37	.27	.10	.02	.28
1965-66	.06	.09	.12	.67	.07	.14	.16	.21	.39	.13

[a]These distributions include both movers and stayers.

white male movers. These relative improvements were again measured by changes in the transition probabilities of the mover matrix. For both white and nonwhite females, the probabilities of moving from L to N and from N to N increased, while the probabilities of moving from N to L and from L to L declined.

Contrasted to male movers, nonwhite females did not always benefit more from growth than their white counterparts. The benefits accruing to nonwhites relative to whites as a consequence of growth depended on age, earning level, and the transition probability used to measure improvement.

Table A-19 presents the female stayer proportions by race, age, and earning level. The stayer proportions are all significantly (at .01) different from zero. Thus the stayer-mover Markov model gives a better description of female earnings mobility than the simple Markov model. The proportion of females who remained in L through 1966 given occupancy in L during 1957 is significantly (at .001) higher for nonwhites than for whites. This result is independent of age and earning level and corresponds to the analysis of nonwhite male stayers relative to whites (see Table A-1). With the exception of the 25-34 age group, the non-low-earning stayer proportions were significantly (at .005) greater for whites than for nonwhites. This was true for all earning levels. For the 25-34 age group, the differences were significant for the $1500 (at .005) and $3000 (at .10) earning levels, but insignificant for the $4500 earning level. The proportion of stayers in L is positively related to age for both whites and nonwhites at all three earning levels.

Table A-19
Female Stayer Proportions, 1957-66 (Age as of 1960)

| Low Earnings | | | Non-Low Earnings | |
Nonwhite	White		Nonwhite	White
		Age Group		
		$1500 Earning Level		
.05	.02	25-34	.34	.30
.11	.04	35-44	.45	.52
.18	.07	45-54	.48	.56
		$3000 Earning Level		
.17	.08	25-34	.30	.27
.28	.16	35-44	.43	.49
.32	.20	45-54	.47	.54
		$4500 Earning Level		
.29	.18	25-34	.28	.26
.41	.31	35-44	.33	.43
.44	.36	45-54	.32	.47

The second stayer probability is the unconditional probability of remaining in L or N for the ten periods. This probability is obtained by dividing the total number of stayers in L or N by the total number in the specific nonincome category, for example, female, white, 25-34. These stayer probabilities are reported in Table A-20 for white and nonwhite females, for each age group, and for each earning level. Note that the probabilities of staying in L are somewhat similar for nonwhite males and white females (compare Table A-2). Within each nonincome category, the proportion of movers is obtained by subtracting the proportion of stayers in N from one. The proportion of movers in each nonincome category is also recorded in Table A-20. It is important to keep these mover proportions in mind when discussing differences in various mover matrixes. In Table A-20 note that the proportion of movers is roughly the same for whites and nonwhites for each of the age categories and earning levels. This was not the case for males.

Analysis of the Mover Matrixes for the 1960 Age Group

The mover matrixes are first analyzed for the 1960 age groups; that is, an individual is placed in one of the three age groups based on his age as of 1960. The behavior of each individual is then analyzed for the ten years. In the

Table A-20

Female Stayers and Movers as Proportions of Each Age-Race Category (1960 Age Groups)

	Nonwhite Stayers In					White Stayers In		
L	N	U	Nonwhite Movers	Age Group[a]	L	N	U	White Movers
				$1500				
.015	.054	.125	.806	25-34	.004	.088	.137	.770
.037	.100	.109	.754	35-44	.008	.163	.113	.716
.067	.114	.104	.715	45-54	.015	.232	.099	.654
				$3000				
.079	.010	.125	.786	25-34	.030	.036	.137	.796
.139	.025	.109	.727	35-44	.060	.072	.113	.754
.180	.025	.104	.691	45-54	.090	.106	.099	.705
				$4500				
.140	.001	.125	.734	25-34	.089	.004	.137	.770
.222	.003	.109	.665	35-44	.156	.014	.113	.718
.264	.003	.104	.629	45-54	.215	.022	.099	.663

[a]In the 25-34 age group, there were 12,161 nonwhites, 103,049 whites.
In the 35-44 age group, there were 10,818 nonwhites, 74,608 whites.
In the 45-54 age group, there were 7,509 nonwhites, 59,258 whites.

Table A-21
Mover Matrixes for Females (35-44) When a $1500 Earning Level is Used (1960 Age Group)

		White			Nonwhite	
	L	N	U	L	N	U
			1957-58			
L	.58	.21	.21	.65	.14	.21
N	.26	.69	.05	.30	.65	.05
U	.17	.03	.80	.20	.02	.77
			1961-62			
L	.53	.25	.22	.63	.16	.21
N	.13	.83	.04	.17	.80	.03
U	.22	.04	.73	.26	.02	.72
			1965-66			
L	.51	.28	.20	.60	.21	.18
N	.12	.85	.03	.14	.83	.02
U	.16	.04	.79	.21	.04	.75

Table A-22
Steady-State Distributions for the 1957-58 and 1965-66 Matrixes of Table A-21

	White	Nonwhite
	1957-58	
L	.33	.40
N	.27	.19
U	.40	.41
	1965-66	
L	.22	.30
N	.49	.44
U	.29	.26

following subsection, the behavior of age groups is analyzed where the composition of each age group varies over time.

Deleting the stayers from the transition matrixes gives the mover matrixes discussed under the empirical findings for males. Mover matrixes are shown in Table A-21 for white and nonwhite females between the ages of 35 and 44 (age as of 1960) for each of the transition periods, 1957-58, 1960-61, and 1965-66, when a $1500 earning level is used. The steady-state distributions associated with the 1957-58 and 1965-66 mover matrixes are also presented in Table A-22.

Table A-23
Population Steady-State Distributions for the 1957-58 and 1965-66 Matrixes of Table A-21

	White		Nonwhite
		1957-58	
L	.26		.34
N	.30		.21
U	.45		.46
		1965-66	
L	.17		.26
N	.47		.41
U	.36		.33

These distributions show the proportion of individuals in each category at any point in time *assuming* that the particular transition matrix persists indefinitely. The corresponding population (movers and stayers) steady-state distributions are shown in Table A-23.

Casual observation of the transition matrixes reveals their nonstationarity; that is, the transition probabilities are not constant over time.[20] For example, the probability of a nonwhite transiting from N to N in 1957-58 is .65, in 1960-61 is .80, and in 1964-65 is .83. As previously hypothesized, one would anticipate that the persistence of high growth rates would affect the mover transition matrix. In particular, it would be expected that for the movers, as GNP increased, the probabilities of transits from L to L and from N to L would decline, and the probabilities of L to N and from N to N would increase. This in fact did occur. Tables A-24 to A-26 show the manner in which these transition probabilities changed over the ten-year period for each of the earning levels and for both white and nonwhite females in the three prime working age categories. Table A-24 displays the changes in the conditional probabilities for the 25-34 age class, Table A-25 for the 35-44 age class, and Table A-26 for the 45-54 age class. In all three tables, improvements in the transition probabilities over the ten-year interval tended to be positively related to the earning level. As the poverty line increased (over the range considered here), people who are more likely to benefit from economic growth are classified as movers.

These tables also reveal that the growth that occurred over 1957-66 did for the most part have the hypothesized effect on the four transition probabilities, that is, L to N and N to N probabilities both increased, and N to L and L to L probabilities both declined. On the basis of these measures, nonwhites appear to have benefited more from growth than did whites. However, this difference is not nearly as strong as it was for males.

To measure the relation between the transition probabilities and growth more

Table A-24

Behavior of Female Transition Probabilities, 1957-66, for 25-34 Age Category (1960 Age Group)

White						Year	Nonwhite					
L-L	L-N	N-L	N-N	U-L	U-N		L-L	L-N	N-L	N-N	U-L	U-N
						$1500 Earning Level						
.52	.21	.25	.69	.19	.04	1957-1958	.60	.14	.33	.64	.21	.02
.48	.22	.21	.70	.21	.04	1958-1959	.61	.16	.26	.69	.24	.02
.49	.21	.20	.72	.21	.04	1959-1960	.59	.17	.22	.73	.24	.03
.49	.20	.19	.72	.19	.04	1960-1961	.59	.14	.21	.75	.24	.03
.50	.22	.16	.76	.20	.04	1961-1962	.58	.18	.17	.79	.24	.03
.50	.22	.16	.77	.19	.04	1962-1963	.60	.18	.17	.79	.27	.03
.49	.24	.15	.79	.19	.04	1963-1964	.57	.20	.15	.82	.28	.03
.51	.25	.13	.82	.21	.05	1964-1965	.55	.23	.13	.84	.33	.05
.51	.27	.13	.83	.16	.04	1965-1966	.54	.26	.13	.84	.27	.06
-.01	+.06	-.12	+.14	+.03	0		-.06	+.12	-.20	+.20	+.06	+.04
						$3000 Earning Level						
.69	.11	.35	.63	.22	.01	1957-1958	.73	.05	.39	.60	.23	.00
.63	.12	.28	.69	.25	.01	1958-1959	.72	.07	.24	.74	.27	.00
.65	.11	.26	.71	.24	.01	1959-1960	.72	.07	.23	.76	.26	.00
.64	.11	.24	.73	.22	.01	1960-1961	.72	.06	.22	.77	.26	.00
.65	.12	.20	.77	.23	.01	1961-1962	.73	.07	.19	.80	.26	.00
.66	.11	.19	.78	.22	.01	1962-1963	.74	.08	.19	.81	.30	.01
.65	.14	.17	.80	.23	.01	1963-1964	.72	.09	.17	.82	.31	.01
.66	.15	.15	.83	.24	.01	1964-1965	.71	.11	.16	.82	.37	.01
.66	.17	.16	.82	.10	.01	1965-1966	.70	.14	.16	.82	.33	.01

$4500 Earning Level

						Year							
.79	.03	.45	.54	.23	.00	1957-1958	.75	.01	.57	.43	.23	.00
.74	.05	.29	.69	.25	.00	1958-1959	.76	.02	.35	.63	.27	.00
.74	.05	.27	.72	.24	.00	1959-1960	.76	.02	.31	.69	.27	.00
.73	.05	.23	.76	.23	.00	1960-1961	.75	.02	.26	.74	.26	.00
.73	.06	.21	.78	.23	.00	1961-1962	.77	.03	.23	.76	.27	.00
.74	.06	.18	.81	.23	.00	1962-1963	.79	.04	.20	.80	.30	.00
.74	.07	.17	.82	.23	.00	1963-1964	.77	.05	.16	.83	.31	.00
.75	.08	.15	.84	.25	.00	1964-1965	.78	.05	.15	.85	.38	.00
.76	.09	.16	.83	.20	.00	1965-1966	.78	.06	.20	.79	.33	.00
-.03	+.06	-.29	+.29	-.03	0		-.03	+.05	-.37	+.34	+.10	0

Table A-25
Behavior of Female Transition Probabilities, 1957-66, for 35-44 Age Category (1960 Age Group)

	White						Year	Nonwhite					
	L-L	L-N	N-L	N-N	U-L	U-N		L-L	L-N	N-L	N-N	U-L	U-N
							$1500 Earning Level						
	.58	.21	.26	.69	.17	.03	1957-1958	.65	.14	.30	.65	.20	.02
	.54	.25	.18	.76	.21	.04	1958-1959	.62	.17	.23	.73	.24	.03
	.55	.24	.17	.78	.22	.04	1959-1960	.61	.17	.18	.79	.25	.02
	.54	.22	.16	.80	.21	.04	1960-1961	.64	.14	1.8	.79	.23	.02
	.53	.25	.13	.83	.22	.04	1961-1962	.63	.16	.17	.80	.26	.03
	.54	.23	.13	.83	.22	.04	1962-1963	.63	.15	.16	.82	.25	.02
	.53	.24	.11	.85	.22	.05	1963-1964	.64	.16	.14	.83	.26	.03
	.53	.26	.11	.86	.24	.05	1964-1965	.64	.17	.13	.85	.28	.04
	.51	.28	.12	.85	.16	.04	1965-1966	.60	.21	.14	.83	.21	.04
	-.07	+.07	-.14	+.16	-.01	+.01		-.05	+.07	-.16	+.18	+.01	+.02
							$3000 Earning Level						
	.75	.10	.33	.65	.19	.01	1957-1958	.76	.05	.35	.64	.22	.01
	.70	.13	.23	.75	.24	.01	1958-1959	.74	.07	.28	.72	.26	.01
	.72	.12	.20	.78	.25	.01	1959-1960	.75	.07	.18	.81	.27	.00
	.71	.11	.18	.81	.24	.01	1960-1961	.76	.06	.21	.78	.25	.00
	.71	.13	.15	.83	.26	.01	1961-1962	.75	.07	.15	.84	.28	.00
	.71	.13	.14	.84	.25	.01	1962-1963	.75	.08	.15	.85	.27	.00
	.69	.14	.13	.86	.25	.01	1963-1964	.75	.09	.15	.84	.29	.00
	.69	.15	.12	.87	.27	.01	1964-1965	.74	.10	.14	.85	.31	.01
	.67	.18	.13	.86	.20	.01	1965-1966	.72	.12	.17	.82	.24	.01
	-.08	+.08	-.20	+.21	+.01	0		-.04	+.07	-.18	+.18	+.02	0

$4500 Earning Level

						Year						
.81	.04	.42	.57	.20	.00	1957-1958	.77	.02	.58	.42	.23	.00
.78	.07	.24	.75	.25	.00	1958-1959	.76	.03	.23	.77	.26	.00
.79	.05	.20	.79	.26	.00	1959-1960	.78	.02	.19	.81	.27	.00
.78	.06	.16	.83	.24	.00	1960-1961	.78	.03	.13	.87	.25	.00
.78	.07	.15	.85	.26	.00	1961-1962	.79	.03	.12	.87	.28	.00
.78	.07	.14	.86	.26	.00	1962-1963	.79	.03	.13	.87	.27	.00
.77	.08	.12	.87	.26	.00	1963-1964	.80	.04	.09	.91	.29	.00
.78	.08	.12	.88	.29	.00	1964-1965	.80	.04	.13	.86	.32	.00
.77	.10	.14	.85	.20	.00	1965-1966	.80	.05	.17	.83	.25	.00
-.04	+.06	-.28	+.28	0	0		+.03	+.03	-.41	+.41	+.02	0

Table A-26
Behavior of Female Transition Probabilities, 1957-66, for 45-54 Age Category (1960 Age Group)

	White						Year	Nonwhite					
	L-L	L-N	N-L	N-N	U-L	U-N		L-L	L-N	N-L	N-N	U-L	U-N
							$1500 Earning Level						
	.61	.22	.23	.74	.18	.03	1957-1958	.70	.13	.32	.65	.20	.02
	.56	.24	.16	.80	.23	.05	1958-1959	.67	.13	.22	.73	.25	.02
	.56	.23	.15	.82	.23	.04	1959-1960	.66	.13	.19	.78	.24	.02
	.56	.20	.15	.81	.20	.04	1960-1961	.67	.12	.18	.79	.24	.02
	.55	.23	.13	.83	.21	.04	1961-1962	.66	.13	.17	.80	.24	.02
	.55	.21	.13	.83	.18	.03	1962-1963	.69	.11	.16	.82	.21	.02
	.55	.22	.11	.85	.17	.04	1963-1964	.66	.14	.13	.83	.22	.02
	.53	.23	.11	.85	.17	.03	1964-1965	.67	.12	.13	.83	.21	.02
	.52	.25	.12	.84	.11	.02	1965-1966	.64	.15	.16	.81	.16	.02
	-.09	+.03	-.11	+.10	-.07	-.01		-.06	+.02	-.16	+.16	-.04	0
							$3000 Earning Level						
	.78	.11	.28	.71	.21	.01	1957-1958	.81	.04	.39	.58	.21	.00
	.73	.13	.18	.80	.26	.01	1958-1959	.77	.05	.20	.79	.26	.00
	.73	.12	.17	.81	.27	.01	1959-1960	.78	.04	.18	.82	.26	.00
	.73	.10	.17	.82	.23	.01	1960-1961	.77	.05	.16	.82	.25	.00
	.72	.13	.14	.85	.24	.01	1961-1962	.76	.06	.15	.85	.26	.01
	.71	.12	.14	.84	.21	.01	1962-1963	.78	.06	.16	.82	.23	.00
	.69	.14	.12	.87	.20	.01	1963-1964	.75	.07	.11	.88	.23	.00
	.68	.14	.12	.86	.19	.01	1964-1965	.74	.07	.14	.85	.22	.00
	.65	.17	.14	.84	.13	.00	1965-1966	.72	.10	.14	.85	.17	.00

$4500 Earning Level

.84	.05	.35	.64	.22	.00	1957-1958	.82	.02	.48	.50	.22	.00
.79	.08	.18	.80	.22	.00	1958-1959	.78	.02	.26	.74	.26	.00
.80	.06	.16	.84	.27	.00	1959-1960	.78	.02	.12	.88	.26	.00
.79	.06	.15	.85	.23	.00	1960-1961	.78	.02	.18	.81	.26	.00
.78	.07	.12	.88	.25	.00	1961-1962	.78	.03	.09	.90	.26	.00
.77	.07	.11	.88	.21	.00	1962-1963	.80	.02	.13	.87	.23	.00
.76	.09	.10	.89	.21	.00	1963-1964	.78	.03	.07	.92	.24	.00
.75	.09	.11	.89	.20	.00	1964-1965	.78	.03	.09	.91	.23	.00
.73	.11	.16	.83	.14	.00	1965-1966	.77	.04	.18	.82	.23	.00
-.11	+.06	-.19	+.19	-.02	0		-.05	+.02	-.30	+.32	+.01	0

precisely, each of the transition probabilities was regressed on percentage change in GNP. For the 35-44 age group and a \$1500 earning level, the following simple linear regressions were obtained:

				Durbin-Watson Statistics
(1)	p_{11}^{w}	= .58	$- .63g, r^2 = .79, t_b = -5$	1.3
(2)	p_{11}^{n}	= .64	$- .23g, r^2 = .16, t_b = -1.1$	1.4
(3)	p_{12}^{w}	= .20	$+ .75g, r^2 = .86, t_b = 6.5$	1.8
(4)	p_{12}^{n}	= .13	$+ .59g, r^2 = .51, t_b = 2.7$	1.8
(5)	p_{21}^{w}	= .23	$- 1.32g, r^2 = .55, t_b = -3$	1
(6)	p_{21}^{n}	= .26	$- 1.35g, r^2 = .43, t_b = -2.3$	1.1
(7)	p_{22}^{w}	= .71	$+ 1.48g, r^2 = .54, t_b = 2.9$	1
(8)	p_{22}^{n}	= .70	$+ 1.47g, r^2 = .40, t_b = 2.2$	1.1
(9)	p_{u1}^{w}	= .19	$+ .19g, r^2 = .04, t_b = .54$	1.5
(10)	p_{u1}^{n}	= .22	$+ .38g, r^2 = .19, t_b = 1.28$	1.7
(11)	p_{u2}^{w}	= .03	$+ .19g, r^2 = .57, t_b = 3.04$	1.9
(12)	p_{u2}^{n}	= .02	$+ .21g, r^2 = .57, t_b = 3.02$	1.2

These regressions yielded mixed results. In some cases, there was no significant relationship between g and a particular transition probability, and in others the relation was significant. Also, in some cases nonwhites were more strongly influenced by g than whites and in other cases the reverse was true.

From the regressions of the nine transition probabilities on growth, the relationship between the steady-state distribution and growth can be calculated. The results are presented in Table A-27 for both whites and nonwhites in the 35-44 age group when a \$1500 earning level is used. As g increases from 0 to 10 percent the white steady-state proportions in L, N, and U change from .33, .27, and .40 to .23, .52, and .25 respectively. Similar changes for nonwhites are from .39, .20, and .41 to .32, .43, and .25. As expected, for both whites and nonwhites the steady-state proportion in L(N) decreases (increases) with g. An interesting finding is that for both whites and nonwhites the steady-state proportion in U is a decreasing function of g. This suggests that the labor-force participation rates of females are strongly affected by growth.

*Analysis of the Mover Matrixes for
the Current Age Group*

The mover matrixes are now analyzed for the current age group. In this analysis, the age intervals 25-34, 35-44, and 45-54 are held fixed over time while

Table A-27

Female Mover Steady-State Proportions as a Function of g, Percentage Change in GNP, 35-44 Age Group, $1500 (Age as of 1960)

	Whites Proportion in				Nonwhites Proportion in	
L	N	U	g (Percentage)	L	N	U
.39	.13	.48	−10	.40	.08	.52
.39	.14	.47	− 9	.40	.09	.51
.39	.15	.46	− 8	.40	.10	.50
.38	.16	.46	− 7	.40	.11	.49
.38	.17	.45	− 6	.40	.12	.48
.37	.18	.44	− 5	.40	.13	.47
.36	.20	.43	− 4	.40	.14	.46
.36	.22	.43	− 3	.40	.15	.45
.35	.23	.42	− 2	.40	.17	.44
.34	.25	.40	− 1	.40	.18	.42
.33	.27	.40	0	.39	.20	.41
.33	.29	.38	1	.39	.22	.39
.32	.31	.37	2	.39	.23	.38
.31	.34	.36	3	.38	.26	.36
.30	.36	.34	4	.37	.28	.35
.29	.39	.33	5	.37	.30	.33
.27	.41	.31	6	.36	.32	.32
.26	.44	.30	7	.35	.35	.30
.25	.47	.28	8	.34	.38	.28
.24	.50	.27	9	.33	.41	.26
.23	.52	.25	10	.32	.43	.25

membership changes. The purpose of holding the age intervals fixed is to measure the influence of aging on the previous analysis.

These modified mover matrixes are displayed in Table A-28 for white and nonwhite females between the ages of 35 and 44 (current age group) for each of the transition periods 1957-58, 1960-61, and 1965-66 when a $1500 earning level is used. The steady-state distributions associated with the 1957-58 and 1965-66 mover matrixes are presented in Table A-29. These matrixes possess approximately the same characteristics as those for the 1960 age group. Both the L to N and N to N probabilities increased.

Tables A-30 to A-32 show the manner in which these transition probabilities changed over the ten-year period for each of the poverty lines and for both white and nonwhite females in the three age categories. Table A-30 presents the changes in these transition probabilities for the 25-34 age class, Table A-31 for the 35-44 age class, and Table A-32 for the 45-54 age class. These changes were very similar to the 1960 age group data. The substantial changes in the UL and

Table A-28
Mover Matrixes for Females (35-44) When a $1500 Earning Level Is Used (Current Age Group)

		White			Nonwhite		
		L	N	U	L	N	U
				1957-58			
	L	.59	.21	.19	.66	.14	.20
	N	.25	.70	.05	.30	.65	.05
	U	.17	.03	.79	.20	.02	.78
				1961-1962			
	L	.53	.25	.22	.63	.16	.22
	N	.13	.82	.04	.17	.80	.03
	U	.22	.04	.73	.26	.03	.71
				1965-1966			
	L	.52	.29	.20	.57	.24	.19
	N	.12	.85	.04	.12	.84	.03
	U	.17	.05	.78	.24	.05	.71

Table A-29
Steady-State Distributions for the 1957-58 and 1965-66 Matrixes of Table A-28

	White	Nonwhite
	1957-58	
L	.34	.41
N	.28	.19
U	.38	.40
	1965-66	
L	.22	.27
N	.50	.50
U	.28	.23

UN transition probabilities (for the 1960 age group) that occurred between 1964-65 and 1965-66 diminish markedly when age is held fixed.

As before, regressions were calculated between each of the four transition probabilities and g. Both ordinary least squares and logit regressions were calculated.

For the 35-44 age group and a $1500 poverty line, the following ordinary least squares regressions were obtained:

(1) $p_{11}^w = .58 - .74g$, $r^2 = .70$, $t_b = -4.0$ 1.7

(2) $p_{11}^n = .66 - .65g$, $r^2 = .49$, $t_b = -2.6$ 1.8

(3) $p_{12}^w = .20 + .76g$, $r^2 = .83$, $t_b = 5.9$ 1.6

(4) $p_{12}^n = .12 + .79g$, $r^2 = .46$, $t_b = 2.4$ 1.7

(5) $p_{21}^w = .23 - 1.23g$, $r^2 = .55$, $t_b = -2.9$ 1.3

(6) $p_{21}^n = .27 - 1.43g$, $r^2 = .45$, $t_b = -2.4$ 1.6

(7) $p_{22}^w = .72 + 1.3g$, $r^2 = .55$, $t_b = 2.9$ 1.3

(8) $p_{22}^n = .70 + 1.5g$, $r^2 = .43$, $t_b = 2.3$ 1.6

(9) $p_{u1}^w = .19 + .29g$, $r^2 = .11$, $t_b = .92$ 1.9

(10) $p_{u1}^n = .21 + .71g$, $r^2 = .39$, $t_b = 2.1$ 2.5

(11) $p_{u2}^w = .03 + .20g$, $r^2 = .63$, $t_b = 3.4$ 1.9

(12) $p_{u2}^n = .01 + .29g$, $r^2 = .52$, $t_b = 2.8$ 1.5

These constant age regressions are for all practical purposes identical to those for the 1960 age group.

The relation between the steady-state proportions and growth were again calculated. These are reported in Table A-33. In moving from a growth rate of 0 to 10 percent, the white steady-state proportions in N and L changed from .28 to .51 and .33 to .23. The corresponding changes in the nonwhite steady-state proportions were .19 to .46 and .40 to .31. For both whites and nonwhites, steady-state proportion in uncovered displayed a dramatic decline, which again suggests that increased growth has a strong effect on female labor participation rates.

Table A-30
Behavior of Female Transition Probabilities, 1957-66 for 25-34 Age Category (Current Age Group)

White						Year	Nonwhite					
L-L	L-N	N-L	N-N	U-L	U-N		L-L	L-N	N-L	N-N	U-L	U-N
						$1500 Earning Level						
.54	.20	.25	.69	.18	.03	1957-1958	.61	.14	.33	.64	.20	.02
.49	.22	.21	.71	.21	.04	1958-1959	.61	.16	.25	.71	.24	.03
.50	.21	.19	.72	.21	.04	1959-1960	.59	.17	.22	.73	.24	.03
.49	.20	.19	.72	.19	.03	1960-1961	.59	.14	.21	.75	.23	.03
.49	.21	.17	.74	.19	.04	1961-1962	.58	.18	.18	.78	.24	.03
.48	.21	.16	.75	.17	.03	1962-1963	.59	.19	.17	.79	.27	.03
.47	.23	.16	.76	.16	.04	1963-1964	.55	.21	.16	.80	.29	.04
.48	.22	.14	.78	.16	.04	1964-1965	.52	.24	.14	.83	.33	.05
.47	.25	.14	.79	.14	.04	1965-1966	.52	.28	.15	.82	.27	.08
-.07	+.05	-.11	+.10	-.04	+.01		-.09	+.14	-.18	+.18	+.07	+.05
						$3000 Earning Level						
.70	.10	.35	.63	.20	.01	1957-1958	.73	.05	.39	.60	.22	.00
.64	.13	.27	.70	.24	.01	1958-1959	.73	.07	.24	.75	.26	.00
.65	.11	.25	.71	.24	.01	1959-1960	.72	.07	.23	.76	.26	.00
.64	.11	.24	.72	.22	.01	1960-1961	.71	.06	.23	.76	.26	.00
.63	.12	.21	.75	.22	.01	1961-1962	.73	.07	.20	.78	.27	.00
.63	.12	.21	.75	.20	.01	1962-1963	.73	.08	.20	.79	.29	.01
.62	.14	.20	.76	.19	.01	1963-1964	.71	.09	.19	.80	.32	.00
.61	.14	.17	.79	.19	.01	1964-1965	.71	.11	.18	.81	.37	.01
.61	.16	.19	.77	.17	.01	1965-1966	.69	.15	.18	.81	.34	.01
-.09	+.06	+.16	+.14	-.04	0		-.03	+.10	-.21	+.21	+.12	+.01

$4500 Earning Level

						Year						
.79	.03	.44	.55	.21	.00	1957-1958	.74	.01	.44	.56	.22	.00
.74	.05	.28	.70	.24	.00	1958-1959	.76	.02	.31	.67	.26	.00
.74	.05	.26	.73	.24	.00	1959-1960	.76	.02	.31	.68	.27	.00
.72	.05	.24	.75	.23	.00	1960-1961	.75	.02	.25	.74	.26	.00
.72	.06	.23	.76	.22	.00	1961-1962	.77	.03	.26	.73	.27	.00
.71	.06	.22	.77	.21	.00	1962-1963	.78	.04	.25	.75	.30	.00
.71	.07	.21	.78	.20	.00	1963-1964	.77	.04	.18	.81	.33	.00
.70	.08	.19	.80	.19	.00	1964-1965	.77	.05	.18	.82	.38	.00
.70	.09	.22	.76	.17	.00	1965-1966	.79	.06	.20	.79	.35	.00
-.09	+.06	-.22	+.21	-.04	0		+.05	+.05	-.24	+.23	+.12	0

Table A-31
Behavior of Female Transition Probabilities, 1957-66 for 35-44 Age Category (Current Age Group)

White						Year	Nonwhite					
L-L	N-L	L-N	N-N	U-L	U-N		L-L	L-N	N-L	N-N	U-L	U-N
						$1500 Earning Level						
.59	.25	.21	.70	.17	.03	1957-1958	.66	.14	.30	.65	.20	.02
.54	.18	.25	.77	.21	.04	1958-1959	.62	.16	.23	.73	.23	.03
.55	.17	.24	.78	.22	.04	1959-1960	.61	.18	.18	.80	.25	.02
.54	.16	.22	.80	.21	.04	1960-1961	.63	.14	.18	.78	.23	.02
.53	.13	.25	.82	.22	.04	1961-1962	.63	.16	.17	.80	.26	.03
.53	.13	.24	.82	.22	.04	1962-1963	.62	.16	.15	.81	.25	.03
.53	.12	.25	.84	.23	.05	1963-1964	.62	.18	.13	.83	.26	.04
.52	.11	.26	.85	.24	.06	1964-1965	.61	.19	.13	.85	.31	.05
.52	.12	.29	.85	.17	.05	1965-1956	.57	.24	.12	.84	.24	.05
-.08	-.13	+.07	+.14	0	.01		-.09	+.10	-.18	+.19	+.04	+.03
						$3000 Earning Level						
.76	.32	.10	.66	.20	.01	1957-1958	.78	.04	.38	.61	.22	.00
.71	.22	.13	.77	.24	.01	1958-1959	.75	.06	.29	.71	.25	.01
.72	.20	.12	.78	.25	.01	1959-1960	.75	.07	.18	.82	.27	.00
.71	.18	.11	.81	.24	.01	1960-1961	.75	.06	.21	.78	.25	.00
.71	.15	.13	.83	.26	.01	1961-1962	.74	.08	.15	.84	.28	.00
.70	.15	.12	.83	.25	.01	1962-1963	.74	.08	.15	.84	.27	.00
.69	.14	.14	.85	.26	.01	1963-1964	.74	.09	.16	.83	.29	.00
.69	.13	.15	.86	.29	.01	1964-1965	.73	.11	.14	.14	.85	.36
.67	.14	.18	.85	.21	.01	1965-1966	.70	.14	.16	.83	.28	.01
-.09	-.18	+.08	+.19	+.01	0		-.08	+.10	-.22	+.22	+.06	0

	$4500 Earning Level											
1957-1958	.82	.04	.40	.59	.20	.00	.78	.02	.53	.47	.22	.00
1958-1959	.78	.07	.23	.75	.25	.00	.76	.03	.25	.75	.26	.00
1959-1960	.80	.05	.20	.79	.26	.00	.78	.03	.19	.80	.27	.00
1960-1961	.78	.06	.17	.83	.24	.00	.77	.03	.14	.86	.25	.00
1961-1962	.78	.07	.15	.84	.26	.00	.78	.03	.13	.86	.29	.00
1962-1963	.78	.06	.14	.85	.26	.00	.78	.04	.13	.87	.28	.00
1963-1964	.77	.08	.13	.86	.27	.00	.79	.04	.11	.89	.29	.00
1964-1965	.77	.08	.13	.87	.30	.00	.80	.04	.12	.88	.36	.00
1965-1966	.77	.10	.14	.85	.22	.00	.79	.06	.17	.83	.29	.00
	-.05	+.05	-.26	+.26	+.02	0	0	+.05	-.36	+.36	+.07	0

Table A-32
Behavior of Female Transition Probabilities, 1957-66, for 45-54 Age Category (Current Age Group)

	White						Year	Nonwhite					
	L-L	L-N	N-L	N-N	U-L	U-N		L-L	L-N	N-L	N-N	U-L	U-N
$1500 Earning Level													
	.62	.22	.22	.75	.19	.04	1957-1958	.72	.12	.29	.68	.20	.02
	.56	.23	.16	.80	.23	.05	1958-1959	.68	.12	.21	.74	.25	.02
	.56	.22	.15	.81	.23	.04	1959-1960	.66	.14	.19	.78	.24	.02
	.56	.20	.15	.81	.20	.04	1960-1961	.67	.12	.18	.80	.24	.02
	.55	.23	.13	.83	.21	.04	1961-1962	.66	.14	.16	.81	.24	.02
	.55	.22	.14	.83	.20	.04	1962-1963	.69	.12	.16	.82	.23	.02
	.54	.23	.11	.85	.19	.04	1963-1964	.66	.13	.12	.84	.23	.03
	.54	.24	.11	.86	.20	.04	1964-1965	.67	.15	.13	.83	.24	.03
	.51	.27	.12	.85	.15	.04	1965-1966	.61	.19	.16	.81	.19	.03
	-.11	+.05	-.10	+.10	-.04	-.0		-.10	+.07	-.13	+.13	-.01	+.01
$3000 Earning Level													
	.79	.11	.26	.73	.21	.01	1957-1958	.82	.04	.31	.65	.22	.00
	.72	.13	.18	.81	.27	.01	1958-1959	.78	.05	.19	.79	.27	.01
	.73	.12	.18	.81	.27	.01	1959-1960	.78	.04	.18	.81	.25	.00
	.73	.10	.17	.82	.23	.01	1960-1961	.77	.05	.17	.82	.26	.00
	.72	.13	.14	.86	.24	.01	1961-1962	.77	.06	.14	.85	.26	.01
	.71	.12	.14	.84	.23	.01	1962-1963	.78	.06	.16	.83	.25	.00
	.70	.14	.12	.87	.22	.01	1963-1964	.75	.07	.10	.89	.26	.00
	.69	.15	.12	.87	.23	.01	1964-1965	.76	.08	.13	.86	.26	.00
	.67	.18	.14	.85	.17	.01	1965-1966	.72	.11	.16	.82	.21	.00
	-.12	+.07	-.13	+.13	-.04	0		-.10	+.07	-.15	+.17	-.01	0

$4500 Earning Level

Year												
1957-1958	.00	.22	.49	.49	.01	.83	.01	.22	.65	.34	.06	.84
1958-1959	.00	.27	.78	.22	.03	.78	.00	.28	.81	.17	.08	.78
1959-1960	.00	.26	.88	.13	.02	.79	.00	.27	.84	.15	.06	.80
1960-1961	.00	.26	.81	.18	.02	.78	.00	.24	.85	.15	.06	.79
1961-1962	.00	.26	.90	.09	.03	.79	.00	.25	.88	.12	.07	.78
1962-1963	.00	.25	.87	.13	.02	.80	.00	.23	.87	.12	.07	.78
1963-1964	.00	.26	.93	.07	.03	.79	.00	.23	.89	.10	.08	.77
1964-1965	.00	.26	.88	.11	.04	.80	.00	.24	.89	.11	.09	.77
1965-1966	.00	.22	.81	.18	.04	.79	.00	.18	.85	.15	.11	.75
	0	-.01	+.33	-.30	+.03	-.04	0	-.04	+.19	-.19	+.05	-.09

Table A-33

Female Mover Steady-State Proportions as a Function of g, Percentage Change in
GNP, 35-44 Age Group, $1500 Poverty Line (Current Age Group)

	Whites Proportion in				Nonwhites Proportion in	
L	N	U	g (Percentage)	L	N	U
.40	.14	.46	−10	.40	.07	.53
.39	.15	.46	− 9	.40	.08	.52
.39	.16	.45	− 8	.40	.08	.51
.38	.17	.44	− 7	.40	.09	.50
.38	.19	.44	− 6	.41	.10	.49
.37	.20	.43	− 5	.41	.11	.48
.36	.21	.42	− 4	.41	.13	.47
.36	.23	.41	− 3	.40	.14	.45
.35	.25	.40	− 2	.40	.16	.44
.34	.26	.39	− 1	.40	.17	.43
.33	.28	.38	0	.40	.19	.41
.33	.30	.37	1	.39	.21	.40
.32	.32	.36	2	.39	.23	.38
.31	.34	.35	3	.38	.26	.36
.30	.37	.34	4	.37	.28	.34
.29	.39	.32	5	.37	.31	.33
.28	.41	.31	6	.36	.34	.31
.27	.44	.30	7	.34	.37	.29
.25	.46	.28	8	.33	.40	.27
.24	.49	.27	9	.32	.43	.25
.23	.51	.26	10	.31	.46	.23

Appendix B: A Theory
of Job Search and
Unemployment

Introduction

In this appendix I apply the theory of probabilistic economics to the study of labor markets. The study emphasizes the role of job search in explaining labor market behavior like "frictional" unemployment and the "discouraged worker" phenomenon.

A probabilistic environment affects economics in two rather distinct ways.[1] The first is that inferences about economic behavior must be statistical. This facet of uncertainty has received considerable attention in the econometrics literature.[2] Second, a reformulation of deterministic economic theory in stochastic terms is necessary when economic agents operate in a probabilistic environment. The blending of economic theory and the theory of probability has been going on for some time, but not until recently has it begun to receive the attention it deserves. The reformulation of economic theory to take account of stochastic components is certainly one of the most important areas of economic research. Pathbreaking work is underway in reformulating the theory of the firm under conditions of uncertainty, in assessing the role of information in general equilibrium theory, in integrating uncertainty with welfare economics, and in designing measures of uncertainty possessing both theoretical appeal and practical importance.

Almost every phase of economic behavior is affected by uncertainty.[3] The underlying determinants of supply and demand have significant stochastic components. Consequently, it is imperative that relative prices be regarded as random variables. The number and arrival times of customers at a store are both stochastic. The number of employees who arrive at their place of work on any given day is a stochastic variable. Research and technology are probabilistic activities; for example, the occurrence of a breakthrough in medical research can be analyzed only in probabilistic terms. Inventory stocks are depleted, key personnel become sick, equipment breaks down, civil wars disrupt trade, cuts in defense spending produce unemployment, and so on.

Human behavior has adapted to uncertainty in a variety of ways. Insurance, futures markets, and stock markets are three institutions that facilitate the reallocation of risk among individuals and firms. Individuals and firms cope with uncertainty using such methods as inventory control, preventive maintenance, and annual physical examinations. Indeed, these adaptations to uncertainty are manifestations of rational behavior. A deterministic economic theory does not provide an adequate explanation of these fundamental behavioral responses to a stochastic environment. Similarly, the information accumulation that characterizes the decision-making of consumers and firms is inexplicable within a purely deterministic model. On these grounds, it is easy to explain and applaud the recent proliferation of articles in the area of probabilistic economics. It is not so easy to explain the long period during which deterministic models have dominated economic theory. When confronted with the stark empirical realities, how could such a theory survive? Undoubtedly part of the answer lies in the manner in which economic theory is tested. In analyzing empirical data, econometricians always include stochastic terms in their econometric models. Hard empirical facts necessitated these additions. However, for the most part, these terms were not grounded in economic theory but merely appended to economic models that had been constructed in a certainty milieu. Furthermore, the stochastic component of econometric models frequently is viewed as an inconvenience that a properly formulated deterministic model would eventually eliminate.

Perhaps a more important reason for the paucity of literature in probabilistic economics is that economic theory has never attempted to explain the behavior of individual firms or individual consumers. Rather the focus has been on the behavior of the *representative* firm and the *average* consumer.

We shall have to analyze carefully the normal cost of producing a commodity, relatively to a given aggregate volume of production; and for this purpose we shall have to study *the expenses of a representative producer* for that aggregate volume. On the other hand we shall not want to select some new producer just struggling into business . . . nor on the other hand, shall we want to take a firm which by exceptionally long-sustained ability and good fortune has got together a vast business. . . . But our representative firm must be one which has had a fairly long life, and fair success, which is managed with normal ability, and which has normal access to the economics, external and internal, which belong to the aggregate volume of production. (Marshall, 1948.)

Since there are so many firms and consumers, a law of large numbers has implicitly been invoked to reduce uncertainty to an agreeable level, namely, almost zero. Although this invoking of the law of large numbers is appropriate for some applications, it is quite misleading for others. The average consumer searches for low prices, purchases insurance, places a positive value on information, and diversifies his holdings of risky assets. The average firm searches for productive employees, insures against fire and other "acts of God," and purchases many kinds of information. None of these actions is consistent with a certainty model.

Another reason for the relatively slow growth of probabilistic economic models is the widely held belief that most of the results of the deterministic analysis remain basically the same when a stochastic model is used: "Instead of equating marginal cost and marginal revenue, equate expected marginal cost and expected marginal revenue." In some problems, substitution of simple expectations for the random variables yields good approximations. In general, however, random variables must be treated more delicately. If the stochastic solution to problems were only slightly different from deterministic solutions, one could seriously question the large investment necessary for designing probabilistic models. However, some of the standard results of deterministic economic theory are false in a stochastic setting. It is sometimes optimal for producers to operate where expected marginal revenue is greater than marginal costs. Fixed costs sometimes have an influence on short-run output decisions. The price-setting and quantity-setting monopolists do not arrive at the same quantity/price solutions.

Distinctive characteristics of probabilistic economics include the value of information and the necessity of search. Searching activity is a fundamental feature of economic markets. Deterministic theories of economic markets encounter severe obstacles when they attempt to explain such basic market phenomena as different prices for "identical" outputs, different prices for "identical" inputs, persistent positive levels of "unemployed" resources, and "underutilization" of employed resources. A probabilistic theory of economic markets can explain these phenomena.

The main problem confronting participants in probabilistic markets is determining the appropriate amount of information to collect before acting— where, in a labor market milieu, action is the acceptance of a particular job offer by a job searcher or the hiring of employees with certain identifiable characteristics by the searching employer. A variety of search models have been constructed to explain the behavior of both employers and employees. All of these models are based on the theory of martingales, of which optimal stopping rules are a special subclass.

In this appendix I apply some well-known results from the theory of optimal stopping rules to labor markets. These applications are performed at the micro level, and the implications of this analysis for macroeconomic phenomena are not investigated. The searching behavior of both job searchers and employers is studied. The analysis described herein could be applied to any economic market in which search plays an important role. However, for obvious reasons my attention is restricted to the labor market. The chapter begins with a brief discussion of martingale theory. Employee search behavior is then investigated. A variety of elementary search models are presented.

The Elements of Martingale Theory

The sequence of sums of independent random variables is basic to the study of stochastic processes. Classical results on laws of large numbers and central limit theorems were derived for sequences with these properties. Two stochastic processes, Markov processes and martingales, are based on simple generalization of this basic sequence. These generalizations invoke different assumptions about the dependence relations among the hitherto independent random variables. For first-order Markov processes, the conditioning is such that the value of the random variable X_t depends on its value at $t-1$ but is independent of earlier realizations; that is,

$$P(a \leqslant X_t \leqslant b \mid X_{t-1} = x_1, X_{t-2} = x_2, \ldots, X_{t-n} = x_n)$$
$$= P(a \leqslant X_t \leqslant b \mid X_{t-1} = x_1).$$

Markov models and their obvious generalizations have been applied extensively in economics. They have been used to analyze consumer choice over time, inventory control, replacement policy, the growth of firms, and income mobility and poverty dynamics. The advantages and disadvantages of Markov models in economics should therefore be apparent.

A martingale as used here has the following structure: Let $x_1, x_2, \ldots$ and $y_1, y_2, \ldots$ denote two sequences of random variables, where

$$y_n = y_n(x_1, x_2, \ldots, x_n),$$

that is, y_n is a function of the first n values of the sequence $[x_i]$. The sequence $[y_i]$ is a martingale with respect to the sequence $[x_i]$ if, for each n,[4]

$$E(|y_n|) < \infty \tag{B.1}$$

and

$$E(y_{n+1} \mid x_1, \ldots, x_n) = y_n. \tag{B.2}$$

If the equality in (B.1) is replaced by $\geqslant (\leqslant)$ the sequence is called a submartingale (supermartingale). A martingale is fair in the sense that the expected gain from the $(n+1)$st trial, $E(y_{n+1} \mid x_1, \ldots x_n)$ is equal to the accumulated gain at n, y_n. This elementary stochastic process has surprisingly rich implications in probability theory.[5]

As an example, let $[X_i]$ be a sequence of independent identically distributed random variables, where

$$X_i = \begin{cases} 1 \text{ with probability } p \\ -1 \text{ with probability } 1-p. \end{cases}$$

Denote the initial fortune by $S_0 = A$, and let S_n be the partial sum

$$S_n = \sum_{i=0}^{n} X_i.$$

Then, assuming the game is fair, that is $p = 1/2$,

$$E(S_{n+1} \mid S_1, S_2, \ldots, S_n) = E(S_n + X_{n+1} \mid S_1, \ldots, S_n)$$
$$= E(S_n \mid S_1, \ldots, S_n) + E(X_{n+1} \mid S_1, \ldots, S_n)$$
$$= S_n.$$

The expected value, $E(\mid S_n \mid)$, is bounded, and the sequence $[S_i]$ is a martingale with respect to the sequence $[X_i]$.

More generally, let $b_n(X_1, X_2 \ldots, X_n)$ be a sequence of functions from the produce space $[-1,1]^{(n)}$ to the positive real line, $(0, \infty)$ denoting the amount bet at the nth trial. As before, the initial fortune is given by $S_0 = A$. Then, the accumulated fortune at the $n+1st$ trial is

$$S_{n+1} = S_n + b_n(X_1, X_2, \ldots, X_n) X_{n+1}.$$

if $p = 1/2$,

$$E(S_{n+1} \mid S_1, \ldots, S_n) = E(S_n \mid S_1, \ldots, S_n)$$
$$+ E(b_n(X_1, \ldots, X_n) X_{n+1} \mid S_1, \ldots, S_n)$$
$$= S_n + b_n(X_1, \ldots, X_n) E(X_{n+1} \mid S_1, \ldots, S_n)$$
$$= S_n.$$

and $[S_i]$ is a martingale with respect to $[X_i]$. If $p \geqslant (\leqslant) 1/2$, $E(S_{n+1} \mid S_1, \ldots, S_n) \geqslant (\leqslant) S_n$ and $[S_i]$ is a submartingale (supermartingale) with respect to $[X_i]$.

The martingale process has been used to analyze the efficiency of securities markets, to investigate the properties of "properly anticipated" prices in futures markets, and to describe the relationships among short-term interest rates.

Some Simple Models of Employee Search

The elementary search model assumes that the employee knows the probability distribution of wages and can search for an unlimited period. The second model of employee search considers the possibility that the searching employee will be bankrupt during his period of search. If bankruptcy occurs, the searcher accepts the next offer given. The third model of employee search assumes that the searcher revises his beliefs about the probability distribution of wages as he accumulates offers. Because of its simplicity, the elementary search model is used to analyze frictional unemployment, the discouraged worker phenomenon, the effects of minimum wage legislation on frictional unemployment and the propensity to drop out of the labor market, and the effects of racial discrimination on job search.

The Elementary Search Model

In this simple job search model, the searching employee is assumed to know both the distribution of wages for his particular skills and the cost of generating a job offer. Job offers are independent random selections from the probability distribution of wages. These offers occur periodically and are either accepted or rejected. There is no limit on the number of offers the searcher can obtain. The amount of search or the period of unemployment depends on the wage rate that the individual knows his services can command in the labor market and on the opportunity cost of the searching activity. If the searcher knows that his skills are highly valued, he will reject offers that fall short of his expectations and remain unemployed. On the other hand, if the cost of search is high, he will tend to limit his searching activities. In these circumstances, the optimal policy for the job searcher is to reject all offers below a single critical number and to accept any offer above this critical number.

To be more precise, a stochastically independent job offer, x, is presented each period, where x is a random variable with probability density function $\phi(x)$. The job searcher is assumed to retain the highest job offer;[6] therefore, the return from stopping after n periods of search is given by

$$Y_n = \max(X_1, \ldots, X_n) - nc,$$

where c is the cost per period of search and includes transportation costs, the psychic costs of rejection, and the value of forgone alternatives.

Let $f(x)$ denote the optimal return when a job offer x has just been observed; then the optimal stopping policy has the following structure. If the searcher stops after searching for n periods, his return is

$$f_n = \max(x_1, \ldots, x_n) - nc = m - nc,$$

where $m \equiv \max(x_1, \ldots x_n)$. The objective is to find a stopping rule that maximizes $E(m-cn)$, where n is the random stopping time. Under these circumstances, if an x is observed initially and the process continues optimally thereafter, the expected return is

$$E[f(x)] = \epsilon = -c + E[\max(m, \xi)].$$

It is clear from this recursive equation that the optimal policy has the following form:

Continue searching   if $m < \xi$

Accept employment   if $m \geqslant \xi$.

Because of the special structure of this process, which will be elaborated below, the searcher can decide to continue or stop based on his comparison of the return from stopping and the expected return from *one* more observation. If he stops he gets m. If he continues for one more period, his expected return from one more observation is

$$m \int_0^m \phi(x)\,dx + \int_m^\infty x\phi(x)\,dx - c. \tag{B.3}$$

An individual is indifferent between continuing and stopping when the return from stopping equals the expected return from continuing,

$$m = m \int_0^m \phi(x)\,dx + \int_m^\infty x\phi(x)\,dx - c,$$

or, equivalently,

$$c = \int_m^\infty (x - m)\phi(x)\,dx$$

from which it immediately follows that ξ is the solution to

$$c = \int_\xi^\infty (x - \xi)\phi(x)\,dx = H(\xi).$$

An alternative derivation of this result proceeds as follows.

The conditional expected value, $E(f \mid N)$, the expected value of the return given that the searcher accepts the Nth offer, is calculated first. Then ξ is obtained by expecting out N. Symbolically,

$$E(f \mid N) = E(x_n \mid N) - cN$$

and

$$E(f) = \xi = E(E(x_n \mid N)) - cE(N).$$

Notice that

$$E(x_n \mid N) = E(x_n x_n \geqslant \xi, x_{n-1} < \xi, \ldots, x_1 < \xi).$$

That is, employment will commence with offer N only if $x_n \geqslant \xi$ and all previous offers have been less than ξ. Further,

$$E(x_n \mid x_n \geqslant \xi) = E(x \mid x \geqslant \xi)$$

by the assumption that the offers are identically distributed. Therefore,

$$E(x \mid x \geqslant \xi) = \frac{\int_{\xi}^{\infty} x \phi(x) \, dx}{P(x \geqslant \xi)}$$

and[7]

$$\xi = \frac{\int_{\xi}^{\infty} x \phi(x) \, dx}{P(x \geqslant \xi)}$$

The term $E(N)$ is the expected waiting time until employment occurs when the prevailing strategy is pursued. The appropriate random variable is the number of trials required to achieve the first success, that is, the number of trials until $x \geqslant \xi$. This random variable has a geometric distribution with parameter $P = P(x \geqslant \xi)$ and expected value $E(N) = 1/P, p > 0$. When these results are combined, given the following relation between x, c, ξ, and $\phi(x)$,

$$c = \int_{\xi}^{\infty} (x - \xi) \phi(x) \, dx = H(\xi).$$

This equation has a simple economic interpretation. The marginal cost of generating another job offer is c. The second member is the expected marginal return from waiting another period. The critical value, ξ, of a job offer is chosen to equate the marginal cost of waiting with its expected marginal return.

It has been shown that $H(\xi)$ is a strictly decreasing function of ξ; therefore, there is a unique value of ξ for every value of c, as shown in Figure B-1.[8]

In this model it can be shown that when

$$E(Y_{n+1} \mid X_1, \ldots, X_n) \leqslant \max(X_1, \ldots, X_n) = y_n$$

the sequence $Y_{n+1}, Y_{n+2}, \ldots$ is a regular supermartingale with respect to $X_{n+1}, X_{n+2}, \ldots$, where $E(Y \mid X_1, \ldots, X_n)$ is given by expression (B.3). The optimal policy for such a process has the nearsighted property described— the individual need look only *one* period ahead. The greater the search cost c, the sooner the process becomes a supermartingale; and, indeed, if c is large enough, it "pays" not to search at all.

The introduction of discounting has no effect on the structure of this policy. Let ρ be the discounting factor

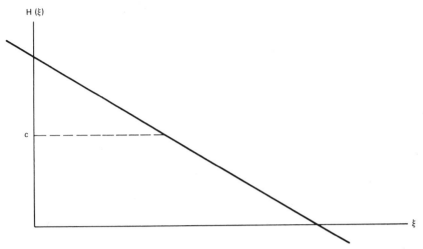

Figure B-1. Relationship between the Function $H(\xi)$ and the Critical Value, ξ

$$\rho = \frac{1}{1 + r} \; ,$$

where r is the appropriate interest rate. Then the critical value ξ is the solution to:

$$(1 - \rho) \xi + c = \rho H (\xi).$$

The more highly an individual values his time (low ρ, high r), the smaller is ξ. Hence, as expected, the introduction of a positive discount rate causes the job searcher to curtail his searching activities.

Interpretation of Labor Market Phenomena
by the Elementary Search Model

The elementary search model is a convenient device for distinguishing the discouraged workers or dropouts from the frictionally unemployed. For this purpose, a distinction will be made between the actual outlay on information accumulation and the returns the individual could make if he remained unemployed. These returns include unemployment compensation, welfare payments, and, perhaps, some leisure benefits.

Remaining unemployed is regarded as simply another occupation, say, the null occupation (leisure) the individual may choose. The optimal policy for people with unattractive employment opportunities and relatively high information costs may be to choose not to search for alternative employment. Those who choose this occupation are called discouraged workers or dropouts.[9] From society's point of view, the continuing presence of significant numbers of discouraged workers is deplorable. The frictionally unemployed are those who are looking for jobs but have not yet obtained a satisfactory job offer for which $x \geqslant \xi$, the probability distribution of wages appropriate to the searcher's skill level.

In Figure B-2, let ξ_0 denote the expected return from remaining unemployed. Note first that since $H(\xi)$ is a decreasing function of ξ, large values of c are associated with small values of ξ, implying that as c increases, the length of search decreases, other things equal. Similarly, small values of c are associated with larger values of ξ and longer periods of search. Consider an individual whose expected returns from remaining unemployed are ξ_0. If this individual is confronted with search costs in excess of c_0, not searching at all is his best strategy. The value of ξ associated with any value of c greater than c_0 is less than ξ_0, the expected return from remaining unemployed. This is another way of saying that the optimal policy for such an individual is to drop out or join the ranks of the discouraged workers.

Alternatively, if the costs of search are less than c_0, the individual will

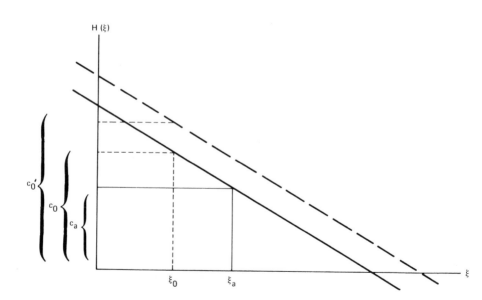

Figure B-2. Relationship between Discouraged Workers and the Frictionally Unemployed

continue to seek employment until he receives an offer exceeding the corresponding value of ξ. The time until such an offer is forthcoming is a period of frictional unemployment.

A description of the structure of the optimal policy is a convenient device for summarizing the preceding discussion. The optimal policy for choosing between dropping out and frictional unemployment has the following form:

if $c \geq c_0$, do not search (drop out);

if $0 \leq c < c_0$, search (choose frictional unemployment).[10]

The expected length, $E(L)$, of frictional unemployment is given by

$$E(L) = \frac{1}{p},$$

where

$$p = \int_{\xi}^{\infty} \phi(x)\,dx.$$

This expected length of frictional unemployment is an increasing function of ξ; that is, the larger ξ, the smaller p, and hence the larger $E(L)$.

The effects of various policies on reducing the number of discouraged workers can be elucidated with this model. Obviously, lowering the cost of search will reduce the number of dropouts. For example, in Figure B-2 consider again the individual whose return from remaining unemployed is ξ_0. If his search costs were reduced from an amount larger than c_0 to c_a, he would begin seeking employment. In other words, the value of ξ, ξ_a corresponding to c_a exceeds ξ_0, and therefore search is worthwhile. The value to the individual of lowering search costs is $\xi_a - \xi_0$, whereas the value to society could be as high as ξ_a if all of ξ_0 were a welfare payment.

Another method for reducing the number of dropouts is to upgrade the skills of the individual's wage distribution, $\phi(x)$, to the right. The skills that an individual acquires during a training program will on the average command a higher wage than his pretraining skills. In Figure B-2, the effect of a successful training program is to shift the solid line representing $H(\xi)$ outward to the dotted line. If the returns from unemployment remain fixed at ξ_0, the individual will drop out only if $c > c_0'$. This inequality is obviously more difficult to satisfy than the previous pretraining condition, $c > c_0$.

The choice between these two methods of reducing the number of discouraged workers depends on the cost of each relative to the induced reduction in the number of dropouts. It seems that lowering information costs is less costly than training programs, but perhaps training has a more salubrious effect on the discouraged workers. An important topic for further research is determining the relative merits of each.

Finally, for one reason or another the individual may be unemployable. Society must then determine whether ξ_0 is an adequate income. If it is not, then an income transfer of some sort is warranted. An individual receiving such a transfer will, of course, shun employment even more than before. Given the original goal of poverty alleviation, however, this is not a serious side effect.

The effects of a minimum wage law on the number of discouraged workers and the number of employed can also be interpreted within this framework. The level of the minimum wage will have no influence on an individual's decision to drop out. Regardless of whether the minimum wage is above or below ξ_0, if it was optimal to drop out before the minimum wage legislation, it will be optimal after. For example, if the minimum wage is less than ξ_0, it has no effect on the individual because he has the superior alternative of remaining inactive with respect to the labor market. On the other hand, if the minimum wage exceeds ξ_0, it is ineffective because it is beyond the range of alternatives he considers.

An individual who is frictionally unemployed and faces a distribution of job offers given by Figure B-3 is following an optimal policy and waiting until an offer exceeds the critical number, ξ_c. If the minimum wage, ξ_m, is less than ξ_c, it will have no influence on his behavior. If, however, ξ_m exceeds ξ_c, offers between ξ_c and ξ_m which the individual previously would have accepted are now excluded by the minimum wage legislation. Consequently, the expected period of frictional unemployment is increased.

In Figure B-3, for example, the expected period of frictional unemployment before the minimum wage was

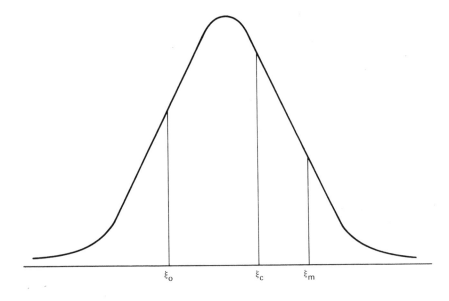

Figure B-3. The Distribution of Job Offers for a Particular Individual

$$E(L) = 1/p, \text{where } p = \int_{\xi_c}^{\infty} \phi(x)\,dx \ .$$

The expected period of frictional unemployment after the minimum wage is[11]

$$E'(L) = 1/p', \text{where } p' = \int_{\xi_m}^{\infty} \phi(x)\,dx \ .$$

Clearly, $E'(L) > E(L)$.

This model also clearly reveals the consequences of either overestimating or underestimating the wage distribution, $\phi(x)$. For simplicity, assume that these errors are always made with respect to the mean of the distribution. Let the true distribution be ϕ' in Figure B-4, and let ξ' denote the critical value of the wage rate. Suppose that the individual overestimates the value of his skills and in particular believes his wage distribution to be given by ϕ. Let ξ be the critical value of the wage rate corresponding to ϕ. Under these circumstances, the anticipated expected search will be

$$E(L) = \frac{1}{p}, \text{where } p = \int_{\xi}^{\infty} \phi(x)\,dx \ ,$$

whereas the actual expected period of search will be

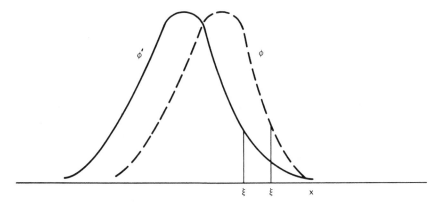

Figure B-4. True and Estimated Wage Distributions for a Particular Individual

$$E(L) = \frac{1}{p'} \text{ , where } p' = \int_{\xi}^{\infty} \phi'(x)\,dx \ .$$

If the individual knew that ϕ' were the true distribution, the expected period of search would be

$$E^*(L) = \frac{1}{p^*} = \int_{\xi'}^{\infty} \phi'(x)\,dx \ .$$

It is instructive to compare the actual expected period of search with the expected period the searcher anticipates. From Figure B-4 it is clear that $E'(L)$, the actual expected period of search, is greater than $E(L)$, the expected period anticipated by the overoptimistic searcher. If the searcher knew the true distribution, he would accept all offers in excess of ξ'. Hence, again from Figure B-4, the actual expected period of search also exceeds the expected period of search if the searcher knew the true distribution. Overoptimism leads to excessively long periods of frictional unemployment. Similar arguments show that overpessimism leads to excessively short periods of frictional unemployment and could indeed cause an individual to drop out. Nonadaptive behavior could also account for persistent unemployment in periods of recession.

The Bankruptcy Search Model

In many cases individuals are unable to search in the elementary manner described above. For example, unanticipated events may cause the searcher to accept the last offer and begin work immediately rather than continuing search. If the job searcher's assets fall below some critical level, then he accepts the last job offer. The random behavior of the searcher's assets can be analyzed using the classical ruin model. Let p be the probability that his assets are increased by one, $X_i = 1$, and q the probability that they are reduced by one, $X_i = -1$, $q > p$. If the individual's assets are unexpectedly increased above a certain level, he drops out to enjoy leisure. The origin denotes the position of his assets when search begins, $-\alpha$ is the reduction that induces him to accept the last offer, and β is the increase in assets that causes him to drop out. Let S_n be the sum of the n binomial variables $X_1, \ldots, X_n$; the function

$$g_n = (q/p)^{S_n}$$

is a martingale[12] with $E(g_n) = 1$. The probability, π, that bankruptcy occurs during search is the solution to

$$(1 - \pi)(q/p)^\beta + (\pi)(q/p)^{-\alpha} = 1,$$

since the expected value of this martingale process is always unity.

For convenience, assume that the probability of ruin is constant during the period of search. Furthermore, assume that if ruin occurs the searcher accepts the last offer. The optimal expected return from one more observation is

$$\xi = \pi E(x) + (1 - \pi)E[\text{Max}(x, \xi)] - c \qquad (B.4)$$

where the individual follows the stop rule:

$$\begin{aligned}&\text{continue} && \text{if } x > \xi \\ &\text{stop} && \text{if } x \leqslant \xi .\end{aligned}$$

It follows that ξ is the solution to (B.4), which can be rewritten

$$\pi(\xi - Ex) + c = (1 - \pi)H(\xi).$$

The Adaptive Search Model

The job searcher seldom has adequate knowledge about the distribution of wages appropriate to his skills. It is therefore important that he revise his estimate of the wage distribution as offers are made. If his initial estimate is high, an adaptive policy reduces the period of frictional unemployment, and conversely if his initial estimate is low.

The job searcher is assumed to have imperfect information about the k parameters, $\gamma = (\gamma_1, \ldots, \gamma_k)$ of the wage distribution $\phi(x)$. He does, however, have a prior distribution, $h(\gamma \mid \theta)$, over the unknown parameters, where θ is a vector representing the parameters of the prior. This prior distribution summarizes the imperfect information that the searcher has about the mean and other moments of the wage distribution. As offers are observed, θ is revised in Bayesian fashion and a new value is calculated, say

$$\theta' = T(\theta, x_1, x_2, \ldots, x_n),$$

where T is a transformation illustrating the dependence of θ' on θ and the n observations. After each observation the searcher revises the prior distribution and then makes a decision either to accept that job offer or to continue searching.

Let $f_n(x, \theta)$ be the maximum expected return when an offer of x has just been made; θ represents the parameters of the prior distribution. The n indicates that a total of n offers will be forthcoming. If none of these offers is accepted, assume that a return of amount a is realized. Then

$$f_n(x, \theta) = -c + \max \ [x, \int\int f_{n-1} (x,\theta) \phi (x \mu) (\gamma \theta) DX d\gamma] \ .$$

Let ξ_{n-1} denote the second term in the maximization. Then the optimal search policy has the same form as before:

accept employment   if $x \geqslant \xi_{n-1}$,

continue searching   if $x < \xi_{n-1}$.

When the probability distribution of wages is not known for sure, it is important to distinguish between a policy in which offers are accepted or rejected as they occur and a policy in which the best observed offer may be selected. For a discussion of these differences in a normal Bayesian model, see De Groot (1970).

A More General Model of Job Search

Obviously, a searcher in the labor market is concerned not only with the wage rate (be it hourly, weekly, or annual) but also with the anticipated period of employment. If other things are equal, the longer the period of employment, the more favorable the job opportunity. The period of employment is included here as an important variable affecting the job searcher's decision-making.

Each offer is now composed of two elements: a wage rate, x, and a period of employment, T. For simplicity, assume that x and T are independent random variables with probability density functions $\phi(x)$ and $\psi(T)$, respectively. Successive draws from each distribution are also assumed to be independent and identically distributed. As before, job offers occur periodically and are either accepted or rejected by the job searcher. A fixed cost, c, is associated with each offer, (x,T).[13] The individual knows the wage rate when he makes his decision. However, T, the period of employment, is a random variable with a known probability distribution. That is, the cost, c, generates an exact value for x, but not for T. If the job searcher accepts the Nth offer, the return is the discounted value of earning x for T periods less the discounted cost of search. The discount factor is denoted by ρ, where

$$\rho \ = \ \frac{1}{1 + r} \ ,$$

and r is the appropriate interest rate.

Assume that the cost of search is incurred simultaneously with job offers and the decision to accept or reject the offer. Then $f(x,T)$ is the maximum return obtainable when a job offer (x,T) has just been received. More specifically, if (x,T) is the first offer received,

$$f(x,T) = -c + \max(W, \xi),$$

where ξ now denotes the discounted expected value of $f(x,T)$; that is:

$$\xi = \rho E f(x,T)$$

and

$$W = x + \sum_{i=1}^{T} \rho^i x.$$

The optimal search policy has the same form as before and is given by

continue searching   if $W < \xi$

accept employment   if $W \geqslant \xi$.

The expected value of f, if the Nth offer is accepted is

$$E(f|N) = E(W_n|N) - \sum_{i=1}^{n} \rho^i c.$$

The expected value of f is then given by

$$E(f) = \xi = E[E(W_n|N)] - c\rho_n,$$

where $\rho_n = E\left(\sum_{i=1}^{n} \rho^i\right)$. Arguing as before

$$E(W_n|N) = E(W_n \mid W_n \geqslant \xi, W_{n-1} < \xi, \ldots, W_1 < \xi)$$
$$= E(W_n \mid W_n > \xi),$$

Since the Ws are independent, and

$$E(W_n \mid W_n \geqslant \xi) = [E(W \mid W \geqslant \xi)] [E(\rho^{n-1})],$$

Since the Ws are identically distributed and $W_n = \rho^{n-1} W$.[14] Finally,

$$E(W \mid W \geqslant \xi) = \frac{\int_{\xi}^{\infty} W\eta(w)dW}{P(W \geqslant \xi)} \quad,$$

where $\eta(W)$ is the probability density function for W, and

$$\xi = \frac{\int_{\xi}^{\infty} W\eta(W)dW}{1 - \rho P(W < \xi)} - c\rho_n,$$

since

$$E(\rho^{n-1}) = \frac{P(W \geqslant \xi)}{1 - \rho P(W < \xi)}.$$

The distinction between the discouraged workers and the frictionally unemployed, the effects of a minimum wage, and all the other implications of the
elementary search model have analogous interpretations here.

Notes

Notes

Preface

1. A prominent exception is Phelps, ed. (1970).
2. Agee and Evans (1966), pp. 7-8, 13.

Chapter 1
Introduction to the Problems of Poverty,
Racial Discrimination, and Economic Growth

1. See Appendix B.
2. Some of the non-labor-market phenomena associated with poverty can also be interpreted within this informational setting. Informational deficiencies undoubtedly help to explain the phenomenon that the "poor pay more." Family size depends partly on the amount of birth control information available. In a general sense education is a special kind of information enabling households to make efficient use of their limited resources.
3. Watts (1963).
4. Lampman (1971).
5. Ibid., p. 79.
6. See Kosters and Welch (1972).
7. See Prest and Turvey (1965), pp. 683-735. A critique of some recent cost-benefit studies of training programs is contained in Ribich (1968).
8. Ribich (1968).
9. For a critical evaluation of the Coleman Report, see Mosteller and Moynihan (1972).
10. Ribich (1968), pp. 127-29.
11. For a critical appraisal of income maintenance proposals, see Green (1968).
12. Friedman (1962).

Chapter Two
A Theory of Income Mobility, Racial
Discrimination, and Economic Growth

1. See Champernowne (1953), Cramér (1957), and Mandelbrot (1960).
2. A significant exception is Mandelbrot (1962).
3. Brownian motion was first observed in 1827 by the botanist Robert Brown. A formal theory of Brownian motion was first devised by Einstein (1905) and made completely rigorous by Wiener (1923).

189

4. For an excellent survey of the human-capital approach to income distribution, see Mincer (1970).

5. For a more complete description of the problems attendant to measuring and interpreting income distributions, see Kuznets (1955) and Stigler (1966), Chapter 18.

6. See Chapter 5 (Maldistribution?) in Bronfenbrenner (1971).

7. For example, see the path breaking work of Kuznets (1955), as well as that of Schultz (1969) and Atkinson (1970).

8. Recently there has been much research on the economics of discrimination. See the work of Arrow (1972), Gilman (1965), Hanoch (1967), and Pascal (1972). The pioneering study of this topic was Becker (1957). A critical survey of this literature that emphasizes the influence of governmental policies in explaining racial discrimination has been composed by Freeman (1972).

9. Actually, employer discrimination may be measured by much cruder variables such as the number of friends and relatives that have been hired or are employed by a particular firm.

10. For a discussion of black job searching behavior, see Sheppard and Belitsky (1966), Liebow (1967), and Lurie and Rayack (1968).

11. This assumes that the experiments do not yield perfect information.

12. See Appendix B.

13. The desired number of successes will again be dictated by the profit maximizing criterion.

14. In terms of the profit maximizing criterion, successes will have some explicit value to the firm, say $V(np)$. Then, the appropriate criterion is to sample from that distribution so as to maximize $V(np) - n\bar{c}$.

15. When this is the case, the posterior distribution of p given sample information is also beta.

16. A model could also be devised in which an employer is considering the possibility of hiring a fixed number of nonwhites. This experiment will provide him with sample information about nonwhite productivities. Such an experiment will be performed when the expected value of sample information exceeds its cost. See Pratt, Raiffa, and Schlaifer (1965).

17. For an analysis of search behavior when the searcher is uncertain about $\phi(x)$, see Appendix B.

18. In the analysis of income mobility, I expect the chain to be nonstationary because of the influence of economic growth. Furthermore, the chain describing nonwhite income mobility should display a higher degree of nonstationarity than the corresponding white chain. This expectation is based on theory of discrimination outlined above.

19. For a detailed discussion see Hoel, Port and Stone (1972).

20. For a discussion of the stayer-mover model, see Blumen et al. (1955) and Goodman (1961).

21. For a derivation of the exact maximum likelihood estimators, see Goodman (1961).

22. See Aaron (1967), Anderson (1964), and Batchelder (1963). An individ-

ual is immune to growth if he remains in poverty during periods of sustained growth.

23. Note that there are

$$\sum_{k=2}^{20} \binom{20}{k}$$

possible tests and they are not all independent.

24. If the process has been observed for N periods, then

$$p_{ij} = \frac{\sum\limits_{t=1}^{N} n_{ij}(t)}{\sum\limits_{k=1}^{2} \sum\limits_{t=1}^{N} n_{ij}(t)} = \frac{\sum\limits_{t=1}^{N} n_{ij}(t)}{\sum\limits_{t=0}^{N-1} n_{i}(t)} \quad,$$

where $n_{ij}(t)$ is the number going from i at $t-1$ to j at t, and $n_i(t)$ is the number in i at $t-1$.

25. A Markov chain is called ergodic if it is possible to go from every state to every other state.

Chapter 3
Description of the Social Security Data
and a Summary of Empirical Findings

1. The percentage was probably higher in earlier years of the period covered. Social Security numbers are now being assigned to many people, especially children, for reasons other than Social Security accounting.

2. Excluding self-employed farm workers, whose reported earnings were not included in this file. For a complete discussion of sample design, see *Workers Under Social Security*, 1960.

3. One of the critical concerns of the Social Security Administration in releasing these files to the "research public" was to insure the anonymity of individual cases. The identification numbers used in our files are not SSNs, although the true SSN is altered consistently. This makes it possible to trace a case through all files. The identification of digit combinations used to select the sample was not divulged.

4. *Workers Under Social Security*, 1960, pp. 7-8.

5. For a more complete description, see U.S. Department of HEW (1970).

6. For a detailed discussion of the sample design, see "The Current Population Survey—A Report on Methodology," Technical Paper No. 7, Bureau of the Census. Also see Schultz (1965).

Chapter 4
An Empirical Study of Income Dynamics

1. The limitations of this data file are considered more thoroughly in Chapter 3.

2. Note that all these measures are invariant to changes in the mean of the distribution.

3. For a complete discussion of this statistic, see Theil (1967).

4. This is strictly true only if the income distribution is lognormal, in which case the Theil measure is one-half the variance of the log income. See Theil (1967) and Atkinson (1970).

5. Schultz's data are based on the Current Population Surveys for the years 1947 to 1965.

6. The truncation of the income distribution introduces a downward bias in these coefficients *and* it is undoubtedly more pronounced for whites than nonwhites.

7. The reporting distribution includes individuals who only wish a casual relationship with the labor market. The proportion of individuals with these casual commitments may increase with economic growth.

8. The full coverage distribution excludes individuals who want an increased participation in the labor market but for one reason or another are denied full access. It also excludes full-time workers who retired during the period and those full-time participants who entered the labor market after 1957.

9. For a discussion of these tests, see Hays and Winkler (1971).

10. For a description of this estimation procedure, see Chapter 3.

11. All incomes were transformed in log incomes. Hence, whenever "income" is used in this subsection it should be read log income.

12. Assuming that the income distribution is log normal, let X_{it} denote the log income for individual i in year t. By definition of the lognormal distribution, X_{it} is normal with parameters μ_t and σ_t^2 $i = 1, 2, \ldots, N$. By the convolution property of the normal distribution, $\bar{X}_{i\cdot}$ is also normal with mean, $\mu_1 + \mu_2 + \ldots + \mu_T / T$ and variance

$$\frac{\sigma_1^2 + \ldots + \sigma_T^2}{T^2}$$

The estimated variance s^2 is the natural estimator of $\Sigma \sigma_i^2 / T^2$, which in turn is twice the Theil measure of inequality for this distribution.

13. A simple one-way analysis of variance also revealed something already known: that average income per year is significantly different among years.

14. This is proportion who remained covered in eight of the nine following years given coverage in 1957.

15. The unemployment coefficient is significantly positive for white males and insignificantly positive for nonwhites.

16. These inequality measures will rank income distributions (with the same mean) in the same way provided the Lorenz curves of these distributions do not intersect. This assumes that the social welfare function, $U(y)$, is concave and increasing y. No other information about U is needed. However, if the Lorenz curves do intersect, then these inequality measures may rank the distributions differently. A stronger consequence of intersection is the ability to construct inequality measures that *will* rank the distributions differently. Since Lorenz curves frequently intersect, it is necessary to find additional conditions on $U(y)$ that guarantee invariant rankings.

17. In the literature on probabilistic economics, the utility function $U(y)$ is said to possess constant relative risk aversion, with ϵ measuring the degree of aversion. The utility function displays risk aversion if and only if it is concave; that is, if and only if $\epsilon \geqslant 0$. In this setting, Atkinson interprets ϵ as a measure of society's inequality aversion. Replacing the work "risk" by "inequality" allows one to apply the standard results of probabilistic economics. For a survey of this literature, see McCall (1971).

Chapter 5
An Empirical Study of Poverty Dynamics:
First Application of the Stayer-Mover Model

1. See *Social Security Bulletin*, January and July 1965, April, May, and December 1966.

2. The movers of this study are analogous to Metcalf's "low income families which are labor-force oriented." See Metcalf (1969).

3. Approximately 90 percent of nonwhites are black.

4. The following test was used to evaluate these differences. Let p_1^i and p_2^i be, respectively, the proportion of nonwhites in nonincome category j who were in poverty (nonpoverty) in 1962 and remained poor (nonpoor) through 1965, and the proportion of whites who did likewise. To test the null hypothesis that $p_1^i = p_2^i$ against the alternative $p_1^i > p_2^i$, form the matrix

	Stayers	Nonstayers
Nonwhite	n_{11}	n_{12}
White	n_{21}	n_{22}

and calculate

$$n = \sum_{i,j} n_{ij}, n_{1.} = \sum_{j} n_{1j}, n_{2.} = \sum_{j} n_{2j} \text{ and } n_{.1} = \sum_{j} n_{j1}$$

then form the ratios $r_1 = n_{11}/n_1 .$, $r_2 = n_{21}/n_2 .$, and $r = n \cdot 1/n$. Under the null hypothesis, the test statistic,

$$u = (r_1 - r_2)/[\sqrt{r(1-r)}(1/n_1 . + 1/n_2 .)] ,$$

is approximately normally distributed with mean zero and standard deviation 1. For a complete description, see Brownlee (1965).

5. The nonstatistical "significance" of these differences must, of course, be determined by other criteria.

6. It is important for policy to distinguish between these two probabilities. The conditional probabilities of staying in poverty (nonpoverty) could be quite high, while the unconditional probabilities of staying in poverty for all four years could be quite small. Calculation of the unconditional probabilities also facilitates the derivation of the mover proportions. The estimates of both the unconditional and conditional probabilities are biased upward.

7. Statistical tests verified these casual observations. Using the χ^2 tests developed by Goodman, (1962) the hypothesis of stationarity could be rejected at very high levels of significance.

8. In the distinction between stayers and movers, only those who remained in poverty (nonpoverty) for the entire four-year period were stayers. Hence, for any two successive years the mover matrix can have transitions from poverty (nonpoverty) in the year t to poverty (nonpoverty) in year $t + 1$.

9. This semblance was tested by using the χ^2 tests developed by Goodman (1962).

10. However, there are cases in which white females do "better" than nonwhite males.

11. For a discussion of job discrimination, see Chapter 2.

12. In 1966, 24 percent of nonwhite families were headed by females, whereas the comparable percentage for whites was 9 (see *Social and Economic Conditions of Negroes in the United States*, BLS Report No. 332, October 1967).

13. This is consistent with the findings of Anderson (1964), Batchelder (1963), Gallaway (1965), and Wohlstetter and Coleman (1972).

Appendix A
Empirical Study of Poverty Dynamics—
Second Application of the
Stayer-Mover Model

1. This is the 35-44 age group (age as of 1960) using a $3000 earning level. In calculating these regressions, it might seem that the restriction on the column transition probabilities (they must sum to one across rows) would be included in

the estimation procedure. However, since the row data satisfy this restriction, the simple ordinary least squares procedure yields estimates of the transition probabilities that also sum to one across rows. See Cook (1971).

2. Three alternative explanations of these differences are (1) the South to North and rural to urban migration rates were higher for nonwhites than for whites, (2) improvements in the quality of education was greater for nonwhites than for whites, and (3) civil rights legislation and the subsequent reduction in job discrimination caused nonwhites to improve faster than whites. None of these alternative explanations is investigated here.

3. This is the 35-44 age group using a $1500 earning level.

4. The subscript 1 denotes state L.

5. The subscripts 3 and 2 denote U and N, respectively.

6. These results are for the 1960 age group.

7. The Goodman test described earlier was applied to these data. The null hypothesis of equality with zero was rejected in every case at significant levels above .01.

8. The annual percentage changes in GNP over this period were: 1957-58: 1.4; 1958-59: 8.1; 1959-60: 4.1; 1960-61: 3.3; 1961-62: 7.7; 1962-63: 5.4; 1963-64: 7.1; 1964-65: 8.3; 1965-66: 9.2. The price level was relatively constant over the whole period with 1965-66 marking the onset of inflation.

9. The Goodman test was used to measure these differences. The null hypothesis of equality was rejected in every case at significance levels above .025.

10. For these differences, the significance level was always greater than .001.

11. See Chapter 5, footnote 6.

12. For a more complete description of the properties of Markov chains, see Chapter 2.

13. Statistical tests verified these casual observations. Using the χ^2 tests developed by Goodman (1962), the hypothesis of stationarity could be rejected at very high levels of significance.

14. The distinction between stayers and movers is that only those who remained in L(N) for the entire year period were movers. Hence, for any two successive years the mover matrix can have transitions from L(N) in year t to L(N) in year $t + 1$.

15. Throughout this study it is assumed that constant values of g do not cause changes in the transition probabilities; that is, the process is stationary for fixed growth rates. Obviously this is a very crude approximation. Persistently high values of g will undoubtedly influence these transition probabilities. There are many exogenous factors affecting the equilibrium value of g, the value of g such that no changes in the transition probabilities are induced. These include population growth and the rate of inflation. The assumption made here is that each of the observed g's is an equilibrium value.

16. Sample regressions were also calculated between the uncovered transition

probabilities and growth. There are five of these probabilities: U to N, U to N, U to U, N to U, and N to U. For the most part these regressions had very little explanatory power.

17. The Durbin-Watson statistic was calculated for each of these regressions. However, the sample size is so small that it is difficult to detect correlation of errors. See Malinvaud (1966).

18. These are actually pseudo steady-state distributions in that the underlying stochastic process is undoubtedly nonstationary. If for cyclical reasons, the transition matrixes repeated themselves every p years, the process would be p-stationary and steady-states could be computed. See Solow (1951).

19. The method assumes that emergence from uncovered gives information about the income distribution of the uncovered category. The procedure may be biased, but given the paucity of information on the uncovered category, the bias cannot be measured. All those who were ever uncovered are covered for at least one of the ten periods. Their income during this covered period is our measure of uncovered behavior.

20. Statistical tests verified these casual observations. Using the χ^2 tests developed by Goodman (1962), the hypothesis of stationarity could be rejected at very high levels of significance.

Appendix B
A Theory of Job Search and Unemployment

1. A survey of the literature on probabilistic economics is contained in McCall (1971).

2. For a discussion of econometric procedures, see Dhrymes (1970) and Theil (1971).

3. "The laws of economics are to be compared to the laws of the tides, rather than with the simple and exact law of gravitation. For the actions of men are so various and uncertain, that the best statement of tendencies, which we can make in a science of human conduct, must needs be inexact and faulty. This might be urged as a reason against making any statement at all on the subject; but that would be almost to abandon life." Marshall (1948).

4. A more formal definition is: A sequence of random variables $[x_n]$ and Borel fields $[F_n]$ constitute a martingale $[x_n, F_n]$ if and only if, for each n,

$$F_n \subset F_{n+1}$$
$$E(|x_n|) < \infty$$

and

$$E(x_{n+1} | F_n = x_n,$$

where the Borel field is the σ-algebra generated by $[x_1 \ldots x_n]$.

5. The concept was first introduced by Levy, but it was Doob who systematically developed martingale theory and demonstrated its manifold applications.

6. Surprisingly, there is no difference in the analysis between the assumption of retaining the highest of past job offers and the assumption of retaining only the last offer. If $\phi(x)$ is not known for sure, these two assumptions *do* give different results. See DeGroot (1970).

7. This equation is easily interpreted. ξ is the return from stopping when ξ is observed. The first term on the right is the expected return from continuing; the second is the expected cost.

8. Notice that the derivative of $H(\xi)$, the slope of the curve in Figure B-1, is equal to $-P$.

9. Nonparticipants in the labor force (dropouts) constitute two very distinct groups' those with attractive employment opportunities and large personal fortunes who would always choose the null occupation regardless of the cost of search, and those who are truly discouraged workers and choose the null occupation in desperation. The theory developed here applies to both groups of dropouts, but our concern is for the latter.

10. This analysis can be generalized to explain individual choice among industries (occupations). Before searching, the job searcher calculates ξ_i, $i = 0,1,\ldots,n$, for each of the $n+1$ industries (occupations) where search is contemplated. He initiates search in that industry (occupation) with the highest ξ_i.

11. This assumes that the minimum wage eliminated all job offers less than ξ_m and has no effect on those greater than ξ_m. This means that the density function $\phi(x)$ is truncated below ξ_m and acquires mass at $x = 0$. If more firms are above minimum wage (after its imposition) than were above ξ_c before, then the expected period of frictional unemployment would be reduced.

12. $E(g_{n+1} \mid g_n, \ldots, g_1) = E[g_n(q/p)^{X_{n+1}} \mid g_n, \ldots, g_1]$

$$= g_n[(q/p)p + (q/p)^{-1}q] = g_n; \text{ see Feller (1966)}.$$

13. In fact, different costs are probably associated with different job offers. In this case c should be interpreted as the average cost. Also job offers may not arrive periodically. The introduction of a continuous model does not seriously affect the results. Finally, job offers may be accumulated with the job searcher always holding on to his best offer to date. This factor can be introduced without altering the analysis.

14. Since

$$W_n = \sum_{i=n-1}^{n+t-1} \rho^i X.$$

Bibliography

Bibliography

Aaron, Henry. "Foundations of the 'War on Poverty' Re-examined." *American Economic Review* 57 (December 1967): 1229-40.

Agee, James, and Walker Evans. *Let Us Now Praise Famous Men*. Boston: Houghton Mifflin, 1966.

Alchian, Armen, "Information Costs, Pricing and Resource Unemployment." In *Microeconomic Foundations of Employment and Inflation Theory* E.S. Phelps, ed. New York: W.W. Norton and Co., 1970.

Anderson, T.W., and Leo A. Goodman. "Statistical Inferences about Markov Chains." *Annals of Mathematical Statistics* 28 (March 1967): 89-110.

Anderson, W.H. Locke. "Trickling Down: The Relationship Between Economic Growth and the Extent of Poverty among American Families." *Quarterly Journal of Economics* 78 (November 1964):511-24.

Arrow, Kenneth J. "Models of Job Discrimination." In A.H. Pascal, ed., *Racial Discrimination in Economic Life*. Lexington, Mass.: D.C. Heath, 1972.

Atkinson, A.B. "On the Measurement of Income in Equality." *Journal of Economic Theory* (1970): 244-63.

Batchelder, Alan B. "Decline in the Relative Income of Negro Man." *Quarterly Journal of Economics* 77 (November 1963): 525-48.

Becker, Gary S. *The Economics of Discrimination*. Chicago: University of Chicago Press, 1957.

_____, *Human Capital*. New York: Columbia University Press, 1964.

_____, "Human Capital and the Personal Distribution of Income." *W.S. Woytinsky Lecture No. 1*, University of Michigan, 1967.

Blumen, Isadore, Marvin Kogan, and P.J. McCarthy. *The Industrial Mobility of Labor as a Probability Process*. Ithaca: Cornell University Press, 1955.

Breiman, Leo. "Stopping Rule Problems." In *Applied Combinatorial Mathematics*, E.F. Beckenbach, ed. New York: John Wiley and Sons, Inc., 1964.

Bronfenbrenner, Martin. *Income Distribution Theory*. Chicago: Aldine-Atherton, 1971.

Brownlee, K.A. *Statistical Theory and Methodology*. New York: John Wiley & Sons, 1965.

Cain, Glen G. *Married Women in the Labor Force*. Chicago: University of Chicago Press, 1966.

Champernowne, D.G. "A Model of the Income Distribution." *Economic Journal*, 1953.

Chung, K.L. *A Course in Probability Theory*. New York: Harcourt, Brace and World, 1968.

Cook, Alvin A. *A Note on Estimating Proportions by Linear Regressions*, The Rand Corporation, P-4712, 1971.

Cramer, H. *Mathematical Methods of Statistics*. Princeton University Press, 1957.

Cramer, J.S. *Empirical Econometrics*. Amsterdam: North-Holland Publishing Co., 1971.

David, Martin. "Welfare, Income and Budget Needs." *Review of Economics and Statistics* 40 (November 1959): 393-99.

DeGroot, M.H. *Optimal Statistical Decisions*. New York: McGraw-Hill, 1970.

Denardo, Eric V. and Bennett Fox. "Multichain Markov Renewal Programs." *SIAM Journal on Applied Mathematics* 16, no. 3 (May 1968): 468-87.

Dhrymes, Phoebus J. *Econometrics*. New York: Harper and Row, 1970.

Feller, William. *An Introduction to Probability Theory and Its Applications*, New York: John Wiley and Sons, 1966.

Fox, Bennett. *Markov Renewal Programming by Linear Fractional Programming*. P-3257-1, Santa Monica: The Rand Corporation, April 1966.

Freeman, Richard. "Labor Market Discrimination: Analysis, Findings and Problems." Unpublished paper, 1972.

Friedman, M. *Capitalism and Freedom*. Chicago: University of Chicago Press, 1962.

Gallaway, Lowell. "The Foundations of the War on Poverty." *American Economic Review* 55 (March 1965): 122-31.

Gilman, H.J. "Economic Discrimination and Unemployment." *American Economic Review* 55 (December 1965): 1077-95.

Goodman, L.A. "Statistical Methods for the Mover-Stayer." *Journal of American Statistical Association* 56 (December 1961): 841-68.

_____ , "Statistical Methods for Analyzing Processes of Change." *American Journal of Sociology* 68 (July 1962): 57-58.

Green, C. *Negative Taxes and the Poverty Problem*. Washington, D.C.: Brookings Institution, 1968.

Hanoch, G. "An Economic Analysis of Earnings and Schooling." *Journal of Human Resources* 2 (Winter 1967): 130-329.

Hays, W.L., and R.L. Winkler. *Statistics: Probability, Inference and Decision*. New York: Holt, Rinehart and Winston, Inc., 1971.

Hoel, Paul G., Sidney C. Port and Charles J. Stone. *Introduction to Stochastic Processes*, Boston: Houghton Mifflin Company, 1972.

Howard, Ronald A. *Dynamic Programming and Markov Processes*. Cambridge: M.I.T. Press, 1960.

Jewell, William S. "Markov Renewal Programming I and II." *Operations Research* 2 (November-December 1963): 938-71.

Kosters, Marvin, and Finis Welch. "The Effects of Minimum Wages by Race, Age, and Sex." In A.H. Pascal, ed., *Racial Discrimination in Economic Life*. Lexington, Mass.: D.C. Heath, 1972.

Krueger, Anne O. "The Economics of Discrimination." *Journal of Political Economy* 71 (October 1963): 481-86.

Kuznets, Simon. "Economic Growth and Income Inequality." *American Economic Review* 45 (March 1955): 1-28.

Lampman, Robert J. *Ends and Means of Reducing Poverty*. Chicago: Markham Publishing Company, 1971.

_____ , Joint Economic Study Paper No. 12. *The Low Income Population and Economic Growth*, 1959.

Liebow, Eliot. *Tally's Corner*. Boston: Little, Brown and Company, 1967.

Lurie, Melvin, and Elton Rayack. "Racial Differences in Migration and Job Search: A Case Study." *Southern Economic Journal*, July 1966; reprinted in *Negroes and Jobs*, edited by Ferman, Kornbluh and Miller, Ann Arbor: University of Michigan Press, 1968.

Malinvaud, E. *Statistical Methods of Econometrics*. Chicago: Rand-McNally and Company, 1966.

Mandelbrot, B. "The Pareto-Levy Law and the Distribution of Income." *International Economic Review*, May 1960.

_____ , "Paretian Distributions and Income Maximization." *Quarterly Journal of Economics*, (1962): 57-85.

Marshall, A. *Principles of Economics*, New York: Macmillan Company, 1948.

McCall, John J. "Probabilistic Microeconomics." *The Bell Journal of Economics and Management Science*, Fall 1971.

_____ , "An Analysis of Poverty: A Suggested Methodology." *Journal of Business* 43 (January 1970): 31-43.

_____ , "An Analysis of Poverty: Some Preliminary Findings." *Journal of Business* 44 (April 1971): 125-47.

_____ , "Economics of Information and Job Search." *Quarterly Journal of Economics* 84 (February 1970): 113-26.

Metcalf, Charles E. "The Size Distribution of Personal Income During the Business Cycle." *American Economic Review* 59 (September 1969): 657-68.

Miller, Bruce L. "Finite State Continuous Time Markov Decision Processes with a Finite Planning Horizon." *SIAM Journal Control 6*, no. 2 (February 1968): 266-80.

Miller, Herman P. "Poverty and the Negro." In Leo Fishman, ed., *Poverty Amid Affluence*. New Haven: Yale University Press, 1966.

Mincer, Jacob. "The Distribution of Labor Incomes: A Survey with Special Reference to the Human Capital Approach." *Journal of Economic Literature* 8, no. 1, (March 1970): 1-27.

_____ , "Labor Force Participation of Married Women." In *Aspects of Labor Economics*, NBER. Princeton University Press, 1962, 63-105.

_____ , *Schooling, Experience and Earnings*. National Bureau of Economic Research, 1972.

Mood, Alexander and Franklin Graybill. *Introduction to the Theory of Statistics*. New York: McGraw-Hill, 1963.

Mortenson, Dale. "Job Search, the Duration of Unemployment and the Phillips Curve," *American Economic Review* 60 (December 1970): 847-62.

Mosteller, F. and D.P. Moynihan, eds., on *Equality of Educational Opportunity*. New York: Random House, 1972.

Pascal, A.H. *The Economics of Housing Segregation*. RM-5510-RC, The Rand Corporation, November 1967.

Pratt, John W., Howard Raiffa, and Robert Schlaifer. *Introduction to Statistical Decision Theory*. New York: McGraw-Hill, 1965.

President's Commission on Income Maintenance Programs. *Poverty Amid Plenty, The American Paradox*. Report of the Commission, Washington, D.C., November 1969.

Prest, A.R., and R. Turvey. "Cost-Benefit Analysis: A Survey." *Economic Journal* 75 (December 1965): 683-735.

Ribich, Thomas. *Education and Poverty*. Washington, D.C.: Brookings Institution, 1968.

Scheffe, Henry. *The Analysis of Variance*. New York: John Wiley & Sons, 1959.

Schultz, T.P. "Secular Trends and Cyclical Behavior of Income Distribution in the U.S." In L. Soltow, ed., *Six Papers on the Size Distribution of Wealth and Income*. New York: Columbia University Press, 1969.

_____, *The Distribution of Personal Income*. Joint Economic Committee, Congress of the United States, Washington, 1965.

_____, "Secular Trends and Cyclical Behavior of Income Distribution in the United States—1944-1965." In *Six Papers on the Size Distribution of Wealth and Income*. National Bureau of Economic Research, 1969.

Sheppard, Harold L. and A. Harvey Belitsky. *The Job Hunt*, Baltimore: Johns Hopkins Press, 1966.

Solow, Robert M. "On the Dynamics of the Income Distribution." Ph.D. dissertation, Harvard University, 1951.

Stigler, George J. "The Economics of Information." *Journal of Political Economy* 69 (June 1961): 213-25.

_____, "Information in the Labor Market." *Journal of Political Economy* 70 (October 1962): 94-104.

_____, *The Theory of Price*. New York: Macmillan Company, 1966.

Theil, H. *Economics and Information Theory*. Chicago: Rand-McNally, 1967.

_____, *Principles of Econometrics*, New York: John Wiley and Sons, 1971.

Thurow, Lester. *Poverty and Discrimination*. Washington, D.C.: The Brookings Institution, 1969.

Tobin, James. "On Improving the Economic Status of the Negro." *Daedalus* (Fall 1965): 878-98.

U.S. Bureau of the Census. *Current Population Survey*. Ser. P-60.

U.S. Department of Health, Education and Welfare (HEW). *Workers Under Social Security 1960*. Social Security Administration, Washington, D.C.

_____, *Longitudinal Employer-Employee Data*. Social Security Administration, Washington, D.C., April 1970.

Watts, Harold W. "An Economic Definition of Poverty." Institute for Research on Poverty, University of Wisconsin, April 1963.

Wohlstetter, Albert, and Sinclair Coleman. "Race Differences in Income." In

A.H. Pascal, ed., *Racial Discrimination in Economic Life*. Lexington, Mass.: D.C. Heath, 1972.

Zellner, Arnold and Tong Hun Lee, "Joint Estimations of Relationships Involving Discrete Random Variables," *Econometrica*, 33 (April 1965), pp. 382-93.

Index

Index

About the Author

John J. McCall is a Professor of Economics at the University of California, Los Angeles and a consultant to the Rand Corporation. He received the Ph.D. from the University of Chicago in 1959. He has written numerous articles in labor economics, probabilistic economics and operations research. He is co-author of the book, *Optimal Replacement Policy*.

Selected List of Rand Books

Arrow, Kenneth J. and Marvin Hoffenberg. *A Time Series Analysis of Interindustry Demands*. Amsterdam, Holland: North-Holland Publishing Company, 1959.

Bellman, Richard E. *Dynamic Programming*. Princeton, N.J.: Princeton University Press, 1957.

_____. *Adaptive Control Processes: A Guided Tour*. Princeton, N.J.: Princeton University Press, 1961.

Coleman, James S. and Nancy L. Karweit. *Information Systems and Performance Measures in Schools*. Englewood Cliffs, N.J.: Educational Technology Publications, 1972.

Dantzig, George B. *Linear Programming and Extensions*. Princeton, N.J.: Princeton University Press, 1963.

DeSalvo, Joseph S. (ed.) *Perspectives on Regional Transportation Planning*. Lexington, Mass.: D.C. Heath and Company, 1973.

Dorfman, Robert, Paul A. Samuelson, and Robert M. Solow. *Linear Programming and Economic Analysis*. New York: McGraw-Hill Book Company, 1958.

Downs, Anthony. *Inside Bureaucracy*. Boston, Mass.: Little, Brown and Company, 1967.

Dreyfus, Stuart. *Dynamic Programming and the Calculus of Variations*. New York: Academic Press, Inc., 1965.

Fishman, George S. *Spectral Methods in Econometrics*. Cambridge, Mass.: Harvard University Press, 1969.

Ford, L.R., Jr., and D.R. Fulkerson. *Flows in Networks*. Princeton, N.J.: Princeton University Press, 1962.

Gouré, Leon. *The Siege of Leningrad*. Stanford, Calif.: Stanford University Press, 1962.

Hirshleifer, Jack, James C. DeHaven, and Jerome W. Milliman. *Water Supply: Economics, Technology, and Policy*. Chicago: University of Chicago Press, 1960.

Jorgenson, D.W., J.J. McCall and R. Radner. *Optimal Replacement Policy*. Amsterdam, The Netherlands: North-Holland Publishing Co., 1967.

Kecskemeti, Paul. *Strategic Surrender: The Politics of Victory and Defeat*. Stanford, Calif.: Stanford University Press, 1958.

McKinsey, J.C.C. *Introduction to the Theory of Games*. New York: McGraw-Hill Book Company, 1952.

Meyer, John R., Martin Wohl, and John F. Kain. *The Urban Transportation Problem*. Cambridge, Mass.: Harvard University Press, 1965.

Nelson, Richard R., Merton J. Peck, and Edward D. Kalachek. *Technology Economic Growth and Public Policy*. Washington, D.C.: Brookings Institution, 1967.

Novick, David (ed.) *Current Practice in Program Budgeting (PPBS): Analysis and Case Studies Covering Government and Business.* New York: Crane, Russak and Co., Inc., 1973.

Pascal, Anthony H. (ed.) *Racial Discrimination in Economic Life.* Lexington, Mass.: D.C. Heath and Company, 1972.

Pascal, Anthony (ed.) *Thinking about Cities: New Perspectives on Urban Problems.* Belmont, Calif.: Dickenson Publishing Company, 1970.

Sharpe, William F. *The Economics of Computers.* New York: Columbia University Press, 1969.

Williams, John D. *The Compleat Strategyst: Being a Primer on the Theory of Games of Strategy.* New York: McGraw-Hill Book Company, 1954.